❖

IMPACT
OF
NARCISSISM

❖   ❖   ❖

IMPACT
OF
NARCISSISM

THE ERRANT THERAPIST
ON A CHAOTIC QUEST

Peter L. Giovacchini, M.D.

JASON ARONSON INC.
Northvale, New Jersey
London

This book was set in 11 pt. Berling Roman by Alpha Graphics of Pittsfield, NH and printed and bound by Book-mart Press, Inc. of North Bergen, NJ.

Library of Congress Cataloging-in-Publication Data

Giovacchini, Peter L.
    Impact of narcissism / the errant therapist on a chaotic quest /
Peter L. Giovacchini
        p.   cm.
    Includes bibliographical references and index.
    ISBN 0-7657-0234-7
    1. Narcissism. 2. Psychoanalysis. I. Title.
RC553.N36G54 2000
616.89' 17—dc21   99-35668

Printed in the United States of America on acid-free paper. For information and catalog write to Jason Aronson Inc., 230 Livingston Street, Northvale, NJ 07647-1726, or visit our website: www.aronson.com

To Louise, Philip, Sandra, and Daniel

❖ ❖ ❖

Contents

❖ ❖ ❖

Preface

The end of the twentieth century is characterized by the end of many of our cherished beliefs and institutions. It has been a turbulent century, but, at its end, the world is enjoying prosperity.

As Charles Dickens wrote about the era of the French Revolution, it was the best of times and the worst of times. In the United States, we are enjoying the "best of times," but we are surrounded by distrust, hypocrisy, corruption, and a government led by a president who has suffered the disgrace of impeachment. As will be discussed in Chapter 1, moral standards have deteriorated and our culture has become crass and materialistic.

There always have been incidents of immoral behavior and corruption, but, at least during most of the twentieth century, they were not so flagrantly exposed. Today, everything seems to be on the surface. The public revelation of corruption and sexually inappropriate behavior is not accompanied by guilt on the perpetrator's part and, in a short time, the public becomes indifferent. We have become accustomed to what would have been totally unacceptable, outrageous, and shocking during the early parts of the twentieth century.

A statement such as "I am not a crook" by Richard Nixon or Bill Clinton's outrageous sexual conduct initially evoked shock because of the abysmal lack of dignity, among other factors, associated with a high office that is admired and respected.

I bring up these incidents because I wish to explain how psycho-analysis fits in such a context. Lack of guilt and the fact that many events have been publicly aired might indicate that repressive forces are not as operative as they have been in the past and in other cultures, such as the Victorian era.

Psychoanalysis came into existence during Victorian times when hysterical neuroses were commonly encountered. Perhaps there was as much corruption and sexual misconduct then as there is today, but it was kept hidden. The Victorian superego might have been better structured or it was more severe than the typical superego of our modern society. However, in both cultures, hypocrisy abounds.

What was shocking in the past, such as the brutal treatment of children and the outrageous conduct of some of our elected officials, is accepted today with equanimity. For instance, the popularity of our president had never been higher than it was after he was impeached.

What was kept hidden in the past is now being consciously experienced and acted out. If the aim of treatment is to make the unconscious conscious, then in-depth treatment would be superfluous. This would account for some of the confusion about what psychoanalysis is. Delving into a stratified psyche does not often happen in psycho-analytic treatment today, but Freud described it as the essence of his treatment method.

In Chapter 1, I emphasize how such changes affect the status of psychoanalysis, which I often refer to operationally as the intrapsychic focus. Throughout this book, I purposely avoid the word *psychoanalysis*, because psychoanalysis within recent years has been viciously attacked and because of the confusion about what it means. Psychoanalysis is often misunderstood or has been given arbitrary meanings. In addition, some psychoanalysts attack what I am describing as not being psychoanalysis. However, whatever it is called, I am emphasizing the intrapsychic focus, which no longer seems to be in synchrony with our culture. Whether this is an outcome of "the best of times" or "the worse of times" is a debatable issue. Dickens, in *A Tale of Two Cities*, placed his plot in the setting of the French Revolution, a movement that was supposed to achieve "liberty, equality and fraternity." The public, in its desire for revenge and retribution, created a reign of terror that was as tyrannical as the monarchy it overthrew. Has psychoanalysis found itself in the center of a reign of terror?

By asking such a question, I realize that I am indulging in hyperbole. But as societal values change, they do not necessarily change for the better. Perhaps an indicator of better or worse is whether psychoanalysis flourishes or declines with the changes.

This is undoubtedly a biased speculation, but I will pursue it further in a clinical context. Viewing feelings and behavior in terms of an intrapsychic focus constitutes a sensitive, humanistic approach to the study of character. By contrast, the lack of the intrapsychic focus restricts understanding of behavior and psychopathology to the phenomenological level. People are viewed as computerized robots, the product of vague mechanical processes and various genetic constitutions.

The concept of unconscious motivation in some quarters is not only ignored, it is assiduously avoided. In fact, even to suggest that the source of patients' emotional disturbances resides within the psyche is considered offensive and demeaning. Patients are viewed as victims of traumatic infantile environments. Organic factors are also implicated, and the participation of the patient's psyche is vehemently denied.

Besides sociocultural forces, there are other factors that have contributed to the unpopularity of the intrapsychic focus. It is easier to attribute the cause of mental illness to organic factors and neurochemical imbalance. This viewpoint frees caregivers from any responsibility and guilt for the fate of their children. Clinicians do not blame; they simply want to understand the dynamics underlying psychopathology. Nevertheless, parents often feel guilty and will rally around movements that support their need to feel that they had nothing to do with their children's problems. I believe that since the majority of patients seen today have structural defects, due to faulty psychic development, the role of the nurturing sources becomes a major force in determining the type and extent of psychopathology.

This book emphasizes a different outlook regarding the decline of the intrapsychic focus. In Chapters 2 and 3 I stress that, as happened with the Roman Empire, there have been serious internal movements that have had a major impact on the stability of psychoanalysis. One of my purposes in writing this book is to express my dissatisfaction with the direction psychoanalysis has taken as the intrapsychic focus has eroded.

It is difficult to assess how much the attacks on psychoanalysis from scholars outside the profession have generated attacks within the ranks. Attacks from within could be the result of an identification with the aggressor or, in a more scientific context, a recognition of the inadequacies of classical theory and technique to deal with a patient population that has structural defects rather than the problems associated with the psychoneuroses Freud described.

My reactions to classical theory are not entirely negative; rather, they are ambivalent. In this book I point out what I believe are constrictions and rigidities associated with strict Freudian orthodoxy and the quasi-religious esoteric cult that was created by the early adherents of psychoanalysis. In a later chapter, I describe a countertransference reaction as being due to regression to the classical position.

However, I believe some clinicians have thrown out the baby with the bathwater as they have strayed from the basic clinical principles Freud formulated. These therapists undoubtedly believe that their theories represent advances and improvements that are more clinically relevant than orthodox approaches, and in many instances this is true. However, I believe that often so-called innovations represent change for its own sake. Some clinicians seek to change and attack the status quo because of a need to be creative and achieve narcissistic enhancement. I believe that many of the efforts to advance the intrapsychic focus are ill-advised and I refer to them as a "chaotic quest."

This does not mean that there has been no progress made since the early days of psychoanalysis. Quite the contrary, there have been many innovations and improvements in clinical and technical principles. The most important advancements have been made in an object-relations context, an area that has been called object relations theory. Some classifications lead to unnecessary polarizations. For example, Hartmann (1939) introduced the era of ego psychology, but many clinicians then created a clash between id psychology and ego psychology. This divisiveness did have some meaning in determining therapeutic approaches. In the domain of id psychology, the therapist's primary purpose was to explore the contents of the unconscious and convey them to the patient with interpretations. In ego psychology more attention was paid to the understanding of the upper levels of the psyche as they created defenses and adaptations both to the inner and outer worlds.

Although Freud concentrated on what he called the transference neuroses, he was certainly aware that often psychopathology involved the ego and its relationship with the outer world. The whole personality is involved in the therapeutic endeavor, and insights include knowledge about all psychic systems, especially the self representation. Some clinicians believe ego psychology and object relations theory are radically different facets of psychoanalysis that discard Freud's ideas, whereas in actuality they are extensions of his formulations that dealt with a wide variety of topics, discussed as early as 1895 (Breuer and Freud), including transference.

From a therapeutic viewpoint, the transference–countertransference axis has gained prominence. Although Chapter 5 discusses countertransference and Chapter 6 discusses the therapeutic process, in fact every chapter deals with countertransference and to some measure with the therapeutic process. Most clinicians who are dedicated to the intrapsychic focus are aware of the importance of countertransference feelings as they struggle to achieve therapeutic resolution. This often means being honest with ourselves and with our patients. Struggling with such feelings may create disturbances of narcissistic equilibrium that have to be understood in order to make countertransference useful to therapy rather than a hindrance as Freud (1910) postulated.

Freud viewed countertransference as an unwanted and negative response. He suggested that therapists who had countertransference feelings seek further analysis so that the feelings could be eliminated as quickly as possible. Still Freud must not have been too rigid in his opinions. When asked about his self-analysis, he humorously replied that he had to be careful about his countertransference.

The technical handling of countertransference is an involved topic that I discuss in the context of numerous clinical interactions. By examining clinical situations and the transference–countertransference axis, it is possible to extend concepts about the treatment process. The intrapsychic focus is deepened as it is explored in the context of the transference and countertransference elements of the relationship between patient and therapist.

This book could be considered an object relationship perspective of the treatment process. But all levels of the patient's and therapist's personality are operating in a transference–countertransference interaction, which I have called the transference-countertransference axis. I do not believe that this is a different view of the therapeutic relationship, inasmuch as Freud emphasized the importance and central position of the transference. However, at least on occasion, he failed to recognize the transference and most likely was unaware of his countertransference feelings that led to a termination of treatment (Freud 1904), as in the famous Dora case.

The orderly sequence of analyzing from the surface downward is rarely possible in the treatment of patients who seek therapy today. The role of the transference is more important than ever and the countertransference has gained a greater dimension.

The progress that has been made in the technique of treatment can be viewed as a three-dimensional expansion of the understanding of the transference–countertransference relationship rather than as a new paradigm (Kuhn 1962). The "chaotic quest" of the title refers to the seeking of new paradigms, which usually consist of clothing the concept of the transference–countertransference axis in the esoteric wrappings of philosophy. The development of intersubjectivity theory is a prominent example of how such an expansion has been elevated to the level of a new paradigm.

These so-called new approaches have very little clinical data to support their theoretical constructs. In one main instance designed to support the therapeutic superiority of the self-psychological approach, the validity of the data has to be questioned in view of recent revelations. The paucity of relevant databases for many of the technical innovations that I will be discussing is noteworthy. This paucity stands in contrast to Freud, whose writings are replete with case histories. *Studies on Hysteria* (Breuer and Freud 1895) is a series of case histories as well as an extensive theoretical treatise. It is the first thorough and remarkably complete psychoanalytic exposition.

Similarly, this book is also replete with clinical material and there are many similarities between the various case reports and the therapeutic interaction as it is discussed in the context of the transference–countertransference axis. Countertransference is a rich subject that can be looked at from various perspectives that help illuminate subtle treatment interactions. In addition, this book discusses narcissism from a relativistic viewpoint, both culturally and characterologically. Formulations and character assessments often threaten the patient's narcissistic balance. Many patients deny the existence of psychopathology, and what may have been considered psychopathology in one group is an alternative lifestyle in another. For example, homosexuality as a diagnosis or as a manifestation of psychopathology has been removed from the *Diagnostic and Statistical Manual* (*DSM*). Concepts about psychopathology are highly relativistic, but the residual narcissistic components that are associated with various characterological constellations can still cause emotional disruption or overcompensatory stances that may disrupt the world surrounding them.

Even though the homosexual behavior of certain patients is not the therapeutic focus, the accompanying narcissistic conflicts are very much involved in psychopathology and are a subject of treatment. Narcissism plays an increasingly important role as a defensive adaptation and a characterological trait in the various forms of emotional disturbances that confront clinicians. It is also a powerful force that often dominates the treatment interaction and that often threatens both the patient's and the therapist's psychic balance. As counter-transference has been stressed, so has been its narcissistic components.

I also stress the impact of narcissism on the construction of theory and on the fervent attachment of some clinicians to what they consider to be new schools. On occasion such idolatry frequently involves a denunciation of the classical approach in contrast to a fierce attachment to it. Chapter 4 presents clinical material that can be interpreted in radically different fashions, the "correct" one depending on what concepts are fashionable at the moment.

Finally, I discuss narcissism in the context of creativity. Different types of narcissism are embedded in the human character. Commonly, they are associated with psychopathology, but as character traits they may serve many purposes.

The creative act is a narcissistically enhancing activity, and this is one reason that many persons find the act of creating and the creative process fascinating. In the construction of theory, such a narcissistic investment may misfire, as I discuss in this book. I also investigate the various degrees of narcissism involved in some of the characters George Bernard Shaw described as they related to their narcissistic achievements in the plays *Pygmalion*, *Major Barbara*, and *Caesar and Cleopatra*. A special type of narcissism is involved that can be referred to by the oxymoron *humble narcissism*.

This book's consistent focus is on the interplay of narcissism and countertransference, the dominant movement in the therapeutic interaction. This viewpoint can facilitate the resurrection of the intrapsychic focus.

The Decline and Resurrection of the Intrapsychic Focus

To this day, the treatment of patients by the psychoanalytic method, other than those patients considered to have transference neuroses, remains controversial. In fact, the treatment of any patient from the perspective of the intrapsychic focus is also debatable. Although biological psychiatry has become dominant and somewhat successful in the achievement of the elimination of symptoms, there is nevertheless considerable dissatisfaction with the treatment of emotionally disturbed patients, both from the therapist's and the patient's viewpoint.

A young schizoid patient in his mid-twenties lived with an older brother who took care of him. They inherited a modest sum of money that their parents had intended for their children's upkeep, knowing that the children's capacities to care for themselves were limited. This had been a fairly comfortable arrangement until the younger brother had a panic attack, accompanied by threatening voices.

He was hospitalized at the Illinois State Psychiatric Institute and prescribed a new drug that at the time was considered a major breakthrough in psychopharmacology—Thorazine (chlorpromazine). To everyone's delight, it worked. In three days he no longer had auditory hallucinations. Everybody was happy except the patient, but he did not say anything.

After discharge, he came to see me. He appeared calm but subdued and emphasized how miserable he felt. Basically, he missed the voices and wanted them back. Without them he felt he had lost parts of himself, that he was no longer a whole person.

Following his lead, I recommended he discontinue the Thorazine and I set up a four-times-a-week therapy schedule. The voices returned, but rather than persecuting him, they kept him company. He continued in analysis for eight years, at which time he was successfully engaged in theatrical enterprises.

Symptoms are not just bothersome nuisances that have to be eliminated by whatever means available. Rather, they are part of the structure of the personality and patients need them even if they are painful to themselves and more often to others. My patient needed his voices, and when his treatment reached a stage where they were no longer adaptive, he was able to exist without them.

The above treatment occurred before major neurochemical discoveries and drugs reduced mental illness to a chemical imbalance. Computed axial tomography (CAT) scans and other imaging techniques had not yet been invented, and specific genes for particular types of psychopathology had not been identified, and they still have not been discovered. Nevertheless, I recently heard a presentation in Carmel, California, stating that the future of psychiatry is in psychogenetics, and mental illness will be explained by alleles and treatment directed to changing genetic constitutions as well as altering mood states with increasingly sophisticated drugs.

Other than a *DSM-IV* cluster of symptoms, where is the patient? On a consultation at the venerable Menninger Clinic, one of the patients presented to me was taking twelve different drugs over a period of three months. I had no idea how to find the human nidus that was submerged in a primordial, elemental morass, creating a miasma that engulfed all attempts at discovering the troubled person, who must have been buried somewhere in that biochemical bog.

Residencies have emphasized less and less the intrapsychic focus as biological psychiatry has gained increasing prominence. Psychiatry has lost its mind as psychotherapy is occupying less or no time on the teaching schedule.

Psychiatry has undergone many changes in a cyclical course in which it has shifted from biology to psychology in a back and forth fashion. Whatever progress the intrapsychic focus had made at the beginning of the century plummeted when Noguchi discovered the spirochete *Treponema pallidum* as being the causative agent for what had been called general paralysis of the insane (paresis), a condition that filled many beds in mental hospitals and was believed to be another form of psychosis. This discovery proved that these patients were suffering from an organic disorder, syphilis of the brain, and currently such patients are seldom if ever seen. Clinicians more than ever returned to Virchow's concepts of pathology, which stressed that if investigators exerted sufficient effort, eventually a cause within the realm of biology would be found for every disease, including emotional disturbances.

Nevertheless, over the years such enthusiasm waned and the mind was studied in terms of processes rather than exclusively in terms of anatomy, physiology, and neurochemistry. Finally, about twenty years ago, there was another shift back to organicity. The cycle will probably continue, and the intrapsychic focus will again gain ascendancy.

To summarize, prior to World War II, mind and brain were equated. This was followed by a period in which the mind was studied in terms of psychological processes. Now, investigators and clinicians are once again trying to bring mind and brain back together, which means obliterating the mind and creating a mindless society.

I cannot help but compare current training with my residency and many similar ones at the time. The prestige of a residency in post–World War II days was, at least in Chicago, determined by how accessible psychoanalytic training was. Certain residency programs had an agreement with the Chicago Institute for Psychoanalysis, guaranteeing that their residents would be accepted as candidates for analytic training. The highest position a clinician could achieve was to be a certified analyst and then a training and supervisory analyst. In many quarters, such achievement ranked above professorships and certification by the American Board of Psychiatry and Neurology. Although psychoanalysis was not considered by the mainstream of psychoanalysts a suitable method for the treatment of schizophrenia, institutions such as Chestnut Lodge, Austen Riggs, and the Menninger Clinic were held in high esteem because if they did not exactly practice psychoanalysis, their treatment philosophies were based on psychoanalytic principles.

THE GOLDEN ERA OF PSYCHOANALYSIS
AND SOCIETAL FACTORS

This postwar period was the golden era of psychoanalysis, as the discipline seemed to emerge and spring free from the previous rejection and skepticism aimed at it. It seemed liberated from the ambivalence that had shackled it.

The rise of psychoanalysis is an interesting phenomenon. In my undergraduate psychology classes, it was reviled for being unscientific and an elaborate fantasy springing from Freud's sexually obsessed mind to explain bizarre behavior that could be easily understood by theories that dealt with conditioned behavior, not necessitating the fanciful formulations of unconscious mental processes.

Our society had been in the midst of the Depression, from which it was gradually emerging. Then Hitler dominated the world scene, eventually acquainting us with horrors that we could not have possibly imagined. The world that we finally saw as a result of the war went against the grain of human feelings, compassion, and concern for the welfare and well-being of our fellow men. The European scene shattered all moral standards and created a world in which kindness and charity did not exist, and love, for the most part, had been reduced to manipulative materialism. We were faced with the shocking realization that a world based on cruelty, bestiality and ruthless narcissism was not only possible, but in fact existed.

This was the soil from which the popularity of psychoanalysis sprang. Why it emerged and flourished in what was, in essence, a posttraumatic war environment, is an interesting question. It has implications for the future of the intrapsychic focus as it is relevant to an interpersonally based therapy aimed at psychic synthesis and development, and the integration and maturation of our culture as it impacts on the inner world of the psyche.

There is a reciprocal relationship between the environment and the acceptance of the intrapsychic focus, each shaping the other, optimally in a positive feedback sequence. The two, however, do not exist in a closed system. A multiplicity of variables can change cultural factors as well as attitudes about the treatment of mental illness. Psychoanalysis has approached the brink of the precipice of self-destruction as it became a tyrant in the posttraumatic world that spawned it, a posttraumatic world that followed the cruel, narcissistic world of unrelenting totalitarianism.

In the meantime, the surrounding culture has changed considerably and is different from the society that greeted our returning war veterans, many becoming our future psychoanalysts.

RIGIDITY OF THE CLASSICAL POSITION: CHANGING CULTURAL SCENE AND THE CLINICIAN'S DILEMMA

As occurs with all movements, there were countermovements. The Chicago Institute for Psychoanalysis, for example, extended its focus to psychosomatic problems (Alexander 1961) and the modification of therapeutic technique in order to shorten the treatment process (Alexander and French 1946). These movements met with considerable opposition and only served to increase the rigidity of so-called classical analysis (Weber 1956). The politics of psychoanalysis became increasingly complicated and convoluted, both within its ranks and in clashes with other disciplines dealing with mental phenomena and health. It seems that psychoanalysis had created for itself a microcosm patterned after the turbulent chaotic situations that our nation and allies fought to destroy. Such comparisons are risky and simplistic, but similarities between the conflicted culture from which psychoanalysis became popular and the various degenerative changes that took place within it afterward are noteworthy. They indicate that adaptive defensive mechanisms, in this instance identification with the aggressor (A. Freud 1936), can be applied to groups and institutions, such as psychoanalysis, as well as to persons (Freud 1921).

Freud could not be challenged or criticized. The bearded, cigar-smoking analysts who sought shelter on our shores to escape and survive the brutality and madness of Hitler's paranoia in turn created their own icon—Freud and his writings. To a milder degree, they treated both the young neophytes and the young Turks in a similar way to how they had been persecuted in Europe (Weber 1956), but they had been, for the most part, able to escape the horrors of the Holocaust.

Classical analysis could not hold the Freudian edifice together for many reasons, but the main one was that it was clinically too narrow. Young therapists found Freud's ideas compelling and brilliant, especially the concept of unconscious motivation, which can be extended from the individual patient to society in general. Freud's (1911–1914) recommendations about technique were also appealing, but the types of patients Freud wrote about were rarely seen (Reichard 1956).

The relationship between the shape of the surrounding world and therapeutic approaches needs further exploration. The manifestations of psychopathology had changed in the postwar period and have continued to change. No longer do clinicians see the clear-cut transference neuroses (Freud 1914a) described with circumscribed anxiety, phobias, and obsessive-compulsive symptoms. Rather, patients complain of their lack of purpose, feelings of alienation, and existential anxiety.

As the years have gone by, patients' descriptions of their early environment became more and more horrible, brutal, and sexually and physically assaultive. They are punctuated with shocking and unspeakably cruel experiences. These infantile environments that lack boundaries, compassion, and decency come to our attention during an era in which the intrapsychic focus has been abandoned. This is a paradox, an ironic one, because it would seem obvious that the cataclysmic, violent, irrational behaviors clinicians encounter cannot be understood on a phenomenological level because they make no sense. They should be explored and understood in terms of irrational unconscious factors. Yet the only method we have to achieve such insights has been denigrated and abandoned, and this has happened principally among psychiatrists.

It is true that much of what Freud has written is anachronistic in the face of the clinical problems that confront mental health workers. Analyzing the return of the repressed seems almost farcical when the character disorders and psychoses commonly seen would imply that some repression would be helpful in making behavior manageable. Nevertheless, investigators have to look beneath the surface and try to make sense of what is going on within the psyche.

Society does not care about unconscious motivation. It seems to have regressed to a concrete, crass, materialistic orientation that seeks simple linear etiological sequences. Everything is reified and whatever happens is attributed to an outside source.

Psychiatry does not care to know anything about patients except their biological constitutions. This is similar to blaming outside sources in that explanations are outside the psychic sphere, and personal responsibility for the difficulties patients suffer is abnegated.

Though psychotherapists do not wish to blame anyone, they want to focus on salient experiences that are instrumental in shaping the personality. They wish to study a process in a nonjudgmental fashion. Caregivers, on the other hand, find it easier to believe that some factor outside their relationship with their children is the cause of mental illness. I recall that in one of the first movements promulgating an organic etiology for childhood autism, groups of parents banded together to insist to themselves and the world that they were not to blame for their children's plight. Their problems were the outcome of organic factors for which they were not responsible.

These movements are characteristic of concretely minded societies and persons. Psychiatrists are also members of and influenced by the social-cultural milieu they live in, and it is understandable that they bring their cultural heritage into their professional lives. Cultural heritage, in turn, reinforces the surrounding world's bias, a feedback moving further and further away from humanistic, empathic concerns that are the essence of the intrapsychic focus.

I believe this is where we stand today—a society that was formed after being subjected to the traumatic threat of being enslaved and that bears the imprint of posttraumatic stress. Under these traumatic conditions culture as well as the mind exteriorizes in order to deny responsibility for what occurs. The interpersonal factor, constructive or destructive, has been minimized and trivialized, its significance denied. This is absurd, ironic, and incredible, a travesty assaulting any vestige of rationality, in view of the incest, sadistic abuse, and all the other horrors our patients seemed to have suffered during childhood. These early assaults are irrelevant, as we search for genes we have never found and chemical processes that cannot consistently explain and ameliorate the course of mental illness.

MULTIPLE PERSPECTIVES AND MENTAL PHENOMENA

I am not denying that biological psychiatry and the neurosciences have much to contribute to our understanding of the human condition. In fact, Freud himself (1914b, 1940) predicted that we could discover cogent issues about mental events at the chemical level. He began his career in the laboratory, and early on he wrote a treatise describing the mental apparatus in a neurological context (Freud 1895). However, he found it difficult to continue in that direction and switched to a purely psychological perspective.

I believe that his masterpiece, *The Interpretation of Dreams* (Freud 1900), demonstrates this shift as he de-emphasizes linear stimulus–response models, such as his "picket fence" model, and focuses on the intricacies of the primary process and secondary revision as they become fundamental to a hierarchal model of the mind that acquired its final form when he proposed the structural hypothesis (Freud 1923, Giovacchini 1979, 1998).

It is important that mental phenomena be pursued from various frames of reference, but this does not mean that clinicians give up understanding their patients as sensitive persons who are immersed in misery, and that their aberrant behavior and symptoms have meaning and adaptive features and are not simply the products of chaotic neurological degradation, as some extremist laboratory scientists have described dreams. Whatever discoveries are made, it is vital that practitioners maintain an intrapsychic focus, and concentrate on unconscious motivations, which simply means that we are dealing with people and not just complicated anatomy, mysterious chemical processes, and inordinately complex genetic constitutions.

The philosophers give man a soul in order to elevate him above just a concatenation of matter and energy. Similarly, our patients have minds that are more than just the sum of their parts. The mind is a supraordinate phenomenon that transcends its organic constituents. Psychiatry has to regain the mind it has lost, and the discoveries that are rapidly accumulating will be more meaningful and enriching.

The resurrection of the intrapsychic focus infuses humanism into scientific creativity, humanism that in my mind is intrinsic to creative activity (Giovacchini 1960, 1993) and broadens the scientific outlook as well as the attitudes of the surrounding world. In contrast, there is a negative feedback produced by the reciprocal interaction of organically oriented mental health workers, primarily psychiatrists, and a concrete, mechanistic, and frequently sadistic external milieu. The reintroduction of the intrapsychic focus could lead to a mutually beneficial relationship between the harmony of the mind and a society that enriches the mind. The mind, in turn, playfully and creatively moves into the external world, enhancing itself and discovering hidden elements of reality that serve to expand both object relations and environmental perspectives.

I have emphasized various polarities, primarily the world of the mind and concrete mechanistic orientations, but there are no villains. There are just trends in human nature that over time tend to repeat themselves.

CONFLICT ABOUT AND RESISTANCE TO THE INTRAPSYCHIC FOCUS

Resistance to the intrapsychic focus does not just come from organicists and a materialistic environment. In my early days as a practitioner, I encountered a similar resistance from mentors and some colleagues to conducting psychodynamically oriented therapy, in a more or less classical fashion, for the treatment of patients suffering from characterological problems and schizophrenia (Boyer and Giovacchini 1967, 1980). Those patients were not examples of the transference neuroses Freud described. Clinicians espousing the intrapsychic focus considered it heresy if young therapists attempted to expand the indications for psychoanalytic treatment (Stone 1963). Only such institutions as Chestnut Lodge and therapists with the reputation of Frieda Fromm-Reichmann (1950, 1959) were accepted, because they used the psychoanalytic method for the treatment of patients suffering from structural defects.

From a theoretical viewpoint, even the concept of structural defects was called into question. Most patients were formulated in terms of clashing intrapsychic forces, and structure was pushed into the background, although Freud (1923) had postulated the structural hypothesis. It was somewhat of a turning point in psychoanalysis, one that had been initially vigorously resisted, when the importance of the economic hypothesis was diminished and the structural hypothesis gained prominence (see Kardiner et al. 1959). Nevertheless, there is still resistance to the decathexis of the energic viewpoint, which is attached to purely psychodynamic explanations (Arlow and Brenner 1964).

I am conjecturing that the demise of the intrapsychic focus was not first caused by external factors, such as hard-core scientists. Perhaps, more important, psychoanalysts and practitioners in related disciplines have to look in their own house to determine how much their rigidity, narcissism, and iconoclastic attachment to Freud have led them on a self-destructive course. The rigidity of the establishment was prominent, especially during the years it had great prominence and the movement had reached its apogee.

Although I believe there is, to a small degree, a reactive resurrection of the intrapsychic focus, today there are counterforces that are making it again difficult to reestablish a psychological foothold for the treatment of emotionally disturbed patients. In this instance, the politics and narcissism of those espousing the psychodynamic approach are the main factors that interfere with the growth of a theoretical system and a treatment discipline. Some groups of psychologists and social workers adhering to what they consider to be theories that have progressed beyond Freud have become even more rigid and arbitrary than the cigar-smoking analysts who carried the Freudian banner to the main cities in our country. Again, the politics of psychoanalytic institutes and institutions, and the narcissism of adherents to a particular viewpoint, such as self psychology (Kohut 1971, 1977) and intersubjectivity (Stolorow et al. 1994), have led to continuous and shameful internecine warfare. Thus, the problems facing the resurrection of the intrapsychic focus are both internal and external.

Every science has to progress if it is going to survive. Even in psychoanalysis's heyday, it became obvious that clinicians had to move beyond Freud's recommendations about the indications of treatment, which had to be relinquished if clinicians wanted to maintain their identity as psychoanalysts. The patients Freud allowed them to treat were rarely or never seen, so young clinicians had to learn to treat patients who came to them. Furthermore, they had to modify their conceptual system and expand their therapeutic range. From a broader viewpoint, therapeutic necessity forced an issue, that of moving clinically beyond Freud's orthodoxy, something I believe Freud would have welcomed, and this would represent the progress psychoanalysis needed in order to survive.

I believe the prospect of treating severely disturbed patients (Akhtar 1992, Almond 1995, Giovacchini 1979, 1997, Grotstein 1993, Modell 1990, Searles 1965, 1986, Volkan 1995) created a hopeful, sanguine atmosphere that went along with the popularity of psychoanalysis, which would have most likely plummeted more quickly and precipitously if it had remained totally immersed in the stodgy, religious atmosphere of reactionary Freudian disciples.

This expansion of the psychoanalytic method to the treatment of patients who could not be categorized as transference neuroses began in psychodynamically oriented hospital wards and such institutions as the Menninger Clinic, Austen Riggs, and Chestnut Lodge.

Some of the residents trained in such settings, I concluded, brought this broader orientation to the treatment of patients in their office practice. It is perhaps ironic that one of the best descriptions of the in-depth therapy of a patient diagnosed as schizophrenic was not written by the therapist but by the patient herself. In Joanne Greenberg's (Hannah Green) book *I Never Promised You a Rose Garden*, the therapist is Dr. Frieda Fromm-Reichmann, a warm, sensitive, intuitive pioneer who was not afraid to use her psychoanalytic expertise for the treatment of severely disturbed patients.

The detailed account of the treatment of a 16-year-old patient who had been diagnosed as schizophrenic was written by the patient herself (Greenberg 1964) . This is a remarkable feat, because not only does the author write about her experiences within the treatment, she also gives comprehensive descriptions and sensitive evaluations about the character and motivations of those persons who were emotionally meaningful to her. She is writing both as a talented writer and as a skilled observer about psychopathology and its causes. Many of her insights were derived from her treatment, and she demonstrated the power of the intrapsychic focus and how she embraced it, a truly monumental achievement, which should serve as a hopeful example for professionals involved in treatment and striving to achieve similar goals.

The new wave of therapists who started their practice after they had completed their training shortly after the ending of World War II accepted for treatment most of the patients who sought appointments. Many of them did not think in terms of indications and contraindications or diagnosis; if the patient could automatically walk into the consultation room, even if he had been dragged to the waiting room, that was considered to be sufficient motivation to make the intrapsychic focus a feasible therapeutic approach. Perhaps being dragged to the waiting room is somewhat of an exaggeration, but therapists did not let rigid and established conceptual systems stand in their way of embarking upon a therapeutic journey. Their attitudes were open, and they started treatment with the spirit of hopeful expectation and curiosity.

There was reciprocity in the patient population. I recall many patients calling for their first appointment telling me that they wanted to be analyzed rather than dwelling on their symptoms. Patients complained of general and vague issues, such as feeling alienated, not knowing who they were, and finding no purpose in their lives. They seemed to be having existential problems as highlighted by Gauguin's nine-foot painting in the Boston Museum of Fine Arts with the title *Where Do I Come From, Who Am I and Where Am I Going?* Today, patients still have vague symptoms, but they seldom ask for analysis. Instead, they seek immediate relief and do not take much, if any, responsibility for their emotional dilemmas.

During the decade following World War II, patients tended to be introspective and intrigued with unconscious motivation and intrapsychic factors. The culture was, in general, less materialistic than current society whose values involve being glued to television and watching violent, erotic action movies. That early childhood experiences were influential in shaping the personality and in the production of psychopathology seemed self-evident to both therapists and patients. This etiological connection has been frequently denied or diminished today by many mental health workers.

Several decades ago, although patients openly sought psychoanalytic treatment and were unconsciously committed to the intrapsychic perspective, there were some patients who had to deny such an interest at the conscious level. I believe this is an important observation, because it may be another area that can help explain some of the factors involved in the decline of the intrapsychic focus and perhaps open paths for its resurrection.

The resistance to psychoanalysis, that is, to introspection and the concept of unconscious motivation, can be viewed as a phenomenon that stems from different types of personality organizations. In some instances, such antagonism may be part of a characterological constellation, a rigid personality that is not capable of looking inward. This could be akin to a constitutional defect, or, to explain it from a psychodynamic perspective, a reaction to a severe traumatizing infantile milieu that led to developmental fixations and constrictions.

Clinicians have learned that although the manifestations of psychopathology have changed over time and may have been culturally determined, the underlying structure and dynamics have not changed that much from Freud's era to our own (Reichard 1956). This could mean that in many instances, concrete materialistic attitudes are not necessarily deeply and rigidly ingrained as inflexible characterological defensive constellations. They may be surface defensive adaptations that are not fundamental qualities of character structure and the self representation.

If resistance to the intrapsychic focus is part of a psychodynamic constellation rather than a rigid characterological constriction, the prognosis for in-depth therapy would be improved and every successfully treated patient who embraced the analytic process would help create a weltanschauung that would be more propitious to humanistic values and endeavors.

I saw a patient many years ago when the intrapsychic focus was very popular.

The patient, a single professional man in his mid-thirties, was literally sentenced to psychoanalytic treatment. A detective in a public restroom who had been planted there to entrap homosexuals had arrested him. The patient approached him and was immediately taken to jail.

The judge felt somewhat protective toward him. He saw an intelligent, well-bred, and educated person before him and did not want to ruin him, especially career-wise. In those days, homosexuals remained in the closet, and the public revelation of their sexual orientation could be disastrous. The judge, like many professionals, had been analyzed, and he put the patient on probation if the young man sought professional help. The patient could do nothing but accept this condition, and that is how he happened to become my patient. At first, he seemed resentful of being coerced into treatment.

Nevertheless, he kept his appointments and was never late. He talked freely, and although he was reluctant to enter certain areas of his life, he seemed to be psychologically minded. His initial resentment and resistance to being in therapy were no longer evident.

Throughout the course of treatment, he revealed a passive homosexual relationship toward his father with some sadistic elements.

He found it difficult to directly ask his father for anything, because if he did, he would be violently reprimanded and sometimes beaten. Several days later, however, his father would give him a present, but never what he asked for. For example, if the patient asked for a baseball bat, his father would give him a pair of roller skates.

As he grew older, the patient became quite skillful in predicting how his father would react. He learned not to ask for what he wanted. He would purposely ask his father for something he did not want. As usual, his request would be angrily rejected, but then his father would buy him what he really wanted.

His resistance to being analyzed was similar to not asking for what he wanted. He very much desired to be analyzed, which meant being understood and relating to someone, something he had never experienced in childhood except in the devious way he manipulated his father. It may seem uncanny to believe that he manipulated the judge in a similar fashion, but the patient was convinced that he did. He wanted to be "forced" into being analyzed, something he did not dare to ask for directly.

Perhaps segments of our culture have a similar type of resistance to the intrapsychic focus. Underneath a surface concreteness, there may be a capacity for psychological mindedness that is waiting to be released. In this chapter I have stressed crass materialism and violence. However, every movement generates a countermovement, as Hegel (1801) postulated in his dialectic.

The Many Faces of the Errant Therapist on a Quixotic Quest

Was Don Quixote an example of a narcissistic character disorder? Certainly he set himself high goals and had a grandiose attitude about his talents and prowess. His ambition was to change the world, rescue maidens in distress, and achieve the highest levels of chivalry. He did not succeed in his pathetic efforts to accomplish heroic feats that would bring him glory and honor. No, he did not fulfill the "impossible dream."

Don Quixote's narcissism may strike us as arrogant, but nevertheless our compassion is stirred, and at the end of Cervantes's novel, the reader feels affectionate sorrow for the defeated, misguided, clumsy adventurer. His narcissism is a thin mantle that barely covers a frail torso.

Don Quixote's fantasies and behavior are so outlandish that they might cause him to be labeled as psychotic. To put it in more human terms, however, he presents himself as an odd character full of lofty ambitions and ideals, that is, an inadequate misfit, unable to adapt himself to the world he lives in. He is similar to the borderline character Adler (1983), Boyer (1983), Kernberg (1975), Kernberg et al. (1987), Masterson (1976), Searles (1986), and I (Giovacchini 1979, 1997) have written about.

Briefly, I view the borderline patient as having a type of character disorder. Character disorders are the outcome of defects in structure, distinguished from the psychoneuroses, which emphasize internal conflicts recognizable by the symptoms they produce. Whether the latter exist or are abundant is a question that is not particularly relevant in this context.

The character neuroses, however, are commonly seen, perhaps the product of our culture, as discussed in Chapter 1. Rather than being understood as the outcome of clashing inner forces, which would involve theoretical constructions based on the energic hypotheses, these conditions and their ego defects can be viewed as disturbances between the ego and its executive system and the exigencies of the outer world.

Borderline patients, who have been widely written about but poorly understood, are borderline in two ways. They can easily move back and forth between a psychosis and, instead of a neurosis I prefer to a state, a relatively stable organization, in which reality testing is basically intact (Kernberg 1975). Just as important is the borderline's inability to cope with reality, as Don Quixote demonstrated, that is, to have the psychic equipment that enables the patient to meet both inner needs and the demands of the outer world. As one of my borderline patients aptly put it, he was trying to deal with a world of calculus complexity with just an arithmetic mentality.

In patients with structural defects, narcissism plays a greater role than in the so-called psychoneuroses. In our era, Narcissus has, indeed, replaced Oedipus. Don Quixote dealt with his alienation and failure to integrate himself with his current milieu by moving up into a grandiose world of his own creation, a narcissistic aggrandizement that included his self-image and external objects. At the end of the novel, when he is forced to confront reality, which means to recognize himself as he basically is and the real world as shorn of his narcissistic enhancements, and, for example, his beloved Dulcinea is what she always was, a whore, he dies. It is interesting that his narcissistic defenses were shattered when he was forced to view himself in mirrors that rejected his projections, thereby reflecting his basic personality.

Don Quixote's pilgrimage and journey can be viewed as a therapeutic endeavor (trips in dreams frequently refer to the treatment process) but he does not stop or limit himself to the achievement of autonomy. The "impossible dream" is impossible because he is pulling himself up by his bootstraps, an impossible task even in conditions of extraordinary strength, and Don Quixote and our patients are enfeebled to begin with. The impossible dream cannot be fulfilled by the "impossible profession" (Freud 1933).

If Don Quixote's quest for chivalry was a therapeutic endeavor, it is obvious that it was misguided and self-defeating, and once again, narcissism was the villain, if villains are necessary, and for our knight-errant they were. Unfortunately, he did not have a mentor, as Dante had his Virgil in his journey into the depths of Hell or various levels of the unconscious. Don Quixote emphasized, however, that any self-healing process requires interactions with the outer world, or more precisely, therapy has to be object directed.

The treatment of patients with character defects is directed to the achievement of maximum autonomy, and they learn to be comfortable with both the outer world of reality and the inner world of the psyche. As therapy becomes more object directed, our theoretical foundations for the understanding of psychopathology and the therapeutic process are based on an object-relations perspective.

Theoretical shifts have to follow clinical conditions. This would seem to be a logical sequence, one stating the obvious scientific maxim, that theory has to follow and conform to the data. Though most theoretical systems have encompassed in a wide sense an object-oriented perspective, they have not necessarily followed the data that our patients present.

Don Quixote tried to create a world that had long ago ceased to exist. He had to move from his reality to one of the past, and his journey consisted of a series of humiliations.

Is something similar happening to the intrapsychic focus? Psychiatry has left the world of mental processes to that of neurochemistry, genetics, and other biological areas. Those who continue espousing the intrapsychic focus are also moving in different areas, which I will soon discuss, but many therapists have moved into areas that do not belong in the clinical arena, similarly to Don Quixote, who had to move outside the world he lived in.

NEW DIRECTIONS AND CHANGES

Grinker (1975) some years ago wrote that psychiatry was riding wildly in many directions. He was referring mainly to the psychopharmacological revolution I discussed in Chapter 1. But he was also aware of the wider implications of the changes in theoretical orientations on concepts about mental phenomena and the treatment of psychopathology. He did not believe that all the changes that were occurring were beneficial or that they would lead to any stabilization for the field of psychiatry. Wandering off in different directions, as Don Quixote did, in the long run accomplished very little, if anything.

Thompson (1994) reminds us that the Latin word *errare* means wandering from the main path. In some instances, this could be considered a creative achievement, transcending accepted beliefs and moving into and exploring new realms and novel vistas. This is what the knight-errant strives for.

Thompson also states that to wander from the path also means to be lost without knowing it. Here *errare* assumes its common meaning of "to err," and the quest of the knight-errant is ill-advised and fanciful but not necessarily bound to fail. The intensity of narcissistic commitment is a basic element in the determination of the outcome.

Heidegger (1977) believes that errors are the outcome of a stubborn commitment to a system of thought or a modus operandi. He states, "Error is not just an isolated mistake but rather the realm (the domain) of the history of those entanglements if all kinds of erring get interwoven" (p. 136). As Freud (1933) remarked, philosophers are hard to understand (perhaps obscurity and convolution is an intrinsic element of philosophical discourse). Heidegger, in his own way, is emphasizing that the seeking of new creative dimensions can lead to the belief that something new has been created, whereas in reality, the investigator has stripped what has been conceptually useful of any meaning.

The treatment process is designed to seek the truth, not necessarily the objective or historical truth that Spence (1982) wrote about. He emphasized narrative truth. Rather, what patients present as irrational and inchoate is subjected to examination, and as it is considered in terms of unconscious processes, meaning is ascribed to what at first appears to be meaningless. Deconstruction reverses this process and makes what was thought to be meaningful into a subjective, nonvalid experience.

Some neuroscientists have joined the ranks of the postmodern group as they assert that dreams and in many instances symptoms are the waste products of neurological degradation, and therefore meaningless. Their purpose, rich symbolism, and connections with past and current experiences are entirely missed. These scientists pay no attention to the content of patients' fantasies and dreams.

For example, a 6-year-old boy was the subject of a clinical presentation in a course in preparation for the American Boards of Psychiatry. He was diagnosed with an obsessive-compulsive disorder. His chief symptom consisted of tying his shoelaces dozens of times a day, which was disconcerting because of the inordinate amount of time that was involved in such apparently meaningless activity. Also, because of this behavior, his hands were becoming chafed and he was developing a serious and painful skin condition.

The clinical discussion revolved around the elimination of symptoms. The consultants reviewed what drugs might be appropriate, ranging from Ritalin to anxiolytic agents to selective serotonin reuptake inhibitors (SSRIs). There was also considerable discussion about diagnosis, obsessive-compulsive disorder being foremost in their thinking, but as good physicians they had to include other conditions in their differential diagnosis such as Asperger's syndrome and Pervasive Developmental Disorder. The prescription of Ritalin was based on the possibility of Attention Deficit Hyperactivity Disorder, although there was little evidence of attention deficit or hyperactivity.

The point is that no effort was made to understand the meaning of the symptoms because these psychiatrists never considered that they had any meaning, or at least they acted as if they had no meaning.

The symptoms simply represented phenomenological clusters that could be stamped by a diagnostic label and then a drug that is associated with that label could be administered.

It is ironic that although clinicians attempt to find a drug of choice, often drugs from various categories are selected and the therapy is a shotgun treatment. Efforts to follow the medical model or to be scientific often miss the obvious, but to do otherwise would require some attempt to get to know the patient.

The father of the shoelace-tying patient was a surgeon, and while operating he frequently tied sutures. His son believed that if he did not tie shoelaces, people would die. It is disconcerting that the connection between the patient's frenetic activity and the father's suturing incisions and thus saving lives was not noted; its significance was totally missed.

A psychodynamically oriented therapist would immediately recognize, from a phenomenological and an intrapsychic level, that the behavior of the father and son is similar and that the latter is a symbolic representation of the former. Of the various psychic mechanisms, certainly identification is involved. To go beyond the formulation would be speculative, since there is no further information that would help in this endeavor.

Such information, however, would be easy to obtain simply by getting a history about the development of the symptoms and investigating the infantile environment, especially the relationship between the father and son. Therapy would then not deal with elimination of symptoms, as happened with the patient discussed in Chapter 1, who missed his auditory hallucinations, but with underlying conflicts and anxiety, especially as they related to the father. Optimally, this boy might acquire a stable identity sense and self-esteem enabling him to relate to his inner feelings and relations with the outer world with harmony and equanimity.

This is another example of how two different clinical approaches clash. Perhaps the psychodynamic and the psychopharmacological approach in this clinical example cannot be reconciled, but with other patients these approaches can be cooperative endeavors. This child could be threatened by therapists who strive to eliminate his symptoms, as was true of the patient discussed in Chapter 1. Unconsciously or even consciously, this child may have experienced a medical approach as intrusive and unempathic, complicating the illness by introducing iatrogenic factors. If clinicians are oblivious of psychodynamic factors, they cannot understand the patient's resistance to their curative efforts. In this sense, they are similar to Don Quixote, who has a constricted view of reality and of the outcome of inner needs, but in the case of the psychopharmacologist, there is a similar constriction due to a strict adherence to a biologically oriented system of thought.

I can anticipate a counterargument that makes a similar point about a blind overevaluation of essentially meaningless fantasies. It is hard to believe, however, that the son's behavior was unrelated to his father, and that the apparent similarities are coincidental and meaningless. Similarly, there may be a connection between an infantile environment characterized by rape, incest, and physical abuse and the later violent, disruptive, self-destructive, and self-mutilating behavior of the patient who has been subjected to these horrible conditions.

The postmodern analyst could argue that Don Quixote's behavior was meaningless and find him easy to deconstruct. The knight-errant's orientation was based purely on his constructions and subjectivity. This could lead to the generalization that all mental phenomena are meaningless.

This attitude is bizarre for those espousing the intrapsychic focus, but it is more prevalent among those who consider themselves analysts than I had ever suspected. At a recent meeting of Division 39 of the American Psychological Association in Boston, many of the sessions were directed to a discussion of postmodernism and how it fit with a theory of the mind. Many of the participants were dedicated to the idea that beliefs are constructed and subjective, and therefore suspect and not valid. This philosophy, for that is essentially what it is, seems to apply mainly to mental phenomena and not organic and biological constructs, which may be why it is consciously or unconsciously embraced by organicists.

The conclusion is that there is no objective truth. This could mean that there is no reality, an absurd assertion for a clinician. This would lead to the destruction of the scientific outlook, as will soon be discussed. Furthermore, the dictum that there is no objective truth is a paradox. If the statement that there is no objective truth is an objective truth, then it contradicts the general issue about the nonexistence of truth. It is, in fact, the same as the liar paradox, which deals with the statement, "I am a liar." If he is telling the truth, he cannot be a liar and if he is lying he is telling the truth. Bertrand Russell, in his theory of classes, distinguishes a statement from a statement about statements. This equivalence between a statement regarding objective truth and the liar was brought to my attention by a patient.

Without objective truth, therapy would also be impossible, because there would be no distinction between the inner and outer world, as may happen in psychosis. There would be no points of reference that could contrast mental events with the stable configurations of reality.

Truth deals with and is a characteristic and a quality of language. If a word construction is true, it is consistent with things and occurrences that exist in contrast to imagination, fantasy, and fabrication. If truth and reality are not the same, they are nevertheless interrelated and cannot exist without each other.

Truth is relative and dependent on position and motion, as Einstein discovered. The intersubjectivists would agree, but truth has to be based on a reality that has a degree of internal consistency. The perception of reality is evolving and expanding, but in therapy it has to serve as an anchor so that the participants do not get swallowed in each other's subjectivity.

PHILOSOPHERS AT THE GATE

As the Roman Empire expanded its borders and the scope of its influence, it gradually became vulnerable to barbaric hordes that eventually destroyed it. There were "barbarians at the gate," but within the gate was a civilization that was crumbling because of corruption and debilitating forces that were weakening its inner structure. With some modifications, the decline of the intrapsychic focus can be viewed in a similar manner.

Internal dissension and narcissism weakened the internal structure and influence of the psychodynamic position. At the same time, external factors such as technological advances and the changing culture pounded away at the gates of the empire that an elitist group tried to control.

As frequently happens in these circumstances, idols crumble, and in this instance the scapegoat was Freud. Clinicians and nonclinical devotees of the intrapsychic focus left the ranks and became opponents by attacking the Freudian edifice, beginning with the energic hypotheses and instinct theory. Scholars in related areas joined these former analysts in trying to bring psychoanalysis to its knees. Finally, it almost became fashionable to attack the master and to reject his ideas as anachronistic and self-serving. Today, most of us acknowledge that ad hominem arguments are a travesty of scientific discourse, but they have been particularly abundant within psychoanalytic organizations and among those who have attacked them.

The younger generation, that is, one or two generations following the European analysts who fled Nazi tyranny, maintained their devotion to the basic principles of unconscious motivation and the intrapsychic focus. However, they needed new systems, partly because of rebellious thinking that was to some measure justified in view of the arrogant intractability of their mentors. They wanted to move from a Newtonian overview into the more rarefied realm of Einstein and quantum theory in order to keep up with modern views and to defend themselves against the adherents of what was called the classical position, which included psychoanalysis in general. The young Turks partly rejected Freud and replaced him with new paradigms. Undoubtedly, the need for new conceptual systems was also the outcome of narcissistic needs, a thread that is found in all the movements within the mental health community.

Clinicians found Freudian classical theory to be inadequate for the treatment of patients who sought their services. If new paradigms are to be sought, it would be expected they would be clinically useful, that they would be designed to help the practitioner the next morning when he saw his first patient.

The intrapsychic focus is a powerful treatment perspective, and conceptual systems should be designed to stress the therapeutic interaction. The language of theory has to be explicitly related to what is happening in the consultation room. Although metapsychology is somewhat removed from clinical data, it can be traced back to lower levels of abstraction until formulations refer to transference-counter-transference phenomena.

Most of the new theories have very little clinical relevance and although some of them, such as intersubjectivity, purport to focus upon the clinical interaction, the concepts upon which they are based come from philosophers who have been associated with the existential school, from Husserl's phenomenology to Heidegger's existentialism, although Heidegger objected to being labeled an existentialist. Furthermore, some of the writings of the exponents of the intersubjectivity school, especially those of Stolorow, are couched in a lofty, esoteric, obscure style that could be mistaken for philosophy. Obscurity and convoluted rambling Germanic sentences are also true of Kohut's writing, which can be considered to be an older new school.

The first major extension of Freud's ideas merely involved a shift of emphasis. Instead of focusing exclusively on inner conflicts in the intrapsychic realm, transactions and conflicts with the outer world achieved greater importance. As has been true of all changes and supposed innovations, there was considerable opposition to the proponents of this viewpoint, which was essentially an object relations approach. Horney (1937, 1942), who was the leader of a subgroup of this movement, resigned from the establishment and started her own group (Paris 1994). Again, narcissism seems to have been a stronger factor than scientific considerations.

This shift had to occur because of the changing patient population. Our patients could be better understood in terms of structural defects rather than internal psychodynamic conflicts. The Oedipus complex receded into the background as existential problems and inability to cope with the demands of the world were more frequently seen. The identity sense or self representation and its cohesion became increasingly meaningful in our attempts to understand and treat patients.

Horney (1942) was an early proponent of the object relations approach, and Winnicott (1958a, 1974), who was also initially vigorously resisted, carried it further from a developmental viewpoint and in the treatment context. His developmental impetus and the concept of the holding environment represent major clinical advances. Object relations theory has helped explain many clinical phenomena and developmental processes (e.g., Fairbairn 1941, 1954, Grotstein and Rinsley 1994).

Freud (1911–1914) pointed out that the superstructures of theory could be easily replaced as new discoveries required a modified conceptual scaffold. The basic tenets of the intrapsychic focus, however, remain the same, that is, psychic determinism and unconscious motivation. These tenets meet the fundamental principles of science as D'Abro (1951) outlined them. He emphasized that science is a method, a way of looking at phenomena, and that it rests on only two assumptions: (1) that there is a world (that we are not just the products of solipsism); and (2) that this world is knowable, that it functions on the basis of certain laws, and that there are uniformities that are capable of being discovered. The investigators of intrapsychic phenomena make two similar assumptions: (1) that there is an inner world (the world of the unconscious); and (2) that it is knowable, and that it also functions according to certain laws. I believe this is all the philosophy we need, the philosophy of science.

Many therapists, however, do not find the formulation and expansion of clinically oriented concepts sufficiently enhancing and turn to more esoteric systems of thought, primarily based on philosophical principles. Postmodernism and deconstruction have not achieved the status of a school, at least not yet, although some therapists might argue this point. Spezzano (1993) believes that being aware of our uncertainty and imprecision is not to give in to fuzzy logic. He believes that what we say to patients reflects this imprecision and uncertainty. Bader (1994, 1998), on the other hand, stresses that the postmodern emphasis on complexity, ambiguity, and misunderstanding merely justifies our confusion and pessimism about being able to help patients.

Karasu (1996) explores theoretical systems in a comprehensive fashion and deconstructs them by pointing out their failures as well as their functions. He maintains an historical perspective, as does Lehman (1991) who states "every generation defines itself in opposition to the one before it, in metaphorical acts of patricide" (p. 73).

Is object relations theory still accepted or has it been superseded? I do not believe that it has been superseded or that it, in turn, has replaced Freudian theory. It is a clinically oriented theory that places greater emphasis on structure and function and is particularly suited to the patient population clinicians frequently encounter. As therapists get to know their patients better, there will be further extensions of our concepts about the therapeutic interaction and character structure.

I do not believe, as Karasu (1996) stated, that theory has to end before the practitioner can be set free. He states, I conjecture in an optimistic tone,

> As an ongoing process toward transcendence of theory it is necessary for there to occur not only the natural course of historical dissolution and changes in ideology, but a concerted deconstruction of man's most trusted tenets. This means a systematic undoing . . . of the infrastructures upon which favored theories . . . are founded. Only then can a true reconstruction occur that is not infinitely bound by the tenacity of ideological preferences of the past. [p. 27]

Cushman (1995), however, cautions, "Simply acknowledging that our most cherished beliefs and institutions are constructions and not reality itself, that chaos lurks just beneath our various constructions, is potentially too disconcerting for us to tolerate" (p. 16).

I disagree that paradigms in Kuhn's (1962) sense have to be drastically replaced every few generations. The physicists I have met are not in agreement with him, at least as far as physics is concerned, and although there may be occasional "quantum leaps," there is still an ever-evolving continuum as science progresses. Similarly, pursuing object relations theory to augment our understanding of the psychotherapeutic process does not require a deconstruction of concepts that have had pragmatic value and have proved clinically useful.

For many practitioners simply plodding along a previously constructed path is not enough. Maybe the pace is too slow or it does not hold the promise of exciting creative discoveries. It does not provide sufficient narcissistic gratification. The glory of the Freudian enterprise has faded and the philosophers are at the gate ready, if not to plunder, then to take over and establish their regime whether it is intersubjectivity, interpersonal relations, or self psychology.

I do not consider postmodernism to be a school that can be placed in a clinical context that espouses the intrapsychic focus. It has some adherents among clinicians but it has very little, if any, applicability to clinical practice.

It is also difficult to fit Lacan into an intrapsychic frame of reference. He seems to fit better in a space created by non-Euclidean geometry rather than our simple three dimensions. The number of his adherents is apparently growing, but the effort required to penetrate his obscurity is too exhausting for whatever insights he might provide. Until there is a clear-cut exposition of his ideas, in good writing and simply presented, it is impossible to determine whether we will get crumbs or a whole loaf. I suspect that there is something important to gain from his ideas, but part of the creative product is its capacity to clearly communicate (Roudinesco 1997).

The "schools" I choose to discuss, with the exception of the interpersonal relational, suffer a similar obscurity, but with some energy they are capable of being understood, although the effort that has to be expended is more than it should be. I am particularly referring to intersubjectivity, which has acquired sufficient status to have its own institute, the Institute for the Psychoanalytic Study of Subjectivity, in New York City.

All three theoretical systems were specifically formulated by clinicians who wanted to gain further understanding of patients and to promote the treatment process. Postmodernism, by contrast, was constructed by a professional philosopher, Jacques Derrida, and I have learned it has not been held in high respect by many philosophers. Of the three, I consider the interpersonal relational school the most clearly expressed and clinically relevant. Self psychology is also directed to the treatment process and does not venture outside the boundaries of clinical dimensions, but Kohut's writings are ponderous and implicitly claim to have borrowed from no one, as is evidenced by his short bibliographies. Intersubjectivity has incorporated a philosophical system into the consultation room. Many of our clinical concepts such as transference and countertransference have been buried and resurrected in another context. Often, similar to Lacan, it is difficult to ascertain what Stolorow and his colleagues really mean because their language is so lofty.

The New Faces

INTERSUBJECTIVITY: OLD WINE IN MURKY BOTTLES

In intersubjectivity theory, the philosophers lurk in the background. Hegel (1801) introduced the essence of intersubjectivity as he emphasized what many have called constructionism, which simply means that perception is considered in subjective and moral terms such as perception of the truth or the good. The taking in of an outside stimulus creates a perception, a highly personal experience according to Hegel, but one that defines the truth.

The German word for "to perceive" is *wahrnehmen*, a combination of the adjective *wahr*, which means "true," and the verb *nehmen*, which means "to take." Literally, *wahrnehmen* would mean taking the true or taking in the truth, the implication clearly being that the act of internalizing makes it true, at least for the subject. To perceive, in a sense, is to create the truth, but, for Hegel, truth is a very complex subject as he develops it further in his ideological dialectic, the basis of his epistemology, in which the construction of ideas is a continuous process of thesis, antithesis, and synthesis.

Hegel's subjectivity of perception has introjective and projective elements. He stresses that consciousness creates the object and consciousness "declares observation and experience to be the source of truth" (p. 72). He elaborates: "So in point of fact, the Thing is white only to our eyes, also tart to our tongue, also cubical to our touch. . . . We get the entire diversity, not from the Thing, but from ourselves" (p. 72). This could be a restatement of the conundrum about whether sound exists if there is no one to hear the tree fall in the forest.

Regarding the concept of projection, Hegel discusses how consciousness alters the object, I would assume according to its needs.

"The first object in being known is altered for consciousness; it ceases to be the in-itself, and becomes the in-itself only for consciousness. And this then is the True. . . . This new object contains the nothingness of the first, it is what experience has made of it" (p. 55).

This philosophical direction leads to increasingly higher levels of abstraction that have no clinical relevance. At some point these ideas crossed into the realm of clinical theory, and it did not begin with Stolorow and Atwood's intersubjectivity theory. From a theoretical viewpoint, I believe it first occurred when Melanie Klein (1946) introduced the concept of projective identification. Maintaining her classical perspective, she remained in an instinctual rather than a structural frame of reference, although many of Freud's adherents would hardly call her a classicist.

Klein described a back-and-forth movement that could be compatible with the intersubjective perspective in that subject and object are intertwined and react with each other. She does not remain entirely in the instinctual realm because the subject puts part of the self, even the whole self and not just the bad parts, into the object. The purpose of this projection is to attack the object and to possess and control it.

In recent years, the introjective aspect of projective identification has differed from Klein's initial formulation. She viewed the patient's introjection as the consequence of a counterattack. The patient, according to Klein, experiences the introjection as a forceful entry from the outside into the inside as a retribution for the initial projective assault, a reversal of what occurs during the paranoid-schizoid position (Laplanche and Pontalis 1973).

The sadistic and masochistic impulses that Klein believed were the essential elements of the fantasies of patients who use projective-identification mechanisms are no longer involved in recent formulations about this process. Racker (1968), for example, described projective identification as an attempt to help the subject gain greater control and organization of impulses that are becoming increasingly difficult to manage. In therapy, the patient projects the unruly parts of the self onto the therapist, who, because of greater ego coherence and more solid boundaries, is better able to contain them and render them harmless. Then the patient is able to make them part of the self once again, but now they are, in a sense, tamed and nondisruptive. In these instances, projective identification is a structure-promoting process, involving an intimate two-person relationship in the current setting, although the nature of projections are reflections of the past, reflections that determine the quality of psychic structure rather than instinctual impulses.

From these descriptions, this interaction is an intense intersubjective experience, but Racker and others following him did not find it necessary to wander away from clinical concepts by creating a different language and using philosophical concepts. Many clinicians find it quite comfortable to understand their patients in terms of transference–countertransference interactions that clearly refer to the therapist's participation as well as the patient's.

Ehrensaft (1998) is one of those clinicians who has known for over twenty years that there are two active participants in the consultation room. The therapeutic process is no longer based on a unilateral relationship in which the therapist is a neutral supreme authority. This latter anachronistic model was discarded many years ago, and once again one has to question why a new school or institute is needed. Metaphorically speaking, it seems that straw men are being created and dead horses are being beaten.

Ehrensaft points out that Anna Freud, the co-founder of child analysis with Melanie Klein, was far ahead of her time in being the originator of the two-person model of psychodynamically oriented psychotherapy. It is ironic that two great enemies, Anna Freud and Melanie Klein, might have shared the beginning of an interactional approach to the therapeutic process, with Anna Freud introducing the clinical dimension by postulating the transference relationship and real relationship, and Klein constructing a theoretical position that is based mainly on structural factors, a stance that emphasizes subjectivity.

Years later, Atwood and Stolorow (1984) decided to use the subjective world, instead of a representational world, and later described this subjective world as "the contents of experience and structures of subjectivity to designate the invariant principles unconsciously and recurrently organizing those contents according to distinctive meanings and themes" (p. 177). They seem to be saying something important and profound, but what are they really saying? What are "contents of experience"? I assume the authors mean that what we perceive and feel is internalized and becomes part of our memory system. Then these memories of interactions with the outer world can be worked over, giving them "distinctive meanings and themes." Was not all of psychoanalysis from the beginning concerned with how perceptions about the self, external objects, and relationships with the surrounding milieu have been distorted because of internal conflicts and structural defects? Behavior is affected and memories are twisted according to the laws of the unconscious, laws that are the outcome of the primary process, which remains independent of reality and, in turn, distorts reality.

These distortions are the basis of prejudice and bias as well as the misguided narcissism of the errant therapist. They have "distinctive meanings and themes," which, in essence, define a person, but there is nothing new in the quotation from Atwood and Stolorow.

In fact, Winnicott (1969) frequently wrote about subjective phenomena, and discussed how the subjective object develops in order to achieve the developmental position of establishing contact with the external world.

Changing the lexicon does not create new ideas. It becomes a chore to have to work so hard to come to the realization that what is being expressed is commonplace, even mundane, within a professional purview. Sentences should not have to be parsed if what is being presented is creative and innovative.

From the ideas I have just noted, Stolorow and colleagues (1987, 1994) developed a framework that they call the theory of intersubjectivity.

Intersubjectivity theory is a field theory or systems theory in that it seeks to comprehend psychological phenomena not as products of isolated intrapsychic mechanisms, but as forming at the interface of reciprocally interacting subjectivities. Psychological phenomena . . . cannot be understood apart from the intersubjective contexts in which they take form. It is not the isolated individual mind . . . but the larger system created by the mutual interplay between the subjective worlds of patient and analyst. [Atwood and Stolorow 1984, p. 178]

This is not exactly a tautology, although "subjectivities" and "intersubjective" appear in the definition of the theory of intersubjectivity. The authors are emphasizing relations and connections. The mutual interplay of the analyst's and patient's world suggests that the subjective experience includes different layers of the selves of the participants, an object relationship in a therapeutic context. Similarly, the transference relationship consists of various levels of the psyche, but infantile elements are dominant.

In fact, the authors first used the word *intersubjectivity* in the transference–countertransference context and noted that the treatment interaction occurred at different subjective levels. Object relations theory, which emphasizes structural or characterological constellations, explores the personality as a hierarchal continuum (Giovacchini 1979), and therefore it follows that object relations are viewed in a similar hierarchal fashion. The personal involvement of the therapist is in no way diminished by thinking in terms of transference and countertransference.

Goldberg (1998) states that the transference in intersubjectivity theory has two basic dimensions, what he calls, following Kohut (1971), a "selfobject" dimension and a repetitive dimension. By selfobject (here is another example of a tendency not only to use a made-up word but also to write in poor syntax, in this instance, constructing a neologism by removing a hyphen to emphasize fusion) he means a transference that has occurred perhaps exclusively in the treatment context. The patient is reacting to the person of the analyst rather than to a meaningful figure of the past. The repetitive transference refers to projecting onto the therapist relationships that characterized the infantile environment, the usual transference that occurs in psychoanalytic treatment.

Again, these are not new ideas. They have been presented repeatedly, especially by Greenson (1965) and Zetzel (1956) in their discussions of the working and therapeutic alliance. Both believed that there was an unobjectionable aspect to the transference that could be exploited for therapeutic benefit. They also distinguished between the real relationship to the therapist and the transference that contained infantile elements and produced a transference neurosis, which was a repetition of the infantile neurosis.

The concept of countertransference implicitly stresses that the infantile elements of the analyst's character are involved in the therapeutic interaction. Something in the unconscious may have been provoked by the patient's attitudes, which the therapist finds disturbing. There may have been some similarities in the patient's and therapist's infantile environments. Thus, in all instances of countertransference, a reaction to the patient's transference, clinicians are confronted with subjective experiences. This is almost a redundant statement if we keep in mind the inherent personal aspects of transference.

I took issue with Greenson's and Zetzel's distinction between transference and nontransference reactions (Boyer and Giovacchini 1980) because it implies that we are dealing with qualitatively different phenomena. Rather, I believe that all feeling, reactions, and impulses have to be understood in terms of a hierarchal continuum. They are a blend of primary and secondary process-oriented psychic processes that vary in their proportions. Some of the patient's behavior may be primarily realistically based and have a minimum of infantile or transference elements. In these instances, reality may dominate the clinical picture, although there are still some unconscious factors at work. But analysts may not be able to interpret the unconscious factors, because the patient may find such explanations far-fetched in view of the dominant reality factor.

A middle-aged housewife arrived a half hour late to her session. She was obviously agitated as she explained that she had a flat tire, an aggravation that irritated her as she sought help and caused her to be late.

I knew she was having some anxiety about what her therapy was revealing and suspected that it was related to her tardiness. I did not choose to interpret her being late as due to a hostile transference and ambivalence, because as a resistance she could rely on the reality of a flat tire, which she would have assumed was outside her control and not unconsciously motivated.

To maintain the intrapsychic focus, therapists have to assume that every transaction has some element of unconscious motivation, but whether it can be used for therapeutic purposes is another question. With my patient I learned that she had taken some side streets that were in poor shape and that her tires were worn out. Still, I did not think with this somewhat concretely oriented patient that I could convince her of the contribution of the negative transference in causing her to have a flat tire.

Viewing the psyche in terms of a structural hierarchy fits well in a psychodynamic context. Rather than speaking of levels of subjectivity, a vague formulation at best, it is more clinically relevant to determine which levels of the psychic apparatus are operating, especially in any particular interaction between therapist and patient. This is a transference–countertransference context with varying mixtures of primary and secondary process. There is a blend of the past and current reality in all transference projections, and therapists are also reacting in a similar fashion in their countertransference responses.

Relating to the therapist as he really is is a reaction that is the outcome of the upper reality-oriented aspect of the hierarchal spectrum, but there will always be some tinge to such a response that is reminiscent of the infantile past. On the other hand, if the therapist reacts on the basis of his past to the patient, this could be disruptive to the therapeutic process. I have called this type of countertransference idiosyncratic (Giovacchini 1989). Still, if therapists use their untoward reactions that are the outcome of infantile elements to understand the transference, they are engaging in a productive therapeutic endeavor.

All of these reactions are highly subjective, but subjectivity has to be understood by a variety of components that have been described thoroughly in an object relations perspective. Developmental levels and interactions are frequently formulated as being characterized by projective identification.

Projective identification is, in itself, a redundancy if one carefully scrutinizes this mechanism by concentrating on the concept of a hierarchal continuum. The perceptual system consists of different psychic and developmental levels. It perceives according to its structure, which determines how it perceives. This is not quite the same as Hegel's (1801) belief that the act of perceiving created the object that is perceived, but the perceptual system's operations are based on how the personality is constructed. Consequently, a subjective factor is intrinsic to every perception, and this factor is involved in all significant object relations.

Relating to an external object means that part of the self is involved in the relationship. That self-involvement is an example of identification. Thus, every perception and every relationship has an element of projective identification. The perception is internalized and becomes imbued with elements of our self representation. Similarly, as the external object is perceived as external, it also acquires aspects of the character structure of the subject through projection. Such projections, based on the structure of the perceptual system, occur in all relationships.

Complicated processes such as projective identification and intersubjectivity, when understood in the context of a structural hierarchy, become mundane and even self-evident.

Theory becomes inordinately complex as scholars and clinicians stray from the treatment encounter and from the data. Occasionally, the effort is made to apply these higher levels of abstraction to therapeutic technique, and this can lead to some very bizarre pronouncements. For example, I have heard therapists proclaim that, in the interest of honesty, they have to reveal themselves to the patient and deal with countertransference as thoroughly as they investigate transference. This applies especially to sexual feelings, which admittedly should never be acted out, but frankly revealing them helps control the tendency to physically express them.

This latter point can be debated. I have known of at least two instances in which therapist and patient frankly discussed their sexual feelings for each other. What might have begun as intellectual exploration soon progressed to more elemental feelings, which finally led to sexual transgressions. This was a catastrophic situation, therapeutically and personally.

Revealing nonsexual feelings can also be called into question, even if it can be considered as the exploration of the intersubjective field. Often such revelations are based on the therapist's needs, and the patient may react to them as an unwarranted intrusion and then feel exploited. In Yalom's (1996) novel, *Lying on the Couch*, the therapist thoroughly discusses his personal life with the patient, and even though this is fiction, Yalom does not concisely illustrate how these discussions had any therapeutic relevance. Dominating the consultation room with the therapist's subjectivity may relieve the analyst of some inner tension, but it degrades a professional relationship, enfeebling its therapeutic potential.

Being aware of one's feelings toward patients has become part of our treatment efforts, but if the feelings are revealed, they have to be in context with transference projections and the repetition compulsion. Patients try to reconstruct the infantile environment through their transference projections and assign a role from the past to their analysts. It may be painful for therapists to accept such projections and they may resent the setting up of such a scenario (McDougall 1985).

Therapists may inadvertently react negatively and this may cause some disruption in the treatment. But this disruption would be only momentary if the therapist understands what has happened. In these circumstances, it can be beneficial if therapists admit that they have unwittingly had a personal reaction due to their being unaware that they were resisting their patient's projections. Once they recognize the extent of the repetition compulsion, they regain their analytic decorum, and an honest discussion of countertransference feelings can be beneficial.

This is, however, considerably different from the gratuitous revelation of personal feelings that has no therapeutic purpose, and in fact may take the focus away from the patient as the therapist turns the spotlight on himself, gaining narcissistic gratification. The intersubjectivity inherent in any relationship has to be understood in terms of its component parts, and in a treatment context this always leads to an examination of the transference–countertransference axis.

This does not mean that there are not lighter moments in treatment relationships in which the participants talk about matters that are not directly related to the patient's psychopathology. Conversations about current events, sports, books, and special interests that both patient and therapist share need not interfere with the course of treatment provided that they are recognized for what they are and that the analyst is not trying to manipulate the patient in order to create a positive transference or has any other therapeutic intent. These interchanges should simply represent a relaxed stance, a friendliness that may help establish a holding environment, but nothing more specific than that.

If they are attempts to set up a "corrective emotional experience" (Alexander and French 1946), eventually patients would experience them as intrusive and insincere. This is relevant, because trying to win the patient's favor and developing intimate feelings has been mistaken for insightful understanding and interest in intrapsychic processes, and passes for therapy.

I had an experience with a patient, whom I have discussed in another context (Giovacchini 1979), in which I was accused of having been rude and unprofessional.

I was seeing a professional man in his early thirties four times a week. He complained that I was utterly useless and the only help he had received was from the workouts at a nearby gym after each session. He felt my method of treatment was anachronistic, but despite his complaints he was never late nor did he miss an appointment.

During a particular session, he was visibly angry as he accused me of having attacked him. He said that the previous session I had been rude, my tone of voice was harsh, and I had been sarcastic, demeaning, and condescending. I was taken aback, since I had no idea of what he was talking about. Nevertheless, I felt that I had better heed his words, because as he entered my office, I had an impulse to say something pleasant, perhaps an unconscious conciliatory gesture.

I replied that I was not aware of any such behavior during the previous session, but since I had such an unusual impulse at the beginning of the session, I believed that undoubtedly something was going on that might be important and that we should try to understand. I introduced a collegial, investigative perspective, since I emphasized that our search was a collaborative effort. He lay on the couch and started free associating.

As he spoke, various events of the previous day's session came to mind. I recalled that I was somewhat enthusiastic about an insight I thought I had and I offered him an interpretation that I believed was valuable. Supposedly after my interpretation, I made the unpleasant comments that had upset the patient.

During the present session, I had a fantasy. In it, the patient was talking as he had done the previous day. I fantasized that he was speaking into a tape recorder. When I intervened, he pushed the stop button and waited for me to finish making my interpretation. Then he once again started the machine and continued his associations. I imagined that if we listened to the tape, there would be no way of knowing where I had interrupted because there was no loss of continuity in his discourse. What I had said was completely shut out.

I told him how I felt, a countertransference disclosure, and wondered why he created a situation that made me feel as if I did not exist. He did not resent my giving him the responsibility for my feelings. He preferred looking at our interaction as something occurring within me, although he accepted that he had shut out my contribution, but was more interested in knowing why I reacted as I did.

I thought silently that being annihilated (a dramatic hyperbole) would never be anything but disruptive. I let the investigation be directed toward my unconscious motives because I had the feeling that something would emerge that was in resonance with his infantile past. His first conjecture was that I was having a reverse oedipal reaction toward him, that as an older man I resented his youthful strength and creative energy, while my vigor was waning, and I was feeling jealous and competitive. Since I had been rude, and I had begun to remember an edgy quality to my voice that previous session, I felt I had to give some credence to his formulation, but it did not seem right. I thought of my son, who was a psychiatric resident at the time, and how I felt proud of his accomplishments. Of course, these thoughts may have been the manifestations of my resistance to an oedipal interpretation but I did not believe that I would have reacted so intensely and then repress what I had done. Oedipal factors did not seem to be so intense as to force me to react in what I considered to be an uncharacteristic fashion.

As I dwelled on my tape recorder fantasy, I realized how I repressed the pain of essentially having been annihilated by the patient. Many memories from my childhood came to mind that I had no intention of revealing to him. Instead, since I was convinced that my reaction was not based on oedipal competitiveness, I told him that I felt I had reacted at a more primitive level than the oedipal. I explained that I had suffered from existential anxiety, that I had felt obliterated and this was an extremely frightening experience. I was willing to accept responsibility for what had happened, but we differed as to the reasons for my behavior.

It sounds as if the treatment had been reversed, that the therapist was being analyzed rather than the patient. In actuality, however, this interchange turned out to be a mutual interaction in which the analysis had a back-and-forth quality. We moved from the exploration of my personality to an investigation of his.

This is the essence of the transference–countertransference relationship and its progression. It is an example of intersubjectivity as the various parts and levels of the patient's and analyst's character interact with each other. Something within the patient, in this instance, had an impact on the therapist because of some of the analyst's vulnerabilities. Conceivably, some other analyst might have had a different reaction or none at all. Still, the therapeutic response was not that unusual and it could be worked with. Once I was informed of my aberrant behavior I maintained an analytic attitude as evidenced by my willingness to accept that the patient had made an accurate observation and that we should determine what happened, and the patient was willing to suspend his anger and to return to investigating the material.

I did not share the childhood memories that were stimulated when I realized I had felt annihilated. I did not believe I had to go so far in my self-revelations because I conjectured that they were not therapeutically relevant. They were part of my agenda and not his. If I had revealed them, then the treatment would really have changed direction and I would have been the patient. Though in the past Ferenczi had proposed that the patient and therapist alternate roles, it was never made clear why this was a feasible approach. I believed that to have gone any further in my revelations of my subjective responses, that is, beyond admitting to the patient that I had an untoward response, would have been intrusive, exploitive, and, to put it in the vernacular, dumping on the patient. There have to be therapeutically determined limits to the intersubjective approach in the transference–countertransference frame of reference.

The purpose of investigating what happened in our relationship was to delve further into the patient's mind. We had to know why the patient was able to get me to react as I did. This is a delicate moment in any therapy, because it might sound as if the therapist is denying his responsibility and placing the blame on the patient. I was aware of my contribution, but the patient's provocative behavior had its own etiological chain apart from me.

There was a parallel process operating; we were both reacting to our past and to each other in the current situation. My past, however, was irrelevant, provided I did not continue reacting as I had and did not gratuitously intrude it into our discourse. His reactions to me as well as his past were both relevant. He might have found his need to eliminate me reinforced by my sensitivity to rejection. This is a restatement that every projection has some validity in that the object of the projection has some elements that are similar to what is being projected, that there is some resonance between the projection and the container. The similarities are the products of the infantile environment of the participants.

My past also became irrelevant to me as I further understood the patient's need to obliterate me. I regained my therapeutic perspective as we started the exploratory process, and his associations brought us completely back to the inner world of his mind. At this point intersubjectivity ceased, and the therapist did indeed become a neutral observer. Still, to become a neutral observer required a moderately tumultuous incident in which the subjectivity of patient and therapist were intricately intertwined, again an intense transference–countertransference interaction.

Neutrality has been decried, and recent evidence reveals that it is doubtful whether Freud ever practiced it. Certainly he could not have remained totally detached when he "analyzed" his daughter. If he had understood the usefulness of countertransference as a therapeutic tool, he may not have been as negative about it as he was (Freud 1910). There could be alternate episodes of intersubjective involvement and the more traditional neutral analyst. Therapists may have to submerge themselves in their subjectivity in order to be objective.

What would have happened if I did not need to react to the patient's attempt to eradicate me and had understood that he had unconscious impulses to reject me? Would we have had to engage with each other at a high emotional pitch? Could we not have continued the treatment just by making an interpretation at the time he shut me out and not the next session after I had provoked him?

I conjecture that if I had had immediate insight, it would have achieved the same results without the necessity of having to experience a painful disruption. In other words, the transference-countertransference or the intersubjective experiences are valuable when there is an impasse or some other therapeutic complication. To un-

derstand what has occurred as an enactment of various infantile constellations of the patient with the possible contribution of the analyst's
past can move the treatment forward, but this might have also happened if the therapist simply understood the situation and did not
need any particular subjective response (Shur 1994). Subjectivity
could be a hindrance to therapy if the analyst does not eventually gain
understanding of what he is doing and the unconscious reasons behind his behavior.

Once the patient understood what had transpired between us, he started
reminiscing about certain periods of his past, beginning with a description of his parents and their relationship to each other. He described
his mother as a social climber who constantly denigrated her husband.
He came from Eastern Europe and spoke with a heavy accent and used
poor grammar. She was ashamed of him and did everything possible
to avoid his company.

She doted on the patient, who was her favorite child. Instead of
encouraging him to accept his father as a role model, she extolled the
virtues of her brother during the patient's early childhood. He was
handsome, bright, and charming, whereas the father, a scrap-metal dealer,
was just a coarse, crude junkman. She wanted her son to treat his
father as a nonentity and to idealize his uncle.

In actuality, the father had been quite successful and had made a
considerable sum of money, a sufficient amount to support his wife's
social pretensions. The uncle, on the other hand, had been a failure at
everything he tried and it seemed that he had been involved in some
shady dealings.

The patient believed that he went along with his mother and remembered many conversations with her as a child that consisted of "father
bashing." As an adolescent, he was able to view the situation more
realistically and appreciated how hard his father worked and what he
had done for him. He had paid for the patient's college education and
had supported him during his postgraduate training, whereas his uncle,
from a practical viewpoint, had done nothing for him. In fact, the father
spent a good deal of money getting his brother-in-law out of scrapes.

I could now understand my countertransference feelings and reactions. The patient had succeeded in projecting his father imago, that is, the nonexisting father, into me. As the mother wished to deprecate and dismiss his father, he was treating me in an identical fashion. I felt the pain of being reduced to a nonexistent state, as perhaps anyone might have felt, but my reactions were, to a large measure, determined by personal elements of my past. I did not discuss these elements with the patient, but I interpreted his projections, and this became a pivotal point in his analysis.

This vignette demonstrates the interplay of our personalities in the transference–countertransference context. It could be argued that there were many subjectivities interacting with one another, but that does not add anything to a detailed discussion of the various levels of the personalities of the patient and therapist that were reacting to each other. As the level of interaction went below realistic surface elements, the transference and countertransference aspects of the therapeutic relationship became evident. Better stated, there is a hierarchal sequence to the various feelings between patient and therapist.

Here I have examined various levels of my responses, juxtaposed with those of the patient. His transference projections were the outcome of the infantile relationship with his mother, whereas I was reacting to these projections at two levels, directly feeling the impact of his projections and, by awakening past experiences, special sensitivities were aroused that caused me to react as I did. This is a microscopic analysis of multiple levels of simultaneous interactions that is carried out in a transference–countertransference frame of reference. The intersubjectivity approach does not easily lend itself to such a detailed analysis.

Atwood and Stolorow (1993) have used their theory to conduct psychobiographical studies of Freud, Jung, Reich, and Rank, and the authors conclude that their theories are based on their subjective worlds. The authors emphasize the reparative elements of their theories and how they were used as defensive adaptations to psychopathological constellations. This is an ad hominem formulation that says nothing about the value or validity of the theory. Whatever is created is, in part, related to subjective elements, but there are many other variables involved, and the subjective element may lead to special sensitivities and keener observations than might not otherwise have been possible.

Winnicott was accused by his former analyst, Joan Riviere, of espousing theories that were the result of neurotic fantasies and, therefore, useless. This was an unpardonable breach of ethics in view of her therapeutic relationship with him, but it was also an untenable conclusion. The theory has to be examined as an entity in its own right and not as being connected to any particular person. Subjectivity can be carried too far.

SELF PSYCHOLOGY: THE NARCISSISTIC PINNACLE

Self psychology, in view of its creator's, Heinz Kohut's, personality, could easily lend itself to an ad hominem attack, something I just condemned. First, I will be critical of its content and its overvaluation. Then I will bring personal elements into the discussion which are painful, but there are special reasons that justify my doing so.

Kohut has been accused of straying from standard analytic doxology by such notables as Anna Freud and Kurt Eissler (Cocks 1994). His developmental continuum is sufficiently unique, making it difficult to work out a constant therapeutic approach that would be compatible with his theories. His theory is further vulnerable in that his data have to be questioned, something that has rarely happened when examining psychoanalytic concepts. The fact that he has deviated from standard technique is not necessarily detrimental to the treatment of borderline patients, but clinicians have to judge his ideas on the basis of their merit, clinical applicability, and the validity of the data that support them.

Kohut's system has been called self psychology because it gives the self representation and its vicissitudes central prominence and importance. He and his followers believe this is a unique formulation, although many clinicians, myself included, have put greater emphasis on the ego and what Sullivan (1953) called the self system in our conceptual formulations and therapeutic approach.

Hartmann (1939) wrote about ego psychology and ego adaptations. My therapeutic orientation has leaned heavily on the adaptive hypothesis, viewing symptoms and even regressions as attempts, sometimes failed, at adaptation. This stresses the ego's (or that part of the ego, the self representation) transactions with the outer world rather than the clashing intrapsychic forces. Much of the psychopathology encountered involves identity problems (Erikson 1959) and failures in the ego's executive system, a situation that defines the borderline state.

Freud (1923) placed the ego in a central dominant position and its stability determines the integrity of the psychic apparatus. Following his tendency to anthropomorphize, he stated that the ego served three masters: the id, the superego, and the vicissitudes of the external world. Freud's concept of the ego was extensive. In it resides the subjective sense of being—what we would call the identity sense, the self representation, or simply the self, as Kohut preferred.

Other clinicians have preferred to view the sense of self as a supraordinate organization that is a reflection of the operations of the psychic apparatus. Many of these formulations are reified distinctions that seem to go beyond the field of observation, and they are neither hindrances nor useful for our understanding of the treatment process. It is similar to weighing produce with an analytic balance to the fourth decimal place when all that is needed is to know how many pounds it weighs.

Freud (1924a) was also the first to recognize that object relations were heavily implicated in the production of psychopathology. He stressed the importance of ego–outer world relations in the neuroses and psychoses over and above ego-id conflicts, as the clinician faced more severe psychopathology. In the Schreber case (Freud 1911), he demonstrated how traumatic object relations became involved in very rich and colorful delusions.

Kohut also recognized that psychopathology could not be formulated simply in terms of the standard transference neuroses. Most of the younger generation was struggling with the same problem, that of treating patients who had not yet been formulated from a structural and psychodynamic perspective. I remember how intrigued we felt when we recognized that a particular patient was not suffering from feelings of inadequacy; he was, indeed, inadequate! Then we had to wonder about types of ego defects, their developmental antecedents, the quality of early object relations, and the infantile milieu. Many of us struggled to make sense out of the chaos our patients presented, but most of us did not think we were creating new systems or paradigms.

We were moving naturally and inevitably further along on paths that had already been established. Sometimes we might pause and inspect the surrounding foliage and perhaps find novel ways of handling clinical problems. The importance of the countertransference in addition to that of the transference was the outcome of these clinical journeys.

Others such as Kohut believed that they had made momentous discoveries. I recall talking with a group of analysts including Kohut at a convention of the American Psychoanalytic Association some time around 1970. Kohut told us that his book would be coming out soon. When I asked him what its focus was, he smiled and said that it was solid gold and then he raised his arm, making a gesture indicating that he had something so heavy in his hand that he could hardly lift it. His grandiosity about a work that stresses grandiosity is amusing, but it has nothing to do with the validity of his work. Still, he was claiming that his viewpoint represented a major shift, similar to that of the later intersubjectivists, and his many followers, analysands, and supervisees have supported him in maintaining this belief. It is of further interest that many of his ideas, such as those dealing with transference and idealization, can easily be applied to groups as well as to the individual patient. The group I am specifically referring to comprised those who gathered around Kohut in Chicago at the time of the publication of the book to which Kohut referred, *The Analysis of the Self* (Kohut 1971), who were mainly his analysands and supervisees. Transference elements may have created an enthusiasm that could have been somewhat contagious. Furthermore, Kohut was an excellent clinician and a charismatic teacher, but he was not a good writer. He wrote rambling sentences in a Germanic style. He was not pedantic, as the intersubjectivists were, and he did not coin many new words, but he was ponderous and had to be read carefully. Most of his sentences had to be dissected to extract any meaning from them.

Kohut did not stray from standard analytic terminology, and his concepts, once they are understood, are relatively easy to follow and can be judged for their consistency and clinical applicability. The latter is discussed in his theory of treatment and can be compared with our own experiences.

Some of his readers may feel further dismayed if they are at odds with Kohut's eloquent disciples, who have canonized his works not only for their profundity but for their clarity. They may feel they have missed the point, or that they are suffering from the "emperor's new clothes phenomenon." Some readers find very little that is new. They feel as if they are eating cotton candy—there is nothing there. It is interesting in this connection that at a journal club where Kohut was discussing Sullivan's (1953) book on the concepts of modern psychiatry, he began his review by stating that what was new in Sullivan was not good and what was good was not new.

Kohut, as is generally true of contemporary clinicians, makes the transference relevant from both theoretical and technical perspectives. He puts it in the context of emotional development and the therapeutic process. This may not be altogether feasible, since what occurs in ordinary development cannot be directly carried over in a treatment relationship, although much of the infantile past can be brought into the consultation room but with some important modifications.

Unlike intersubjectivity theory, Kohut, for the most part, used psychoanalytic terminology, although he had some words of his own to replace traditional or common language. Since he does not purport to entirely abandon the psychoanalytic edifice, he should not wildly transgress theoretical boundaries, but he does.

For example, he postulates two subtypes of transference, the mirror transference and the idealizing transference, as being characteristic of early developmental levels. He states that these emerge during the phase of primary narcissism. This is conceptually confusing and inconsistent, because primary narcissism is a developmental stage that precedes the development of object relations if Freud's (1914a) developmental schema is accepted. Using the concept of primary narcissism would indicate that he is, to some extent, accepting Freud's stages of emotional development.

Freud begins by postulating an undifferentiated amorphous phase, somewhat similar to the blastula of embryology. Psychic energy seeks goals and gratifications within the organism, and this is noted as the autoerotic stage in which various parts of the soma are cathected.

As external and internal stimuli impinge on the undifferentiated blastula, they cause structural changes and differentiation at the interface of these incoming stimuli, a nidus that eventually becomes the ego. Psychic energy is now directed toward this ego, a state Freud called primary narcissism. This is a very early developmental phase in which the sophisticated recognition of external objects and even organized internal needs would not be possible.

Transference, as a clinical interaction, means a carrying over (*übertragen*) of feelings, impulses, and even parts of the self onto the person of the analyst. This can, of course, happen with others outside the treatment context, but all transferences require some contact with and recognition of the outer world. Patients may regress to preobject phases and still retain later acquired characteristics, but this does not mean that transference manifestations are intrinsic to the primitive mental state of the regression.

Placing the idealizing and mirroring transference in a preobject phase, that is, primary narcissism, makes no conceptual sense, since transference is a type of object relationship, and as the mind is viewed as a hierarchically ordered continuum, transference would be an element in all object relations.

A clinically relevant theory has to have a consistent, orderly developmental sequence to help understand how the psychic apparatus gains structure and differentiates as it achieves organization through a reciprocal interchange with external objects. The latter occurs in therapy through the process of transference resolution. Therefore, it is important to recognize that if the developmental timetable is turned topsy-turvy, the interpretation of the clinical interaction and the value of therapeutic interventions have to be called into question. Other factors besides the formulations given by self psychologists and their responses to the mirroring or idealizing transferences may have been involved in their therapeutic successes.

This is especially important in the face of the psychopathology seen today. If therapists are confusing developmental levels, this confusion will eventually cause disruption in the patient and create difficulties in the transference–countertransference axis, usually a disturbed balance because of an influx of narcissism or wounded narcissism within the therapist (see Chapter 4).

It is somewhat surprising that self psychologists have been able to get so much mileage from mirror and idealizing transferences and that they have gained so much publicity in the analytic literature. This is especially puzzling because no one has questioned the assertion that these are two different types or subtypes of transference, whereas in actuality, mirroring is a quality of all transferences, and idealizing occurs alongside many other elements commonly found in transference phenomena.

Kohut defines the mirror transference as a transference in which the patient wants to be admired by an external object; in therapy, this is, of course, the analyst. During the beginning of object relationships and the gradual separation of self from the outer world, it is better known as the narcissistic transference. It occurs in a later developmental phase than primary narcissism, and is known as secondary narcissism, which is a developmental phase. Secondary narcissism also means self-object.

All early transferences are narcissistic transferences and are required for psychic survival. The child has to be admired, that is, to be loved in order to thrive both physically and emotionally. In spite of many of its objectionable qualities, narcissism is as fundamental a requirement for human survival as are food and shelter (Spruiell 1975). Spitz's (1945, 1946, 1965) observations of an orphanage where the children's physical needs were taken care of but emotional contact was completely withheld are a tragic reminder, in that most of the children died before their first year, of how essential someone's admiration can be, a point Kohut emphasizes.

The quality of mirroring has been elevated to an entity and defines the phenomenon of narcissism. The original myth of Narcissus is of a youth admiring his image in a pond. He is, in essence, looking at a mirror and admiring the version of himself he sees.

The idealizing transference occurs during a later developmental phase, although this is not stressed in Kohut's writings. But, again, the question has to be raised as to whether this deserves to be considered a type of transference or whether idealization is a quality that is added on to the contents of transference projections.

Furthermore, are we dealing with idealization as an aspect of ordinary development or are we confronted with psychopathological distortions? Mirroring is an important activity required for psychic growth, but can idealization, in the way Kohut views it, be considered in a similar fashion? Certainly idealization is important for emotional development and especially creative activity (Giovacchini 1993), but where does it fit in the economy of early psychic life?

Winnicott (1953) writes about children feeling omnipotent and idealizing themselves as a characteristic of the transitional phase. I do not believe that we can take this literally, because the infant's psychic apparatus is not sufficiently complex to have feelings of omnipotence and to be able to idealize. This type of mentation can only occur during later phases of emotional development. Patients can regress to these earlier levels, and during the regression, as they retain later-acquired constellations, they can idealize. Kohut does not locate idealization on the developmental scale, which might have implications about his treatment recommendations.

Idealization and the need to be admired are commonly encountered phenomena and do not identify any particular school. They are simply aspects of object relationships that can be recapitulated in therapy in transference projections.

Another example of placing complex constructs at early developmental levels, such as primary narcissism, refers to what Kohut calls the *grandiose self* and the *idealized parental imago*. Both, of course, require sophisticated evaluations of the inner and outer world. Again, these distinctions are important because, according to self psychologists, these constructs are the vehicles through which therapeutic resolution occurs.

Kohut acknowledges that an optimal therapeutic outcome of the treatment of borderline and narcissistic patients is the acquisition of psychic structure. This occurs through the process of *transmuting internalization,* a term Kohut invented and to which his followers have attributed great significance. Is there anything new in such an expression? What does it contribute to our understanding of the therapeutic process? *Transmute* means to change, and *internalization* refers to something that was once outside being put inside. If an external object or experience is to lead to a structurally progressive change within the psyche, it has to be smoothly incorporated and integrated. This happens in all learning experiences. I do not believe we need new and pedantic terms to describe familiar processes, as evidenced by the lack of consensus over such terms as *internalization, introjection, incorporation,* and *identification* (Schafer 1968).

Kohut makes some interesting points regarding the working through of the mirror transference. By working through I assume he means that the patient, to some degree, has resolved the need to be admired. Kohut concludes that working through releases constricted aggressive drives. This is not a surprising or innovative conclusion. Winnicott (1960a) wrote about the formation of a false self in order to conform to the external world to gain acceptance and approval. This often requires a repression or splitting off of destructive urges. These urges are often released as the patient attempts to reach the true self. This is a familiar dynamic observed by countless therapists.

The idealizing transference leads to internal regulations and the consolidation of the ego-ideal (Ornstein 1979). Idealization can lead to the acquisition of higher levels of structural integration, and the internalization of the idealized object would naturally lead to the expansion of the ego-ideal. It is interesting that Kohut viewed analytic progression from a perspective based in both camps, those of classical instinct theory and the structural revisionists. The achievement of internal regulation requires a balance of instinctual pressures, and the consolidation of the ego-ideal is a structural acquisition. This might be the direction that the treatment of patients suffering from ego defects is heading toward.

Regarding structure, Kohut again makes up a new word by plastering two familiar words together and then believes he has expressed something novel. Selfobject is a case in point. The words *self* and *object* are well entrenched in the lexicon of object relation theorists, and *self-object* means exactly the same as *selfobject*. The concept goes back to Freud's (1914a) definition of secondary narcissism as a stage in which the libido's first object is the self. Granted that the words take secondary importance to the concept; Kohut was not even the first person to use the term *selfobject*. In reviewing the text of a book Boyer and I wrote together (Boyer and Giovacchini 1967) for a second edition, I found the word *self-object* in a footnote and italicized. This was four years before Kohut published *The Analysis of the Self*. Modell (1963) earlier used the same term and in a similar context.

I wish to introduce some sense of balance when discussing Kohut's contributions to the treatment of patients in general and severely disturbed patients in particular. In addition to being critical about the substance of his writings and his claims to originality, I wish to counterbalance many of the extravagant claims of his followers. For example, Wolf, an avid follower of Kohut, states, "He is revitalizing and reshaping psychoanalysis. . . . Heinz Kohut is the Freud of our time" (Moss 1975). Gedo (1997) writes that another of Kohut's followers, Arnold Goldberg, said to a visitor from Europe, who made some critical statement about Kohut's oafish behavior at a dinner party, that Kohut had to be excused because he was the only national monument we had.

Self psychology has become a school in which personal factors have invaded conceptual and technical domains. In this instance, the ad hominem works in reverse. It idealizes the founder of the school, which then leads to an idealization of his ideas. It is ironic that self psychology, which highlights grandiosity, narcissism, and idealizing transferences, was formed by a group of analysands and supervisees who have elevated their leader to sainthood, and he, in turn, was more than eager to accept their adulation. Classical analysts had a similar relation to Freud. The origins of the movement have nothing to do with its validity, but its acceptance and spread is connected with the ardor of the followers as they eloquently proselytize.

Ad hominem thinking has to be put in its proper perspective, especially when discussing self psychology, because so much of the personality of the founder is embedded both in the theory and technique that follow. The emphasis on narcissism reflects Kohut's monumental narcissism, which I will bring into focus later, and the so-called therapeutic innovations are intimately connected with his personality and often his talents.

Freud has been recognized as having laid down many technical principles, but in the recent past he has been exposed as not being able to practice what he preached (Matthis and Szecsödy 1998). Sometimes this has been considered a denigration of his clinical expertise, and at other times this has been seen as an indication that he was human and let his feelings interfere with the conduct of the treatment. Arguments were usually leveled at his breach of the analytic frame, such as analyzing his daughter (Lohser and Newton 1996).

Relatively early in his career I knew Heinz Kohut well and recognized that he was a person with rare intellectual and clinical gifts. I sat with him through many clinical conferences and was impressed by the depth and quickness of his comprehension. He was a charismatic teacher, and it is easy to understand why some of his students and analysands idealized him. To put these positive personal attributes into a theoretical system underlying therapy neither validates nor invalidates the system. It behooves the clinician to determine whether such talents as empathy, intuition, and sensitivity, certainly relevant talents that cannot be prescribed, can become the conceptual basis of a treatment orientation. Similarly, the idealization of a system of thought does not make idealization a fundamental attribute around which the treatment relationship revolves. Furthermore, what might have been second nature to Kohut cannot be legislated and become part of the clinician's technical armamentarium.

I have mentioned Kohut's positive and creative talents, quite the opposite of implicating Winnicott's neurosis as the basis of his theories. In self psychology, empathy, obviously a highly valued quality for therapists, is the basic hub around which the therapeutic process revolves, and Kohut's clinical sensitivities were well known.

The main contribution of any theoretical system dealing with intrapsychic factors is its relevance to our treatment efforts. Kohut promises us a novel technical approach that he believes is superior to anything that has been proposed. Thus, it behooves the clinician to carefully examine what he offers us and meticulously scrutinize the data upon which he bases his conclusions. The reader should be prepared for some unpleasant surprises.

Kohut's therapeutic principles revolve around the reliving during the treatment of narcissistic developmental stages that are associated with the construction of the grandiose self and the idealized parental imago. By mirroring, the idealized parental imago supports the formation of the grandiose self. Thus, analytic technique is directed to fostering the transference as a developmental stage and then moving further. Kohut stresses that during early stages of treatment fostering the positive transference is essential, whereas Kernberg (1975) believes that the negative transference should not be evaded and that both should be pursued from the beginning.

Presumably the patient has not received sufficient narcissistic gratification as a child. The therapist, by mirroring, satisfies the patient's need for attention and gratification. The chief therapeutic tool is empathy. Empathic comments and interpretations reset the developmental process in motion. The narcissistic phases of development were not adequately dealt with, and the therapist provides or makes up for the lack of parental support that would have occurred with adequate mirroring and, as Kohut put it, by the "gleam in the mother's eye."

Granted that the frustrated transference states Kohut describes are the manifestations of psychopathology, it becomes difficult to understand how attempts at gratifying infantile needs or making up for deprivation can lead to developmental progression. To mirror back grandiosity might, in some instances, be similar to supporting a delusion. Furthermore, no matter how understated, the therapist is still role playing, and this will make the resolution of the transference difficult if not impossible.

Further, how does supporting the patient's defensive narcissistic orientation foster emotional development? From a structural viewpoint, the therapy is dealing with two primary process factors: the patient is displaying primitive aspects of the self, and the analyst, by supporting him and trying to gratify, is reacting in the same frame of reference. The interactions are at a primary process level. *A primary process oriented need and a primary process response cannot by themselves lead to secondary process structuralization.*

Kohut correctly warns us that therapists should neither guide their patients nor admonish them. It is not good technique for the therapist to prematurely confront the patient with reality; otherwise, the therapeutic setting will not be able to create the climate for the remobilization of the grandiose self. He agrees with Freud that the analyst should not be an educator nor should he try to manage the patient's life. These are useful and well-known principles that apply to all analytic patients.

Kohut and his followers, however, are introducing two different stances in dealing with patients. First, the therapist makes active efforts, by being empathic, to make patients feel better about themselves and not prematurely confront them with reality, which implies that finally one must have a comeuppance, a second, if not harsher, then at least practical, stance. Once the therapist has demonstrated a capacity to be empathic, patients form bonds that will help them withstand the less indulgent moments of the treatment relationship.

Prior to reality confrontation, patients somehow gain strength by constructing extensions of the grandiose self. This occurs through the merger transference and one of its variants, the twinship transference, and leads to the formation of a primary identity. Therapists become the carriers of their patients' grandiosity; patients fuse with the therapist, as children project their grandiosity onto their mothers and then fuse with them. These transferences are simply descriptive of various degrees of fusion and projective identification between patients and therapists.

These are adultomorphic distortions if applied to infantile experiences, but there is no question as to the existence of such phenomena in treatment. They have been observed regularly in the treatment of patients with structural ego defects and have been referred to as fusion or omnipotent fusion, which represents a regression to a psychopathologically distorted infantile symbiotic relationship. Primarily, such a regression occurs spontaneously in therapy, but Kohut suggests that the therapist manipulates the treatment in that direction through intuitive and empathic skills.

Nevertheless, Kohut stresses that this merger transference has to have temporal limits. It ends when the therapist confronts the patient with reality, which must mean that therapists have now become critical of their patients because they are indulging themselves with their grandiosity. It is ironic, however, that self psychologists have started this cycle. They have encouraged the formation of this type of transference, which leads to narcissistic aggrandizement, and then they change their posture.

Ornstein (1972), at the divisional meeting of the Western Psychoanalytic Societies, emphatically summarized this transference sequence by stating that the analyst does not "prematurely debunk" what the patient has been led to believe. Debunk means that what had been previously done was bunk, and clearly this turn of events is a deviation from standard treatment, because to encourage first and then to discourage, no matter how gentle the therapist may be in either stance, is manipulative and managerial, and debunking, in no way, sounds gentle.

This sequence of mirroring and later confrontation is the essence of Kohut's innovative contributions to the therapeutic process, and to prove the efficacy and superiority of his technique he presents the two analyses of Mr. Z. (Kohut 1979). This case represents the fundamental data from which he derives his theories about the treatment process. He believes that the best way to prove the superiority of his method is to present the course of treatment of a patient who has been treated by the classical method and then another course of therapy with the same patient that has been conducted according to the principles of self psychology. His position would be strengthened if the first treatment had been unsuccessful, whereas the second course had been effective. Kohut tells us of his therapeutic experiences with Mr. Z., whose reactions to both treatments fit the bill perfectly (Kohut 1979).

Mr. Z., an only child, had two analyses, both with Kohut, the first having lasted four years, after which the treatment was terminated, supposedly successfully, but with some apprehension by Kohut that perhaps not all was well. After five and a half years, the patient, apparently not satisfied, returned to treatment, which lasted another four years. For the moment, I wish to focus on the significance and meaning of Kohut's interventions, with an emphasis on certain subtle interactions that are misleading in that the reader may believe that certain orientations are intrinsic to classical analysis and rejected by the "new" therapeutic method.

The patient, a graduate student in his mid-twenties, complained of vague symptoms and mild somatic difficulties. He had problems getting involved with girls, felt socially isolated, and had difficulties in establishing interpersonal relationships. In essence, he sought treatment because generally he felt alienated and unhappy in his everyday life, common reactions in patients suffering from characterological problems and low self-esteem.

I wonder why Kohut felt this patient was a candidate for classical analysis. At that time, early in his career, Kohut was an ardent Freudian. He was probably as knowledgeable about Freud as anyone I have ever met, and he recounted with pride how he waved good-bye to Freud at the railroad station as Freud and his family were leaving Vienna for the last time. I also recall that when I returned to my residency training from military service, I asked Kohut what he would suggest I read. He said, "Read Freud." Having had plenty of time to read while in the army, I had read everything of Freud that was then available. I told this to Kohut and he replied, "Read him again." He was totally devoted to Freud and his principles.

Kohut accepted Mr. Z. for treatment and did not particularly think in terms of ego defects and pregenital factors. He learned that he was dealing with an only child who lived with his widowed mother. The patient complained about extreme loneliness, which he tried to relieve by reading, or going to movies and concerts alone or with an unmarried friend. Sometimes his mother would accompany them. Apparently, his friend became interested in an older woman, and this caused a breaking up of the triumvirate and it was at this time that Mr. Z. sought treatment.

Kohut reports that in the first analysis, he dealt with the patient's material as if it were a defense against a basically oedipal configuration, a fairly classical formulation for the psychoneuroses that Freud would have deemed treatable by standard techniques. Kohut reports that the main theme during the first year of analysis was characterized by a regressive maternal transference. He focused on the patient's narcissism but he viewed it as a manifestation of oedipal attachments that had been frustrated rather than a manifestation of an early developmental arrest. Mr. Z.'s narcissism was expressed by "unrealistic, deluded grandiosity and his demands that the psychoanalytic situation should reinstate the position of exclusive control, of being admired and catered to by a doting mother" who "had, in the absence of siblings who would have constituted pre-oedipal rivals and, during a crucial period of his childhood, in the absence of his father who would have been the oedipal rival, devoted her total attention to the patient" (p. 5). The patient's arrogance and grandiosity were the outcome of an imagined oedipal victory, according to Kohut.

These formulations seem to refer to psychopathology that is more severe than an oedipally based neurosis, whose existence I have often doubted. Even during this first analysis, Kohut formulated that the mother and child were involved in a narcissistic fusion. He concluded that she fed him immense amounts of narcissistic supplies, but at the expense of not allowing him to move away and establish his autonomy. Developmentally, this was a destructive fusion, but the patient received exclusive attention and satisfaction related to an emergent grandiosity.

Kohut states that he focuses on what he believed was the defensive nature of the patient's grandiosity, which would have been instrumental in maintaining the repression of oedipal strivings. This sounds inconsistent because, in the above quotation, he states that the patient's grandiosity is the outcome of an oedipal victory that he wants reinstated, and now he refers to it as a defense to repress oedipal feelings rather than an attempt to regain them, clearly contradictory formulations.

Nevertheless, Kohut continues describing how he was struggling with the patient to give up his defenses so that the underlying material could be dealt with. He further elaborates the oedipal material by discussing Mr. Z.'s fear of the father and his castration anxiety, but he particularly emphasizes the libidinal tie to the mother. He states that the idealization of the mother was a conscious manifestation of his incestuous wishes toward her.

Technically, Kohut concentrated on interpreting what he considered to be narcissistic defenses against oedipal strivings. How effective this would be is highly questionable because of his fuzzy concepts about the role of narcissism in the patient's psychic economy, but this will soon prove to be a moot point. Kohut mentions that he was not particularly aware at that time that the mother's actions and attitudes emotionally enslaved Mr. Z. and stifled his strivings for independence and autonomy. He expresses his negative countertransference when he admits that the patient's narcissistic defenses, demands, and arrogant sense of entitlement were burdensome.

Briefly, Kohut alludes to certain negative countertransference feelings when he admits that he wished the patient would work through his narcissistic defenses, his imperious demands, and his arrogant sense of entitlement.

Initially, Kohut felt that the patient's eventual positive response to therapy was due to the effectiveness of his interpretations. It was with this thought in mind that the first analysis was terminated, but apparently Kohut had some reservations about its outcome. He felt the termination was unexciting and this could be a sign that something was wrong.

I suppose he meant that there must be good feelings between patient and therapist when treatment has been successfully concluded. There is often a certain amount of sadness, a bittersweet reaction as they say good-bye. The intensity of the feelings that characterize most well-conducted therapies brings about a closeness that is mutually enhancing.

Nevertheless, Kohut asserts that both patient and therapist believed that treatment had been sufficiently successful so that it could be concluded, and he believed they had been involved in a standard analytic interaction. Later, he claims to have recognized that the patient's psychopathology went beyond oedipal problems and included disturbances originating in earlier developmental stages.

The treatment of patients whose psychopathology is based on pregenital fixation rather than an oedipal neurosis presumably would be quite different from the orderly sequence many analysts assume to be characteristic of the typical neurotic patient. In psychoanalytic institutes, candidates are taught there is a treatment sequence beginning with the analysis of defenses characteristic of specific psychosexual stages and finally reaching the oedipal. Seldom do clinicians find patients whose material unfolds in such an orderly manner. In most analyses patients relive early phases of development in the transference context. It would be difficult to treat a patient who had been misdiagnosed with classical technique and to expect such a sequence.

Kohut eventually claims to have questioned the validity of the therapeutic success of the first four years of Mr. Z.'s treatment. He conjectures that whatever improvement the patient experienced was due to a transference cure, and he felt he had to change his therapeutic strategy to suit the patient's needs. To tailor the treatment to the patient's needs does not mean that the clinician has introduced innovations or new treatment paradigms. Long before Kohut, therapists had learned that if they wanted to treat patients suffering from character disorders, they would have to be flexible, accepting, and nondemanding. In spite of Kernberg and colleagues' (1987) recommendations, being confrontational seldom helps.

Kohut states that his attitude shifted when the patient returned to treatment. Apparently, Kohut concluded that the sexual problems had not been resolved, that sexual fantasies had been suppressed, and that there had been no structural change. Kohut decided that the patient returned to treatment in order to get narcissistic gratification through the mirror transference. He reported that the patient formed an idealizing transference followed by narcissistic demands, which I note was exactly what happened during the first course of treatment.

Kohut claims that his therapeutic stance shifted during the second treatment and this apparently means he was less confrontational as implied by Ornstein's (1979) statement that Kohut was spared the "burdensome iatrogenic artifact, namely the unproductive rage reactions and clashing with the analyst could now be avoided" (p. 355). He postulates, using Kohut's language, that the patient's rages and childish demands represented feeble attempts to disentangle the self from noxious self-objects, which I assume to mean that he was struggling to separate himself from a destructive maternal fusion. This would seem to indicate that rage and narcissistic demands are positive and constructive reactions rather than manifestations of frustration because narcissistic demands are not being met.

In his second analysis, Kohut did not begin by analyzing narcissistic needs. He viewed them as analytically valuable replicas of childhood and he did not create an atmosphere in which he expected Mr. Z. to grow up. The patient felt calmed and soothed when Kohut's attitude, at least momentarily, softened. He was more sympathetic than challenging, and he commented that he empathically told the patient that it must hurt when one is not given what is felt as being one's due.

This implies that before Kohut, therapists tended to be challenging, that there was an adversarial relationship between therapist and patient. To some degree that was true, as Freud made the overcoming of resistance the chief therapeutic task, but for years, many clinicians, too many to mention, have viewed symptoms, including resistance, as having positive and adaptive qualities. Instead of feelng challenged, patients feel understood, and self-esteem is enhanced without any deliberate attempt by the therapist to provide narcissistic satisfaction.

Self psychologists have explicitly stated that their therapeutic approaches consist of responses to the mirror transference that are examples of empathic attunements. They represent attempts to supply patients with narcissistic supplies that were not provided when they were children, because of the weakness of, or lack of, the mother–infant bond. These responses are deliberate, consciously conceived interactions initiated by the therapist.

The history Kohut presents to us demonstrates that Mr. Z. did not lack narcissistically enhancing experiences. He was not deprived in childhood. He was the gleam in his mother's eye, and, I happen to know that even in adulthood, he was still the gleam in her eye. She doted on him and continued to do so until she died. So this was not a question of supplying something that was not given in infancy when narcissistic supplies are particularly important and vital.

I am not denying that what the mother gave was destructive. Her ministrations were responsible for the insatiable quality of the patient's narcissism, which created a bottomless pit. Bolstering a narcissism based on primary process factors rather than reality-oriented elements cannot lead to progressive structuralizing changes. Attempting to provide infantile needs for an adult ego does not work. Giving a patient mother's milk does not nourish. Mr. Z. was given nourishment; perhaps he was smothered rather than mothered, and to repeat this process in adulthood could be a therapeutic disaster.

The gratification of infantile needs as an adult is vastly different from the gratification of needs that are appropriate to a developmental stage that is not dominated by stress, trauma, and an engulfing mother. Though the patient may be making narcissistic demands to free himself from a "noxious" self-object, this does not mean that it is an appropriate solution. It is difficult to understand how reactions to frustration can achieve cohesion and autonomy. To some extent, the patient is deluding himself in believing that grandiosity will give him power and freedom, that these are attributes of a cohesive, mature psyche. The therapist would be colluding with unrealistic expectations, and in patients with severe psychopathology he would be supporting and fostering a delusion.

Kohut acknowledges that he cannot go on indefinitely mirroring back grandiosity. He states, "I can still remember the slightly ironic tone of my voice meant to assist him in overcoming his childish grandiosity" (p. 14).

I do not wish to belabor this case any further by continuing to emphasize the technical and diagnostic fallacies of Kohut's formulations. I have gone into considerable detail because this is the main body of data Kohut supplies to support his theories of psychopathology and technique. There are many inconsistencies in his formulations, and it would be impossible to understand how the maneuvers and interventions he describes could lead to any kind of therapeutic resolution. Yet Kohut claims that Mr. Z. was considerably better after his second course of treatment, whereas nothing much had happened after his first analysis.

I conjecture that perhaps Mr. Z.'s better adjustment was due to a transference cure (Giovacchini 1997). Obviously he is an extremely narcissistic personality, and being in treatment with an analyst as famous as Kohut might have sustained him, somewhat in the same fashion as the Wolfman thrived because of his relationship with Freud (1918).

Mr. Z. might not have wanted to step forward while Kohut was alive for fear of embarrassing him, but after he died I wonder why he did not reveal he was Kohut's famous patient, as happened with Little Hans and Freud (Freud 1909a).

I have read this case history several times and after each reading I have felt increasingly uneasy. There are so many similarities between Kohut and Mr. Z. that would have spelled a remarkable coincidence. First, they were both only children whose fathers were away from home during the first years of their lives. They had doting mothers. Kohut's mother, whom I met several times, visibly adored her son and was markedly possessive. In his younger years, Kohut was shy around women. He was comfortable in triumvirates, his best friend at the time being a resident or instructor on the same hospital house staff he was on, and he, his mother, and his friend would frequently go out together to movies and concerts or simply sit together in their apartments and listen to music.

Having disagreed with many of his formulations, I started thinking about Mr. Z. in psychodynamic terms, and my thoughts frequently led me to think about triumvirates, but I found myself speculating about Heinz Kohut rather than Mr. Z. Kohut had dinner with my wife and me about once or twice a week (again a triumvirate of two men and one woman), and he would be completely relaxed as he sang along with records playing operatic arias. At work, he often felt anxious about his performance and sought reassurance, but in our living room he was completely at ease.

Knowing about his background, I wondered if he needed a buffer, another man who might have represented the missing father, to feel comfortable with a woman who doted on him, but whose doting, if it got out of hand, might have become dangerous and painful.

Finally, Kohut married a professional person, as Mr. Z. had, and his social relationships gradually changed in that he withdrew from many of his old friends.

Clearly I was forming the conclusion that there is no Mr. Z., that Kohut and Mr. Z. were the same person. This was a shocking revelation that I dared not voice, because I had no tangible proof. I was simply speculating. Often therapists attract patients who are similar to themselves. Still, the similarities were staggering, especially their narcissistic needs.

The reader may have noted that my presentation of Mr. Z. had some speculative qualities and that I claimed knowledge that did not come from the material Kohut presented. I was moving back and forth in my thinking from a two-person therapeutic relationship to the projections of one person that would have very little if any claim to scientific validity.

In any case, I was stunned and shocked about my conclusions, but I finally had to reveal them in a confidential fashion to several colleagues whom I hold in high esteem. They found it hard to believe, but accepted that my reasoning seemed sound. They also advised me, as I had already decided, not to make my suspicions public, so I just sat on them for several years.

Cocks's (1994) compilation of Kohut's correspondence finally came into my hands, and I was stunned when I read that Mrs. Kohut and her son believed that her husband was Mr. Z. In a sense I felt vindicated, but I was also sad and perplexed.

I wondered why Mrs. Kohut made such a public revelation, that she let the cat out of the bag, rather than keeping the memory of her husband unsullied. I found it remarkable, however, that this information was given in a casual, offhand manner as if there were nothing unusual about faking a case report. Apparently Mrs. Kohut, a sensitive, charming woman, did not believe that her revelation was, in any way, unusual.

Later, at a meeting, my dismay was further intensified when I discussed the revelation in Cocks's book with a self psychologist. He said that he had known for years that Kohut was Mr. Z., and that a fair number of his colleagues also knew. No one seemed to be particularly concerned, although they were not talking about it openly. Ernest Wolf, in a book review, mentioned the possibility that Mr. Z. and Kohut were the same person, but he indicated this was a delicate matter and did not wish to pursue it further. At least, he did not seem to be proud of it.

In this instance, as I anticipated earlier, I have to abandon some of my objections to ad hominem arguments because the situation among the self psychologists is so outlandish that it cannot be explained by rational arguments. It is as if the leader of their movement can do no wrong. He is above the rules of scientific integrity and ethical decorum. Recall Goldberg's words, as quoted by Gedo (1997), that even though Kohut broke the rules of social conviviality, one must remember he is the only national monument we have. Narcissism rules supreme and it does not matter if the data are made up; the theory and technique is so elegant that it does not need the usual scientific evidence to validate it.

Those self psychologists who feel some need for rational support argue that most clinical presentations are not exact replicas of the facts, that case reports are usually disguised because of not wanting to intrude on the patient's privacy and to maintain confidentiality. The other argument usually given is that Freud analyzed himself and wrote about it. Both of these arguments are specious, lame attempts and rationalizations to justify Kohut's false presentation of data.

Regarding disguising clinical presentation, from what I can gather Kohut disguised very little. I and others who knew him well were able fairly easily to recognize Mr. Z. as Heinz Kohut. Besides, what was he disguising, the fact that he was the patient? He did not want to reveal he was writing about himself, but to achieve this he had to invent a fictional patient.

Even though most case histories are disguised, they usually include a patient and a therapist. These are two-person relationships and they focus on the interaction between those two persons. How can one discuss a therapeutic relationship, an interpersonal interaction, when there is no second person, as occurred in the second treatment where he is inventing a narcissistic interaction and calling it an object relationship? Narcissism is a powerful force that spreads from individual ego boundaries to a system of thought.

True, Freud wrote about himself, but this was an entirely different situation. He did not use his self-analysis to justify a system of therapy. He was simply trying to learn about his own psyche, which he must have assumed was pretty much like anyone else's. Though highly varied, our minds have a large degree of commonality, as do our livers, lungs, and other organs. Freud wanted to understand himself, hoping he would discover some universals, as he believed the Oedipus complex to be. Furthermore, Freud was quite careful to reveal the source of his data when he felt it was relevant. He did not conceal, he had a self-analysis, and he frequently wrote about his dreams and fantasies. Freud's observations were not based on a transference interaction. When asked about transference interactions in self-analysis, Freud humorously replied that one had to beware of the countertransference.

The essence of the therapeutic action of the self psychologist's approach is the growth-promoting potential of empathic attunements within the context of a narcissistic transference, which they prefer to call the mirror transference. This type of interaction is obviously impossible in a self-analysis in the Freudian sense. It could not occur with Mr. Z. because Mr. Z. was analyzing himself, and this is tantamount to pulling oneself up by the bootstraps.

In both so-called treatments, the patient was angry, demanding narcissistic gratifications from the therapist. In the second treatment, how can one be demanding and angry for attention from oneself? In the first analysis, Kohut claims he was trying to analyze defenses, presumably narcissistic defenses so the oedipal material would emerge. He indicates that there was a struggle going on between himself and the patient in both analyses as would often occur in analyses in which patients experience resistance. A struggle would also occur if the therapist believes he is dealing with an oedipal neurosis, but the patient is suffering from a structural defect and a narcissistic imbalance.

Some speculate that his first analysis was a report of his analysis with Dr. Ruth Eissler. In that case that would have been a two-person relationship and Kohut is disguising both patient and therapist. However, it is implied that there was a misdiagnosis, that what was thought of as an oedipal problem was really a narcissistic disorder, so if Kohut is reporting accurately, Eissler did not understand her patient and this would have caused complications, accounting for the failure of the treatment. A treatment aimed at resolving an oedipal problem when there is a structural defect is bound to fail and *this is not an indictment of the classical approach.*

At most, the first course of treatment is irrelevant and it does not matter what happened because Kohut's claim that his method of treatment is better is neither supported nor refuted by its presentation. The falsification of data is meaningful in the second treatment where the interventions reported could not have been effective in a one-person self-analysis.

If everything Kohut wrote about is not pure fiction, then we would have to believe that he was having an internal struggle during his self-analysis. This could only happen in a quasi-psychotic ego, which uses massive splitting mechanisms for one part of the psyche to be at war with another, and I do not believe he qualified for such a diagnosis.

Ordinarily, the self-analyses therapists conduct are attempts at exploration. One part of the psyche is not actively fighting against another one and clinging to defensive beliefs. Clinicians might find it difficult to get in touch with hidden parts of the self, but they do not become angry and demanding and feel entitled. Such feelings can be evoked only in an object relations context.

The most ridiculous feature of the narrative of Mr. Z. is Kohut's claim that he made an empathic interpretation and the patient felt calmed and soothed. He said that it was understandable that a person might be disappointed when he felt he did not get what he thought was his due. This remark was intended to make the patient feel better about himself, to bolster his self-esteem and to provide some narcissistic supplies.

If such a mild remark made to the self, especially an angry, needy self, were to have a soothing, reassuring effect and eventually lead to internal changes, then therapists would be entirely superfluous. Kohut was acting as if patients were superfluous. Such a self-soothing remark would be the ultimate of picking oneself up by the bootstraps and brings us back to Coue's daily chant, "Every day and in every way, I am getting better and better." This would be a monumental regression in psychotherapeutic technique rather than an innovative treatment approach.

As appalling as I find Kohut's deception, I find the attitudes of some, not all, of his followers equally, if not more, dismaying. To try to pass it off as inconsequential as some have done or to rationalize that his ideas stand on their own or that Freud used his findings from self-analysis is an attempt at condoning what is obviously a breach of scientific ethics.

I feel indignant and sad because of my early friendship with Kohut and his very obvious talents as a clinician and teacher. To forestall anyone who wishes to impugn my motives for writing such a highly emotionally charged critique, I felt it had to be done. Someone had to speak up and it seemed no one would. No matter what else within me might have been involved, I feel that the integrity of psychoanalysis is at stake, a field that has recently suffered many blows and does not need any hidden skeletons in the closet.

Clinicians can take some ideas from self psychology and then move them forward. Its emphasis on structural factors, its object-relations orientation, and certain insights about narcissism will be retained in any treatment-oriented theoretical system that will help us deal with the different patients commonly seen today, but its flaws have to be acknowledged.

THE RELATIONAL APPROACH—OPEN VISTAS

Mitchell (1980, 1988) is a prominent member of a group that can be considered to be in the avant-garde of an object relations approach. Some of the ideas of the intersubjectivists as well as self psychologists are included in their thinking and clinical innovations, but Mitchell's writings, in contrast to theirs, are comprehensive and lucid, a refreshing change.

There is an open quality to Mitchell's writings and he is very explicit as to how he presents his data. For example, Mitchell (1993) wants to eliminate jargon as much as possible. His aim is to take one definition of psychology as "jargonized common sense" and to dejargonize it. This accounts for the clarity of many of his expositions.

Instead of case presentations, he presents short vignettes to make a specific point, these being fairly direct discussions of his experiences with patients. He realizes that the essence of psychoanalysis is confidentiality, so he makes up composites when he needs to present clinical material in greater detail. What is included in these composites are patients he has seen, and not made-up hypothetical treatment interactions.

As with self psychology the self has a crucial position in the relational approach. The self is a difficult concept to formulate and it can be approached from different vistas. There is a view of the self as consisting of multiple layers, some on the surface and some concealed. Others believe that the self exists only in relations with others, a more current concept that emphasizes the relational context.

Mitchell acknowledges his predecessors and outlines the connections (not necessarily a continuum) between Freud's formulations and those of modern object relations theory. Freud wrote about conflicts emanating within a tripartite model—id, ego, and superego—whereas Mitchell (1993) believes that "the joints of the mind are located at the borders between different versions of the self. Conflict is now envisioned as the clash between contrasting and often incompatible self-organization and self-other relationships" (p. 104). These formulations do not replace classic analytic theory. Rather, they lead to extensions.

Moving into object relational theory has often meant that psychodynamic conflict theories have been replaced. Instead of viewing psychopathology only in terms of intrapsychic conflicts, structural defects have been highlighted as the source of emotional problems. There has been a shift from id-ego conflicts to conflicts between the ego and the outer world. Relational theorists add another dimension to what is not necessarily a dichotomy. Instead of drives, various dimensions of psychic structure, such as different levels of the self, can be observed as clashing with each other. This still maintains an intrapsychic focus, not entirely eliminating clashing internal forces, although now these forces consist of various parts of the psyche and, according to Mitchell, these are different levels of the self.

The healthy ego consists of compatible selves that compose a well-synthesized, cohesive self representation. There may be as many facets to the self representation as there are in a well-cut diamond, which can be examined in terms of individual facets or grossly as a whole.

In the psyche one can view the self as a continuum proceeding from the surface to the interior, as I have written about the identity sense (Giovacchini 1965). First, a person can be identified by appearance, such as height, weight, hair color, race, and so on, followed by nationality and religion, occupation, marital status, and finally internal characteristics such as feeling states, moods, and narcissistic balance. The self is a highly complex variable structure, and Mitchell views it in both spatial and temporal terms. Each facet of a well-constructed self has to be in balance, that is, compatible with other facets, but this does not always happen.

Winnicott (1960a) wrote about true and false selves, a division often required to maintain contact and harmony with the outer world. The false self sometimes hides the true self in order to protect it. This is similar to an ego defense causing repression of a drive whose emergence might be disruptive to the psyche.

The false self also represents a surface adaptation to the external world at the expense of autonomy. I believe the word *false* is an unfortunate choice because it has a pejorative connotation. The false self is simply a structure that tames the expression of instinctual needs as it adapts to the exigencies of the outer world. It may require some sacrifice of autonomy as it conforms to the rules of civilization, and, for the most part, it is compatible with other facets of the self.

In severe psychopathology, widely different selves are often acceptable to each other. I recall a state hospital patient who believed he was the emperor of the universe. This did not interfere, however, with the chores he had been assigned, such as scrubbing the floor. He was comfortable with the oxymoron of royal janitor.

Psychotic patients often clearly reveal how different parts of the self clash with each other, an intrapsychic conflict rather than one that primarily involves a clash with the outer world. From the viewpoint of the patient's psychopathology, the difficulties with reality are secondary. This would seem to indicate that these patients are better understood in psychodynamic terms rather than object relations theory. However, objects are still involved, but they are internal objects (Robbins 1993).

A middle-aged scientist was brought to therapy by his family because he had become an embarrassment to them. He would stare into empty space for hours at a time, but if he was addressed, he would respond. He had never married, but he had a few male friends with whom he played tennis, and he was a member of a group that was immersed in oriental mysticism with an emphasis on karma (fate).

It turned out that when he was staring into space, he was hearing voices. These voices were friendly and teaching him various things such as giving him pointers for his tennis game. They also made observations about other people and his surroundings, which he found helpful in dealing with them, although, for the most part, he kept his distance.

Still, as Mitchell discussed, he defined himself in terms of his experience with people such as the tennis player or the scientist. In his fantasies and hallucinations he was explaining or elucidating what he was doing to someone else inside of him. He did not feel any conflict with external objects, although they began feeling conflicted toward him and they demanded that he get into therapy. This was after he told his parents about the voices. He had also alienated himself at work.

When I first saw him, he was quite animated and told me with great enthusiasm about his karma and soul traveling, reaching different levels and planes bringing him closer to the Grand Master.

I was astonished to learn that the Grand Master did, in fact, exist, and on one occasion came to Chicago for a convention of a group that believed their souls could travel to ethereal heights and that they could communicate through mental telepathy, not requiring any direct sensory contact. Communication, as with everything else, was an internal process and did not require an actual external object, although there was a fantasized object or internal object. The patient was constantly speaking to internal objects and he frequently withdrew and ignored the external world.

Nevertheless, he was friendly with me, although he did not believe he needed treatment. He enjoyed the opportunity to proselytize and to win me over to his viewpoint.

He extolled the virtue of the Grand Master and told me he received 10,000 letters a week and personally answered every one of them. I foolishly asked him how that was possible, to which he calmly replied, "Well, he is omnipotent." Reality, in the conventional sense, had little meaning for him and he was content engrossing himself with internal objects.

He also frequently talked about lengthy discourses he held with Darwin, who was part of his inner world. Darwin apparently was somewhat of a technician and they spoke about electrical problems, wiring, and circuits. I wondered why he had to have such a lofty person as Charles Darwin to discuss what appeared to be mundane and concrete problems. He indignantly protested that he was not talking about Charles Darwin, but Darwin an electrical engineer from the West Coast, who was now residing within himself. I struggled to explain to him that he was reifying and anthropomorphizing feelings and parts of the self, but he insisted he was dealing with internal objects and not intrapsychic phenomena.

All was not well in the inner world. Darwin and the Grand Master were powerful, helpful, and reassuring, but there were evil forces inside him that wanted to tear him apart. Another reason his family brought him to see me was that periodically he would have acute panic states that required his being sedated, but as far as could be determined, there were no precipitating factors to account for them.

He brought me a dream that heralded such a panic state. He was being carried in the arms of a Titan dressed in armor and with a sword and shield. A dark huge lizard somewhat similar to *Tyrannosaurus rex* lunged at the warrior Titan, pulled off his breastplate, and with his sharp teeth tore his heart out, causing the patient to be dropped in a swamp in which he sank. Swamp gases enveloped him and he burned like a will-o'-the-wisp. This was one of a group of panic-producing dreams in which some giant's heart would be torn out and the patient would be dropped and would perish. In this dream, he became a will-o'-the-wisp and gradually fluttered into a state of nothingness.

The patient's dream depicted internal objects around which he had formed a delusion of good versus evil waging a war within him. In a sense, these internal objects can be viewed as different aspects of or various self representations that were far from compatible with each other, a contrast to the royal janitor who could accept contradictory aspects of the self.

This patient, however, could also be described in terms of oxymorons. He believed himself to be powerful and omnipotent as he identified with the Grand Master. Yet he was considered by his family and their friends to be peculiar and inept, and he was treated like a child. He had no difficulty in accepting such demeaning behavior toward him.

The incompatible and destructive internal objects, as they formed varied self representations, were frightening and could not be tolerated, as evidenced by his excruciatingly painful panic states. The external world of objects, however, did not exert such powers over him. He was able to ignore it and maintain his grandiosity. Object relations became damaging only when they were internalized. The same can be said about the production of narcissism and grandiosity. These qualities were acquired when narcissistic enhancing relationships were internalized, but such interactions did not exist, or if they did, they were minimal in his childhood.

Thus, he could maintain an oxymoronic stance between the self and external objects, but not among his various internal objects. The external world was not able to reciprocate. It could not adapt to or tolerate his attitude of omnipotent ineptness and it forced him to be institutionalized. As might be expected, he was given heavy doses of antipsychotic drugs, which, in a sense, killed or drugged his internal objects.

I reached this dramatic conclusion because after he was released from the hospital he continued his therapy with me for a short period of time. Whereas previously he was animated and talked about his internal world with vivacity, he now looked like a zombie and reported feeling dead inside. He denied that the Grand Master and Darwin were inside him and repeated in a parrot-like fashion that these were figments of his imagination and personification of parts of himself, interpretations I had repeatedly made. For me, the present state was more painful than when he was actively delusional.

I doubted that he really believed what he said about the personification of parts of himself, but, obviously, the effects of internal objects had been considerably dulled by phenothiazines and by the fear of being reinstitutionalized if he once again spoke about them. In any case, he had developed sufficient control by having decathected the internal world and this made him more compatible to the external world. This was at the expense of his vitality.

When I questioned him about the sincerity of his convictions regarding the status of the internal world, he felt mildly relieved. He felt mildly about everything and though he still believed in the existence of the Grand Master within himself, it no longer had the impact or gave him the powerful feelings he once had. Grandiosity was vapid.

I believe that what he was expecting from me was to revive and restore his previous internal organizations by discussing and encouraging his delusions. I could not join him in such an endeavor, but I felt sad because of the obvious pain he felt at having lost the vitality and power of his internal world.

I presented in Chapter 1 the young man who wanted his hallucinations back after they were made to disappear by drugs. I suggested that he stop taking his medication and he could have his voices back as long as he needed them.

There are some differences between these two patients. The hallucinatory patient was dealing with voices that were perceived as being outside the self, that is, he did not initially view them as being part of himself. He dealt with them as a segment of the outer world and was able to deal most of the time fairly well with the rest of reality. He could keep the voices segregated from the remainder of the external milieu. Furthermore, his external objects, primarily his brother, were able to tolerate his behavior. The one time the voices intruded into all of his surrounding world he had to be hospitalized.

The situation was markedly different with the patient presented here. His external objects could not accept his inner psychic life. There was no segment of reality that could accept him, except for the organization that was oriented in a similar fashion, but it was not an immediate presence required to support a psychotic inner world.

Although it might have made the patient feel better, I could not support a delusional system, which I believe the self psychologists sometimes attempt to do. I did not disapprove of his internal objects, but I sometimes found his detailed descriptions of the wisdom of the Grand Master and the reflected glory he received somewhat tedious, in part because I felt it was a hopeless situation. Reinforcing primary process demands cannot lead to higher levels of structural organization. That is how I felt about this patient, whereas the patient who needed his voices did not require reinforcement. He could have his voices as long as he needed them and I did not encourage or disapprove. In a sense, I was neutral and could look forward to a time when he would not need them. They were not the essence of his existence, or of the construction of the self, as the internal delusionary objects of the scientist patient were. They were defensive adaptations that could be discarded as the psyche progressed along the developmental pathway.

In both patients, the genesis of psychopathology, as well as its maintenance, depended on relationships. Therapy also depends heavily on the interaction between therapist and patient. I have preferred, along with many other clinicians, to define these interactions in terms of the transference–countertransference axis. Even when conflicts seem to be deeply internalized, relationships are involved in either stabilizing or dissipating psychopathology as well as in determining whether the therapeutic process will be effective in acquiring higher levels of psychic structure or end in a stalemate.

Unfortunately, I was not able to find my way out of the dilemma the scientist patient created because he presented an unsolvable paradox. To make him feel alive, I had to join him in a delusional system that was not always comfortable, but that sustained him because of its grandiosity. The family would have fought me if I had tried. I would have been involved in a complicated network of relationships dealing with the patient's inner and outer world. My sadness about and sympathy for the patient, which could have led me to side with his psychopathology, ran counter to my professional ego-ideal, which, as I will discuss later, would have upset my narcissistic balance.

Freud did not stray beyond the patient's psyche when he discussed clinical situations, as has been made apparent in recent books about his patients. He was aware of transference; in fact, he discovered it, but he did not discuss it as an active dynamic in the treatment process. The patients I have just been discussing focused on intrapsychic processes, but the therapeutic field would have been limited and constricted if relational factors were excluded. The therapist's role is also expanded in that I had to evaluate the forces that impacted on the patient and how they led to changes not only in psychic equilibrium, but also, I suspect to some extent, in the types of introjects and internal objects such patients construct.

The self is determined by its experiences, that is, by how it relates to external objects. It is easy to understand how the self develops and is constructed from experiences with the outer world. Winnicott (1969) describes how the object is used in the process of identification. Identification is a mechanism that leads to a sense of identity, the construction and cohesion of the self representation. He describes in detail how the subjective object is used and finally relinquished on the pathway to establishing external objects as the self separates and recognizes the existence of the external world. In essence, Winnicott's exposition is a detailed account of the progression of secondary narcissism to external object relationships.

Mitchell and his colleagues explore the internal world in terms of relations as they view multilayered and continuous selves. They make their concepts clinically relevant as they demonstrate how they can use them in a treatment context, opening up new vistas on the therapeutic process. In many instances recognizing these widened clinical dimensions can help therapists overcome various obstacles that create impasses. In other situations, therapists find that they cannot work in the context the patient and the external milieu have created, as happened with me and the scientist patient.

CONCLUSIONS

Most theories that deal with in-depth therapy have strayed from paying exclusive attention to intrapsychic factors and give interactions with the outer world a more prominent position. This is not a particularly new or different direction, as the works of Horney (1937, 1942) and Sullivan (1953) indicate. I have discussed three "schools" that have emerged: those of the intersubjectivists, the self psychologists, and the relational therapists. As mentioned in the preface, there are many other prominent contributors I could have discussed but most of them have not pulled together a systematized body of concepts that could be grouped in a category and elevated to the status of a school. Therapists such as Boyer (1983), Giovacchini (1979), Kernberg (1975), Masterson (1976), McDougall (1985, 1989), Volkan (1995), and Winnicott (1958a, 1974), to mention a few, have roamed freely in the realms of object relations but have not forsaken thinking in terms of intrapsychic forces conflicting with each other, which, in some circles, has become politically incorrect. Masson (1988), in particular, has vehemently attacked looking into the patient's mind as being assaultive and demeaning.

Large segments of modern psychology have given up conflict theory. The intrapsychic focus has been abandoned, and many psychotherapists decry instinct theory but also reject the idea that patients may be having internal troubles. Some of the recent schools reflect these attitudes by emphasizing relationships and not accepting that patients have some responsibility in creating their emotional problems.

As happens to society in general there are cycles in mental health movements and swings between biological and psychological theories. I believe there will be a backlash as the emphasis on object relations continues to increase and moves too far away from looking into patients' minds and assessing how they contribute to their emotional difficulties. We are swinging too far in the direction of the environment as we get further away from the mind.

Within the last decade the successful struggle of non–M.D.s to gain admission to psychoanalytic institutes and societies has led to many changes in our thinking and approach to patients. Practitioners have attacked the medical model as being tyrannical and authoritarian. Many good things have resulted from the influx of psychologists, social workers, and nurses, but we have to be careful not to throw out the baby with the bathwater.

Intersubjectivity theory, in particular, has moved away from the clinical arena and has joined the ranks of the philosophers. It seems today that the effort to obliterate the medical model has also obliterated the clinical focus and approach. This is particularly striking during many clinical presentations by nonmedical practitioners. They may, for instance, start their case discussion by talking about the patient's babyhood, and continue along developmental lines before letting us know the gender and age of the patient. These presentations are haphazard and often miss the salient features that would give clues to the genesis of psychopathology or open up avenues for exploration. In some circles, the concept of psychopathology is rejected and denigrated as a taboo subject.

A psychiatrist would be less likely to indulge in such unorganized presentations. There is an orderly and systematized quality to a medical history, a sequence that directs and guides our attention to diagnostic channels.

Taking and presenting a history can be learned. Anna Freud, at the Hampstead Clinic, organized an approach called the index, which is similar to a medical case history. This is interesting because she was neither a social worker, a psychologist, nor a psychiatrist, and yet she discovered one of the most essential ingredients of the medical model.

The main objection to the medical model is that it is a one-sided relationship in which the patient is the passive recipient and the doctor is the supreme authority who cannot be questioned. Freud is sometimes cited as an extreme example. For example, Kardiner (1977) writes about his analytic experiences with Freud. Freud concluded that the material he was listening to was oedipally oriented and that Kardiner wanted to kill his father. He interpreted this to his patient, but Kardiner questioned the validity of what Freud told him. He mildly protested, because obviously he was afraid of Freud, but stated that he did not think the interpretation was correct. He added that perhaps he wanted to kill Freud. Freud became angry and accused Kardiner of being uncooperative and resisting his interpretation. He became so vehement that he threatened to stop his treatment. If Kardiner did not believe him, he could go back to America. Kardiner hastily admitted that Freud was right, that he really wanted to kill his father. It seems strange now that Freud should have reacted so negatively. Kardiner was merely rephrasing Freud's interpretation in a transference context, and this is what is supposed to happen in a well-conducted treatment.

Not all changes in theory and technique are dictated by scientific principles. This book has been stressing the impact of narcissism in initiating movements that are sometimes fads but deemed to be politically correct (Lasch 1991). In the behavioral sciences, there has always been a hierarchy, with the psychoanalyst at the top, the psychologist next, and the social worker at the bottom. Many activities are politically motivated and clearly the inequities psychologists and social workers suffered weighed heavily in their decisions dealing with concepts and technique, decisions about their therapeutic philosophy. It is easy to understand why they would reject what they believed had a medical tinge in view of their having felt unfairly excluded. This is understandable but not necessarily wise for the field of mental health.

The narcissistic thread binding the superior position in the clinical area was held only by psychoanalysts and psychiatrists. It was first broken by psychologists when they succeeded, over the protests of the medical establishment, in getting licenses to practice. They, in turn, resisted social workers when they attempted to achieve the same recognition. These struggles were not based on ethical concerns; each group tried to exclude others because of pragmatic issues involving competing for patients and making money.

These are reasonable issues, but there is some ambivalence about accepting them by the professional members of these various groups. They need more lofty reasons to explain their competitive and perhaps greedy behavior, and they may seek their rationalizations in creating systems of thought that will support their professional status. This may mean destroying the status quo as it had been constructed by physician-analysts for the most part.

Being politically correct has become a rationalization and has gone to ridiculous lengths. For example, the people physicians treat are called patients. Psychologists and social workers treat clients. Now there is a movement to take everything out of the medical model or even out of mental health by calling therapists providers (initiated by insurance companies) and those they treat consumers. Some of the theories I have discussed reflect this tendency to equalize, which unfortunately in some instances brings us outside the professional arena. Consumer and provider refer to services, but providers may also be plumbers, electricians, or any other tradesmen. The psychotherapeutic relationship, in my mind, is at a different level; it has a dignity of its own that is intrinsic to the treatment interaction, a respect that develops in the participants that is mutually enhancing and rewarding. Recently, an article in the "Piece of My Mind" section of the *Journal of the American Medical Association* makes the same point about medicine in general (Jackson 1998).

The theoretical schools I have discussed also stress equality but the therapeutic interaction goes beyond equality as it eschews submission to the severe medical model.

In most schools of psychology the conflict model has been given up. A distinguished former head of a department of psychology told me that if he were starting all over again, he would not choose to enter the field. Clinical psychology has radically changed.

First, it practically ceased to exist as it was replaced by experimental psychology. Now, it has lost all dynamic qualities. To look for intrapsychic factors and to understand the patient in terms of unconscious motivation is, in some circles, tantamount to blaming patients for their plight. Patients are victims of infantile trauma, a victim psychology that precludes any explanation of what the patient's role might be in the production of psychopathology. Even the word *psychopathology* is a pejorative term to some psychologists.

Patients are hapless victims of circumstances, as the repetition compulsion is cast aside, and therapy is aimed at attempts to heal a damaged ego by treating patients kindly and making up for infantile deprivations, an approach that is not particularly different from what is proposed by self psychologists. Acquisition of insight and understanding the nature of inner conflicts and psychodynamic constellations have little, if any, role in most treatment relationships.

Often, there is a limit to how much empathy such therapists can give. As Ornstein (1972) stated, eventually one has to debunk the patient's grandiosity or use an ironic tone, as Kohut presumably used on himself in what, at best, could be called a self-analysis. These therapists who are basically operating in a social context frequently become impatient and end up, in one way or another, insisting that the patient grow up. Usually the patient's dependent needs and demands have become annoying.

For example, a social worker forbade a patient from calling her because the patient was calling frequently and at all hours. In view of the pressure the patient was putting on her, it was understandable that she impose some limits, perhaps to preserve her sanity. The patient, a housewife, would have accepted more frequent appointments rather than calling, but her therapist would not give her extra sessions. She felt she was too dependent and thereby restricted how much infantile gratification she should allow.

Here there is a contradiction that is found in many therapists who have abandoned or who never learned the conflict model, which stresses the intrapsychic focus. These therapists attempt to make up for infantile deprivations and trauma and yet they forbid some infantile and regressed states. By refusing to look for sources of and the adaptive significance of regressed behavior, therapists are telling patients that they have to suppress revealing the manifestations of psychopathology. At times, regressed behavior can become unmanageable and then we call it acting out, but this has to be examined in a transference–countertransference context to determine whether therapeutic resolution is possible.

There is much to be gained by broadening our therapeutic perspectives and including an exploration of the psyche's relations with the outer world, but not at the sacrifice and abandonment of the exploration of intrapsychic conflict. The two go hand in hand and are not mutually exclusive. Unfortunately, much of the present-day practice of psychotherapy has moved away from the patient's mind and limited the treatment process to the creation of what optimally, but seldom, is a restorative relationship.

❖ C H A P T E R 4 ❖

Narcissistic Investments and Clinical Dividends

Many years ago, candidates at psychoanalytic institutes were strongly invested in classical theory, and perhaps by emulating their mentors their dedication became a source of narcissistic supplies. It has been said that patients treated by Freudian analysts dream Freudian dreams and those treated by Jungian analysts dream Jungian dreams. This implies that our orientation is sometimes forced onto the patient, and this is apt to happen when our dedication to a point of view goes beyond scientific consideration and evaluation. Personal involvement obscures our vision and creates biases that are imposed on our patients. When narcissism is involved this can cause clinicians to lose their objective, nonjudgmental stance.

Narcissism is not always deleterious. There are different forms of narcissism that can be placed in a hierarchal continuum, which this chapter discusses. First I demonstrate how a fairly common form of narcissism determined how clinical material was understood, and how a change in narcissistic balance led to formulations that were antithetical to the unanimous consensus that had been reached.

THE TWO ANALYSES OF MRS. A.

Imitating Kohut's description of the two analyses of Mr. Z., I will describe a patient who had only one analytic treatment, but who was first formulated in terms of a classical neurosis; forty years later, another formulation was made that was quite the opposite of what had been agreed upon during a clinical seminar when I was a candidate at the Chicago Institute for Psychoanalysis.

The patient, a 19-year-old married college student, sought analysis because she had free-floating attacks of anxiety and was generally unhappy. She complained of finding it difficult to concentrate, and this interfered with her studying at a highly demanding university. She also had various phobias, such as a fear of heights and of riding on trains and other forms of public transportation. She had nightmares in which she would be falling in empty space. She also considered herself ugly.

Actually, she was quite attractive, but she was dressed in a peculiar and noticeable fashion. She wore a shiny patched blue serge suit coat that she had borrowed from her husband. She also wore a man's white shirt that hung over a pleated tartan skirt. My first impression was that of an abandoned waif.

Her symptoms began several years earlier when she was smuggled out of Europe during the Second World War. She was the only daughter of a wealthy Jewish family. The Nazis invaded her country but the family was able to arrange to have her sent to the United States to stay with an aunt. The patient assumed that her parents had been killed because after the war she was not able to locate them.

Her life here was almost a direct antithesis of what she experienced in Europe. There she was taken care of by servants, lived in a mansion, and could have practically anything she wanted. This all suddenly changed when she arrived in Chicago. Her aunt was living at almost the poverty level, and the patient had to sleep on a tattered couch in the living room. Her meals were bought by food stamps.

Her childhood was not exactly idyllic, either. Though all her material wants were catered to, she did not feel much warmth. Her mother was cold and withdrawn, and apparently quite narcissistic in that she was more concerned with clothes, jewelry, and social status than with her daughter. Her father was a compulsive, managerial type who was very involved with her and took over all facets of her life. Though she was just in early adolescence when she left Europe, he was insistent that she marry a Jewish professional and he took an avid interest in her coiffures and wardrobe. He was sensitive and aware of his humble origins and wanted his daughter to become a member of the aristocracy now that he had amassed a fortune.

Outwardly, the patient seemed to have adjusted well to her new environment. She apparently was better educated and more sophisticated than her peers and was fluent in several languages. She graduated with high honors and won a scholarship to a prestigious university.

I was struck as to how different she looked from her father's idealized version of her. Her hair was disheveled, as was her general appearance. There was a sad, languid quality about her, quite the opposite of the narcissistic Jewish princess.

Shortly after she started at the university, she met another impoverished student who was working at a practically full-time job. (Though this school had high academic standards, it let its students progress at their own pace. They were free to choose the number of courses they wanted to attend beyond the basic requirements.) They married two months after they met. He had secured work as a janitor and they lived in a small basement apartment.

Her life was shabby and drab, but she seemed reconciled to it. She did not complain, but I suspected that her symptoms and seeking analysis were a form of protest. She had become very interested in psychology and was pleased that the Chicago Institute for Psychoanalysis had accepted her as a control patient. They had diagnosed her as a hysterical character disorder, believing that she was one of the transference neuroses Freud (1914a) wrote about, an opinion that lingered for many years.

She started analysis in an animated fashion, but she presented a curious mixture of seductive charm and a joyless, sexless appearance. Her demeanor was quite in contrast to her physical being. It seemed as if she lived in two worlds, as she actually had.

Her first group of dreams reflected her inner duality. She would juxtapose different geographic locations. For example, she would dream of a famous boulevard or avenue in the city of her birth, but on the sidewalk would be the building she lived in now and the entrance to her basement apartment. She would also dream of Chicago's Michigan Avenue and Lake Shore Drive in the midst of dilapidated peasant huts of her home country. I conjectured that her unconscious was still living in both worlds, but she could not decide which one to accept because they each held considerable pain for her.

My supervisor, on the other hand, chose to emphasize that the patient was trying to settle into the analysis. She saw a foreshadowing of a dependent phase. We discussed oral dependent defenses, and soon the patient began having dreams that seemed to confirm such a formulation. She dreamed of receptions being given especially for her, lavish affairs with gourmet foods and wines. She was the center of attention and often her father appeared in these dreams.

The transference motif was also becoming clearer in that some of the persons she dreamed of were poorly disguised versions of me. This phase of treatment lasted nearly three years in which oral and narcissistic elements were becoming clearer.

She also began to feel anger and resentment about her riches to rags transition, and she evinced considerable vehemence about her impoverished state. She separated from her husband and finally divorced him when she was a senior.

She had obtained a fairly lucrative part-time job and was able to move into an apartment that was considerably better than the one in the basement. Finally, she found work as a social secretary; she lived in her employer's mansion in a comfortable apartment of her own. Her wardrobe had also improved and she became an attractive, chic woman.

I had constantly interpreted her oral-dependent defenses as they had been transferred onto me, and as I kept emphasizing the dependent transference, she became increasingly feminine and attractive. At the beginning of treatment, most of her wardrobe was masculine, and although she did not look masculine, she gave the impression of being sexless. This was no longer the case as her behavior also underwent drastic changes.

Previous to analysis, she had led a demure, chaste life. There was practically no sex with what she described as a dull, undistinguished, colorless husband, who remained a janitor, as far as we know, for many years. During the first three years of treatment sex hardly entered her discourse, but now this drastically changed.

With some reluctance, she told me she had met a foreign student on the campus and she became deeply infatuated with him. He was supposedly the son of an Italian count, something that she valued because it appealed to her vanity. I said nothing but thought about her father's ambitions for her to become a member of the aristocracy rather than being just a servant or a social secretary. I felt uneasy about this relationship; she told me a lot about her lover, and I suspected he might be somewhat sociopathic. I suspected that he was an arrogant impostor who could hurt her physically and emotionally.

I evinced some doubts about what she felt was an ideal relationship, but I did not actively discourage her or give her any advice. My suspicions, however, turned out to be correct; she discovered he had been arrested several times for pretending to be of noble blood and then trying to swindle his would-be victims.

The patient felt sheepish when the truth about her lover became known. Just one week later, she had met another Italian student and had slept with him. Then she met more Italians on campus and had affairs with them. She had become quite promiscuous and she seemed to flaunt these experiences in front of me. I tried to be impassive but I had some forebodings.

My supervisor and I came to what we believed to be an obvious conclusion. We decided she was in the throes of an erotic transference, but instead of bringing it into the treatment she was discharging her feelings by acting out with Italian men who represented me since my name is Italian. It is amazing how many Italians were on that campus at the time. We decided that I should be vigorous in interpreting the erotic transference, with the explicit intent of curbing her acting out, which we feared was reaching dangerous and self-destructive proportions.

Here is an example in which a therapist tries to use an interpretation to impose a prohibition, and maybe that is why my attempts at interpretation failed in that they had no effect on her behavior.

She continued being promiscuous. I remember how some therapists had insisted on abstinence of certain instinctual impulses, following Freud's rule of abstinence, and this often led to an adversarial relationship.

Her recalcitrance and her stubborn pursuit of Italian lovers created what we considered to be a stalemate. The analysis was not progressing to what we hoped to be the oedipal phase. Her libido was spread all over the campus rather than in the consultation room, and my supervisor and I felt we were facing a very difficult dilemma.

With reluctance we agreed that I had to be firm and prohibit her from any further sexual acting out. I believe my reluctance was greater than that of my supervisor, but I agreed with her that it had to be done or the treatment would have been doomed. I had to tell the patient that if she continued her behavior, there was no point in continuing the analysis, since there would be no hope of resolution. Her feelings had to be mobilized in the transference. I explained all of this as best I could, as gently as possible, and without the use of technical jargon.

She accepted what I said quietly, agreed to do as I asked, and did not request any further explanations. Nevertheless, I was uneasy about what I had done. Although she acquiesced without protest, I felt she was quite angry and that something had happened in our relationship that might change the tenor of the treatment. Something vital had been lost.

My supervisor was delighted about the way I had intervened and predicted that once again the treatment would get moving. Still, for a while we were both on tenterhooks because, although the patient agreed to curtail her behavior, there was a change in her mood that to me spelled disappointment and distance.

Nevertheless, she continued doing well both in school and on her job. While employed as a social secretary, she made many friends and her social circle widened. She graduated with honors and then started a business of her own.

In the treatment, she stressed her need to be independent, her desire to have a husband and a family. She had met a young man, a Jewish physician, and at the end of the analysis, they married. It was this event that ushered in the termination phase, and she clearly was anxious to end her treatment. She felt that her analysis had been completely successful, that she was now a grown-up, independent woman and had found the man she loved. She accentuated this with her final dream in which she was getting married and I was acting as a father-surrogate giving the bride away. She seemed grateful and we parted on good terms, but I have never heard from her again.

My supervisor was pleased and believed that the successful outcome of this treatment indicated that classical analysis, which in this case meant emphasizing the analysis of the transference and not letting it be dissipated by acting out, was an effective method of treatment that led to character changes. She derived personal gratification for her contribution to the treatment, which, in retrospect, I admit was considerable. I do not believe I would have been able to prohibit the patient's acting out without my supervisor's prodding me.

The patient's final dream was especially impressive. We believed it indicated the resolution of the Oedipus complex. She was dreaming about transferring her oedipal wishes toward me as representative of the father in the transference to the young man of her choosing. The fact that he was a Jewish doctor, supposedly the ideal choice of Jewish mothers, only in this case it was the father, was also a sign of success. To us it meant that she was no longer rebelling against her Jewish background or against her parents' ideals as she had done at the beginning of treatment when she was married to a gentile failure who would not be able to supply her with the luxuries her parents had provided for her. She was able to achieve what her parents wanted for her and still preserve her autonomy without needing to self-destructively rebel. She could now reconcile herself with her father's wishes and accept them as her own.

The promiscuous acting out with Italian students represented a rebellion with self-destructive elements as well as a defense against the erotic transference.

Our wrapping up of this case was neat, and I believe that my supervisor and I felt, if not smug, at least somewhat self-satisfied.

My supervisor felt pleased because the worthiness of analytic dedication was once again proven, and her skills as a teacher were further confirmed. My narcissism, in turn, was also boosted for a job well done and the mild applause I received from my teachers and peers.

I had periodically presented this patient at the clinical seminars that were the core of the curriculum at the psychoanalytic institute. The case presentation had been well received, but the last one, which dealt with the termination phase of analysis, was particularly memorable. The leader of the group, Eduardo Weiss, a pioneer and experienced clinician, was particularly impressed with the sequence of events as they unfolded in the treatment relationship. At the same time, he displayed some confusion and puzzlement and then he asked me why the treatment had been so successful. At first, I was startled. What kind of question was that? If something had gone wrong, then pursuing what happened, how the process had derailed, would have made sense. But to ask why something had gone right seemed paradoxical. Still, part of me believed this was a meaningful question and I did not have an immediate answer.

My colleagues and I had many reactions to this seminar; some threatened our narcissistic balance and made us question our faith in the intrapsychic approach. Here was a patient who seemed to have an optimal treatment experience, and our suspicious reactions would cause us to believe that a successful treatment experience was so rare or nonexistent that when confronted with one, we had to explain what happened over and above understanding the process from a technical perspective.

For a while, the group sought reasons other than therapeutic resolution to explain why and if the patient got well. Outwardly it seemed as if she did, unless she was lying, but this seemed hardly credible. One of the candidates conjectured that maybe she wanted to give me a gift of a successful analysis and went through the motions of achieving psychic help. This discredited the role of interpretation and the technical handling of transference projections, and the group agreed that the handling of the transference was correct. The question of why she would want to grant me such a gift was raised, but no one was able to answer it.

Finally, the success of the treatment was attributed to the patient's characterological strengths. She had been able to withstand the traumas of displacement, the descent from riches to rags, and the move to a strange new country. She was perceptive, psychologically minded, and had a good capacity to integrate insights. We were all happy about the conclusions we had reached, and our narcissism and the security of our professional ego ideals remained intact. Our faith in the classical approach was renewed, and I was given credit for a control case that enabled me to graduate from the institute and become a member of the American Psychoanalytic Association and the International Psychoanalytic Society. All had gone well for the patient, the psychoanalytic movement, my colleagues, and me.

It should be clear to the reader that the fact that I am discussing this patient in such detail hints that I do not believe all was well. Throughout the years, I periodically thought about this patient and found it increasingly difficult to rest on my laurels. Two events kept nagging at me.

First, I still felt uneasy about my instituting a prohibition. Those were different times and reactions to her behavior today would not be as shocking. Several years ago, I presented this patient to the Dallas Psychoanalytic Society and they asked what difference did it make if she had been promiscuous as long as she exercised some caution. In the 1950s, sexual mores, although they had relaxed considerably, were much tighter than they are now. The Dallas analysts were able to separate her behavior from psychodynamic factors, although they were also able to connect it to the transference. They avoided the pejorative term *acting out* and were nonjudgmental. They reinforced my doubts about my intervention by giving me the impression that they would have acted differently. Still, how to overcome her resistance to acknowledging the erotic transference was a question that was difficult to resolve.

I conjecture that if therapists of the past had the same attitudes about sexual behavior as those of today, there might not have been a problem. In this patient, sexual acting out could well have been an iatrogenic notion absorbed by the patient in the service of resistance. Our expectations that we would encounter resistance might have become a self-fulfilling prophecy. Several decades ago, therapists had more fixed criteria as to what might be the manifestations of successful treatment. They were often formulaic in nature, usually including material success and a good heterosexual adjustment.

By contrast, current attitudes about good therapeutic outcome have changed considerably. There is less focus on behavioral change and more on the establishment of internal equilibrium and autonomy. Patients make a choice as to what adaptations they will use to relate to the external world. As long as they are more or less acceptable to the milieu, patients are free to relate as they please. Homosexuality is an example of what in the past was considered a defensive, psychopathological mode of relating. It has become, in most circles, an acceptable adaptation and is considered an alternate lifestyle.

Perhaps if my attitude had been more relaxed and not implicitly prohibitive, my patient might have been able to allow herself to experience erotic feelings toward me and discuss them more freely. Still, many patients developed and revealed their erotic transferences. It is a question of degree of how intense internal prohibitions of oedipal sexual feelings might be. My patient undoubtedly had severe superego pressures against incestuous impulses that could be discharged in potentially self-destructive relationships. If she had experienced her therapy as more relaxed and accepting, she might not have found it necessary to evade them by her promiscuous behavior.

Another source of my uneasiness was the speculation made by a peer that perhaps the apparently successful analysis was a gift that the patient gave me. The group had some hesitation in accepting how well things went. The analysis started with oral dependent defenses that protected her from emerging incestuous feelings. These pregenital impulses were analyzed and then she went through a period of intense resistance sustained by sexual acting out. The Oedipus complex was finally resolved when she stopped acting out, and then she achieved freedom and heterosexual harmony. This is a formula, a simple sequence of analytic progression, first the analysis of pregenital defenses, followed by facing the oedipal complex and then working it through, which results in release of libido, which is then directed toward external objects.

All of this sounds contrived, especially the dream in which I am giving her away as she is being married. It does not even sound as if it were a dream. It sounds more like a made-up story or a daydream because it seems to lack any primary process elements. This would support the thesis that she was giving me a gift.

All patients' material has some significance beyond conscious intent. It has been said that no one can make up a dream that is not significant and indicative of processes going on at deeper levels of the personality. Still again, it is a relative question, and a contrived dream may have been motivated by more secondary process elements than an ordinary dream that begins at deeper unconscious strata. With my patient, making up a dream to please me could very well have been part of the gift-giving process.

Finally, I accepted the gift-giving conjecture of my fellow student and the reason for such behavior became obvious. I recalled how the patient's demeanor had changed after I gave her the ultimatum of discontinuing treatment if she did not stop her promiscuous behavior.

As a child she felt extremely insecure. It was dangerous to identify with her mother, who was so vulnerable and needy. She was nurtured by maids, who took care of all of her material needs. The mother seemed to require whatever energy she had to hold herself together.

Her father treated her like a porcelain doll, which only reinforced her feelings of fragility, but she also received tremendous narcissistic gratification from his idealization of her. Her feelings alternated between seeing herself as an abandoned waif and as a princess. Oddly enough, she achieved a degree of comfort with both roles, which served her well when her status was drastically altered as she arrived in the United States. She was fairly comfortable as an abandoned waif.

I now believe that she decided to leave treatment to get away from my dominating influence. This was a recapitulation of her relationship with her father, who tried to run her life according to his needs.

I now turn to the "second" analysis of Mrs. A. As far as I know, she did not have a second analysis, but I wish to formulate her dynamics and treatment from a different perspective than that of classical theory. I believe she can be viewed in terms of object relations theory with an emphasis on structural factors, narcissistic balance, and the integrity of the self representation.

This shift in the theoretical frame of reference will give different meanings to the behavior and the material she presented. This does not totally invalidate the formulations we made many years ago, because behavior is multidetermined and can be understood from different levels. Nevertheless, this "second" analysis, that is, its formulation, gives the clinical material and therapeutic outcome a different slant.

When she started treatment, she had dreams in which the new country and the old country were juxtaposed. I believed she was trying to bring her past life into the current setting. She was also trying to convert the treatment setting into her home. The consultation room was being made into a transitional space, literally by spatial manipulation as manifested in dreams that had a playful quality. This could have indicated that she was attempting to create a setting in which problems could be worked out and the developmental process set in motion, which meant moving into the new culture, and she seemed to adapt well.

The analysis of the passive-dependent transference as a defense against oedipal feelings can be looked at in a different light. Instead of being such a defense, it could have represented an attempt to establish a relationship with her father—the positive side of the ambivalence she felt toward him. Parties, banquets, and receptions, as they occurred in her dreams, rather than simply referring to regressed oral needs were symbolic of the narcissistically gratifying relationship she had had with her father. He had related to her in such a manner during childhood and especially puberty when he gave her many debutante-type parties. Psychically, she was trying to cast me in such a role as she transformed me into the giving father, but there were conditions to what she was receiving.

What he gave her was not totally fulfilling. It made her feel tranquil but it was not basically satisfying. She sensed that something was missing and she probably recognized that his interest was tendentious, that he was catering to his own needs by aggrandizing her. I do not believe she felt genuine love from him, and her mother could not supply emotional nurture. I believe that the so-called oral dependent dreams were wish fulfillments in which she was expressing her needs for love and acceptance. In the dream setting, as in the playful activity of the transitional space, she could symbolically depict what she felt she lacked. This is a different dynamic from that of an intrapsychic conflict between incestuous desires and superego prohibitions that took the form of defensive regressed oral impulses.

I recall a dream that, at the time, I believed was another incident of dependent defenses, because it involved eating. She dreamed of a large banquet hall. In one corner was a quartet playing soothing chamber music. She was half reclining on a couch, feeling languid contentment. In the center of the room was a long buffet table overflowing with delicious dishes and sweets. She had eaten a considerable amount, but she was in no way full. All the food was diet food with practically no calories, so she felt as hungry as ever, even after she had eaten amounts that would otherwise have satiated her. Nevertheless, she was appreciative of the soothing music, but she also felt sad because the food appeared attractive but had no sustenance.

Since then, I have divided the nurturing experience into two compounds, a foreground consisting of the nurturing substance, primarily nourishing food, and a background in which the child is being comfortably held as the food satisfies needs and soothes internal agitation. Instinctual needs are gratified in a calm, tranquil environment, what can be called the holding environment. The patient in the dream indicated that she had formed a transference in which I could soothe her, like the quartet in the corner, but I could not feed her. More precisely, she could let me soothe her but did not want me to feed her.

Everything in her family was at the surface level. Her mother and father were both concerned with appearances and did not care about what lay beneath the surface. As with the diet foods, there was no substance. She could not trust me as she could not trust her parents, especially her father, who seemingly reached out to her although she never felt that he really cared for her.

I felt that if she allowed me or her father to symbolically feed her, we would have become too important and therefore dangerous because she would have found herself vulnerable to our whims and caprices. She would be cared for, but at the expense of her autonomy.

At times during her analysis, she spoke of feeling as if she would be swallowed up, but these associations were regarded as her fears of her oral dependent impulses getting out of control. A defense, in itself, could become dangerous. In this revised analysis of Mrs. A., I conjecture that she was trying to let me care for her but was afraid that she would lose all semblance of autonomy as she would feel herself being destroyed by fusing with me, the noxious selfobject Kohut wrote about. This was depicted in the dream by letting me soothe her, but the food that I was offering her was as shallow as her family's values.

To carry along this line of thinking, her promiscuity was not a defense against an erotic transference. It was, albeit self-destructive, an attempt to get what she could not allow herself in the transference interaction, and at the same time it was a reaction against what she experienced as the burdensome aspects of her father's possessiveness. Though she had never previously acted out, she had fantasies of rebelling, of unchaining herself from the shackles her father put on her. These fantasies were a current that continued to run through her thoughts and might be considered a fantasized version of the repetition compulsion, which finally was translated into sexual behavior.

Her relatively quick adaptation to impoverished circumstances, paradoxically, could have been part of her rebellion, as previously hinted. Her marriage to a poor gentile student and her odd manner of dressing were as far off the mark as she could get, considering her father's interest in how she should dress and his wanting to place her high in the social hierarchy.

I have written very little about her mother because in the treatment she was practically nonexistent. I did, on occasion, question the lack of material about her, but the patient shrugged it off, indicating that there was little feeling between the two, that they had an ephemeral relationship. My supervisor and I believed that oedipal guilt might have forced the patient to repress her feelings about the mother, but it is equally possible that because of the lack of nurturing experiences she had an imperfectly formed maternal introject.

These formulations, which stress object relations and adaptations to the outer world but do not eliminate intrapsychic conflict, put a different slant on my intervention of prohibiting her sexual behavior. Unwittingly, I would have been playing into the manipulations of the repetition compulsion. I placed myself in the cast of characters, and not only was I the receptacle of the patient's projections of the father, but I had become the father when I told her to stop acting out or else I would have to stop the therapy. This was a harmful countertransference enactment about which I had no insight. It was harmful because I had no insight.

As I repeatedly emphasize, countertransference always occurs and can be useful if the therapist recognizes that it is operating. My narcissistic attachment to the classical position and my wish to please my supervisor so that I could graduate and because she was, in fact, a decent person, might have blinded me to what was really going on.

Hitler's invasion of my patient's country, in an odd way, provided her with the opportunity to free herself from her father's dominance. She was a passive participant in the liberating process and did not have to display open signs of rebellion. As with her father she had to get rid of me and she had to achieve this in a passive fashion because she still carried within her a primitive terror of actively tearing herself away from a nurturing source, even though it was threatening and far from satisfactory. She could not openly take the initiative to leave me or her father. It had to appear as if she had nothing to do with leaving. If she disobeyed me, she would be actively rebelling, and she did not have the courage to defy me because of superego pressures, among other factors. This was another vestige of the father transference.

I believe that she unconsciously decided to have me send her away as her father had done. She wanted to please me, which she could do by giving me the gift of a successful analysis, as my peer many years ago believed might be the case. The final dream, in which I was giving the bride away, was not so much my giving her away as it was her leaving me as she had to leave her father to find her autonomy. I hope she has found it.

If the therapy had been as successful as we thought it was, it was strange that I have never heard from her. I usually hear something from my former patients. If she had moved she might have sent me a note or announced the birth of a child if she had one. Perhaps she might have sent a Christmas card, but there were no messages indicating that she had some good feelings about our therapeutic experience. Maybe her analysis was so thorough that she completely worked through the father's transference, but I doubt it.

I have given this fairly detailed account of this patient's dynamics because I wanted to demonstrate how the clinician's theoretical orientation may determine how patients are understood, and this can vary considerably, dependent upon that orientation. I am not to this day certain which formulation is the most correct. I state the question in such relative terms because the complete picture of Mrs. A. could include elements from both of her analyses (the first actual analysis and formulation, and the second formulation).

The two formulations cannot be completely reconciled and it is more than a question of emphasis, although there are some factors that are not mutually exclusive. Mrs. A., who needed to liberate herself from her father, may have had incestuous wishes toward him at another level. As is well known, behavior and feelings are multidetermined. Still, the trends in the two formulations are different and the various transference phenomena take on other meanings than those we formulated during her treatment.

There is internal consistency in both viewpoints. Our narcissistic attachment to the conclusions derived from the classical approach must not have been too secure. There was considerable doubt, not necessarily about the success of the treatment but as to why it was successful. These concerns, including my own, caused me to reexamine the clinical material and seek other explanations that may be more plausible. Since then, I have seen many patients whose psychopathology could best be explained as examples of structural defects, so I applied these concepts to Mrs. A.

The dedication to this latter point of view may also be determined by narcissistic factors, but it has nevertheless proved clinically useful. It is a balanced approach as it explains many phenomena that emphasize problems with the self representation and adaptations to the external world. The object relations approach is less fixed to a rigid theory than the classical approach and more flexible and modifiable as new clinical material is gathered.

NARCISSISM: ITS EXTENT AND VARIABILITY

Concepts of psychopathology have turned from Oedipus to Narcissus. This shift focuses on two points of view. First, it attaches greater significance to psychic structure, particularly the self representation, rather than on clashing intrapsychic forces. Second, it focuses on developmental factors, inasmuch as narcissism is in the minds of some clinicians a vital developmental phase, and defects on that level lead to the psychopathology that is so frequently encountered today.

Unfortunately, the term *narcissism* has acquired a pejorative meaning. It has been used to demean, and it has been frequently leveled against psychoanalysts, who have been considered to be a particular species of narcissistic characters. I realize that I have also used the concept in a negative sense, especially when I assert that the weakness of many theories and formulations can be attributed to a narcissistic attachment to them or that certain theoretical concepts are compatible with the narcissistic needs of the leaders and followers of a particular movement. The negative connotation of narcissism, however, is very narrow, and the concept is basically rich and varied.

Narcissism is an essential ingredient of creativity and humor. When it is being used defensively, it can be offensive and felt as arrogant. I believe how one responds to a narcissistic display can immediately tell us what type of narcissism we are dealing with.

Other types of narcissism are not experienced as arrogance. Persons in the midst of creative activity may often brag about the significance and extent of their discoveries, but their listeners do not feel threatened; instead, they may be amused and sometimes even share in the enthusiasm. They may resonate with the innovator's good feelings. For example, Archimedes boasted that if he were given a spot to stand on, he could move the earth. Most people are happy to agree with him, because they know what he says is hypothetically true. Having discovered the principle of the lever, what he said was feasible, and undoubtedly there was a playful quality to the way he said it.

Einstein and Bohr playfully argued with each other using hypothetical experiments that could never be replicated. Their back-and-forth banter and claims were sometimes outrageous, although they were dead serious about their beliefs. The accounts of their interactions are amusing and awe inspiring, as we realize that we are witnessing the interplay of great minds and in no way do we feel that they are trying to enhance themselves by exclaiming their superiority. Feynman, a Nobel prize-winning physicist, was well known for his sense of humor and his pranks, but he was also known as a brilliant, intuitively sensitive person (Feynman 1989a,b, Gleick 1992).

I recall a patient, a creative scientist, who while lying on the couch would gently wave his hand back and forth. It was a graceful nonoffensive movement. I asked him what he was doing and he told me that he was causing a building that was in his view to rock back and forth. The patient had had a brief psychotic break but his gesticulating did not seem portentous of psychic disintegration. It seemed whimsical, playful, and amusing rather than grim and megalomanic. Following his lead I kept looking at this particular building and I could imagine it was swaying. The effect of this behavior was pleasant and amusing and the patient was able, despite his temporary loss of psychic equilibrium, to continue with his creative work.

I recall another occasion of a blatant display of narcissism that created no particular response except to note that I was witnessing a curious and interesting phenomenon. A celebrity was a member of a panel, in which I was included, on a popular television talk show that was discussing important current events. Before the cameras started rolling, the participants were sitting around a huge coffee table, drinking coffee and chatting amiably as we were getting acquainted with each other. This celebrity was slumped in a chair, his eyes closed and totally withdrawn from the group. He looked like an abandoned puppet with no muscle tone, and since he seemed to need to withdraw from the rest of us, no one paid any attention to him.

As soon as we were on the air with the camera focused on him, he came to life. He straightened out his body, sat forward, and became increasingly animated. He asked brilliant questions, made cogent comments, and in general dominated the discussion. As soon as the camera was turned away from us during commercials, he once again collapsed into a puppet. It was if the focus of the camera was his life force. He had to be on display and the center of attention to give him a sense of aliveness. Still, no one was threatened by his behavior. The group's response was neutral and the other members were perhaps somewhat amused. Somehow he managed to maintain his self-esteem but at no one else's expense.

Generally, narcissism can be classified into two categories: (1) as an accompaniment of normal developmental stages that expresses itself in heightened self-esteem and self-confidence, and (2) as a defensive adaptation usually associated with psychopathology.

Freud (1911, 1914a) included narcissism in his developmental pathway. He compared the beginning psyche to a blastula embryonic stage in which there is very little differentiation. There is no distinction between the internal and external worlds. The libido, essentially an energic force, is autoerotic, that is, various organs are libidinized without acknowledgment or recognition of the surrounding milieu.

As briefly discussed, when external stimuli impinge on the periphery of this undifferentiated mass, it achieves a degree of organization leading to the formation of a rudimentary ego. Psychic energy is directed to this peripheral structuralization, and this Freud called primary narcissism, a stage along the progression of the psyche into the outside world.

Both Winnicott (1969) and Freud (1920) believed that the early formation of object relations, which simply means that the external object is acknowledged as external, involves many subjective elements. Winnicott wrote about the external object being created by the baby, a belief that was fostered by the mother by not intruding her presence. This early stage of a subjectively created object is called secondary narcissism, a concept that has been minimized by the intersubjectivists and the self psychologists who underplay the equivalence of secondary narcissism and the self-object.

This balance between subjectivity and objectivity persists through all later developmental phases, even when object constancy is achieved. This is a narcissistic balance that determines the well-being of a person who maintains self-esteem as he becomes involved and gives of himself in intimate relationships and other psychic investments involving considerable expenditures of psychic energy.

Freud (1905a) described emotional development in terms of libidinal satisfaction. To avoid irrelevant controversy I will bypass the discussion of the sexual nature of psychic energy or even the concept of psychic energy per se. Basically, he viewed developmental progression as a series of psychosexual stages determined by various parts of the body that participate in the achievement of instinctual satisfaction, stages such as the autoerotic, oral, anal, phallic, and finally a sexual desire for the opposite sex. For many reasons this sequence has been challenged, particularly by Fairbairn (1941, 1954). The important point is that Freud, after he left the phase of autoerotism, was describing psychic development as dependent upon relations with the outer world, essentially an object relations approach.

Rather than relating various organ systems to relations with external objects, I prefer to conceptualize psychic development as a continuum from relatively amorphous perceptions of reality to sophisticated, sensitive assessments of the external world. This approach focuses on sensory elements. However, alongside the development of perceptual sophistication the ego's executive systems learn about methods of adaptation, enabling it to relate better to the exigencies of the surrounding milieu. This is a narcissistically enhancing process promoting heightened self-esteem. Thus, developmental progress is the outcome of a hierarchal sequence of adaptive mechanisms containing both sensory and motor elements.

I have outlined the first stage of development as a prementational state, one that preceded psychological processes, and, at this stage, the concept of self does not yet exist. This is also a prenarcissistic phase because there can be no balance between the outer and inner world. The child's orientation is basically physiological, as feeling states vacillate between calmness and internal disruptions that are devoid of psychological content. The neonatologists find as they delve further that this phase becomes shorter in duration as infants presumably can be aware of elements of the external world very soon after birth. It is an important phase because it is related to some very primitive forms of psychopathology.

As the child matures, the early beginning amorphous perceptions of reality become more structured, but there seem to be two trends simultaneously operating. The first is similar to an inertia in which the infant wants to maintain a subjective stance, a position of narcissistic invulnerability. Alongside this inertia is an innate push to explore the surrounding world, an exploratory curiosity that moves away from self-preoccupation but that can be even more gratifying. This movement toward the exterior reaches its peak after the consolidation of the transitional phase, as Winnicott (1953) formulated.

Within the transitional space the psyche moves back and forth from the inner to the outer world. Narcissism becomes coherently organized as the self fuses with external objects and reciprocal interactions are the outcome of such fusions.

Winnicott describes how illusion is responsible for the creation of the transitional space. The infant believes he is the source of his nurture because the mother is so perfectly attuned to her child's needs that she satisfies them as soon as they are felt. The child then believes that wishes have a built-in mechanism for their satisfaction that therefore is under his control.

The child's perception of the world is subjective. Children during the transitional stage blend the exterior world with their inner life, and they create transitional objects by bringing them into their perceptual sphere and possessing them. Winnicott believed the child felt omnipotent because he could be totally self-sufficient. I doubt that children of 6 months of age could form a construct as complex as omnipotence. The feeling of omnipotence has to be formed at a later age, but in regressed states it can be retrospectively placed into the transitional space.

I believe that during the transitional phase, children acquire a mechanism in which they create an internal harmony that is felt to be under voluntary control. This is a mechanism associated with primordial narcissism that later becomes elaborated into complex feelings of self-confidence, and by exaggerated distortions it is transformed into states of grandiosity.

Each developmental phase can be scrutinized in terms of narcissistic balance, roughly a ratio of how much a person is involved with the self to how much psychic energy is directed toward the outer world. With cholesterol levels, absolute quantities are not as important as ratios between good and bad lipids to determine risks of cardiac problems. Regarding the psyche, we can only calculate in relative terms about quantities, and ratios will inform us as to risk of decompensation, but even then some persons are capable of immense expenditures of feelings toward others and yet retain significant quantities of self-involvement, helping them preserve considerable self-esteem.

The situation with the mind is considerably more complex than cholesterol levels. The experiences of giving and being intimately involved in external object investments can, for certain persons, be self-enhancing. The ratio between self and object interactions may remain constant, but the level of good feelings about the self rises in both the self and object as a consequence of their interaction. Another person does not necessarily have to be involved; this enhancement can occur when the self is involved in creative activity as the subject explores the outer world and changes it by adding something—the creative product—to it.

In psychopathology, this positive feedback does not occur. Often, self-esteem is not generated by object relations. Rather, interactions with reality frequently lead to feeling depleted and, for the most part, patients with narcissistic problems cannot profit from potentially helpful experiences. These patients are often the offspring of narcissistic parents and they tend to become involved with narcissistic characters.

An attractive divorced professional woman lamented that all the men she encountered were incapable of forming intimate relationships. She stressed that both her parents were narcissistic, and her former husband and her bosses were narcissistically oriented. These were insights that she acquired during a lengthy analysis. She sought treatment shortly after her divorce when she generally felt anxious and depressed. She had lost her sense of direction, and was unhappy at work because her supervisor demeaned her for being a woman, but he took credit for her work. He made her feel as if she were a woman of no importance. Most of the people at work were misogynists, but they tolerated her presence because her contributions were valuable; at times she was able to pull the department she worked for up to acceptable standards. Her co-workers and superiors might have been fired without her accomplishments, but they never acknowledged how important she was.

As a child, she was constantly criticized by her mother. Her father, apparently, was irascible and sometimes physically abusive, and when he was not hitting her for some misbehavior he totally ignored her. Mainly, he ignored her, since most of his physical violence was directed toward a younger brother.

Her father was hardly ever at home and he died when she was 9, so her mother was the dominant figure in her life. Clearly, the mother, by fusing with her daughter, used her for narcissistic gratification. However, this was far from a mutually enhancing experience. During her treatment, the patient described moments with her mother when she felt exhausted and depleted of all good feelings she might have had toward herself. She was then angry at herself for giving in to her mother, primarily by letting her get to her, and then she would feel inadequate and self-critical.

The mother always favored the patient's sister, who was the ugly duckling, whereas the patient was the belle of the family. Even today at a party or family gathering the mother would begin her conversation with the patient by making a disparaging remark about her clothes, her facial expression, and her appearance in general. She was projecting her self-perceptions into the patient, as if she were getting rid of the hated parts of herself. Nevertheless, she clung to her and would brag to her friends about her professional accomplishments and beauty. It seemed that she wanted the good aspects of her daughter for herself and wanted to deposit what she found reprehensible in herself into her daughter. This is another example of a destructive fusion, and the patient was getting the worst of it as the narcissistic flow, in terms of self-enhancing exchanges, was a one-way stream that moved from the patient to the mother. There was no mutuality or reciprocal interaction and my patient felt that her mother was her nemesis.

As an adult, she developed various somatic symptoms that involved the gastrointestinal system. All the members of her family were obese, except the patient, who is slender and trim. Her symptoms were often the outcome of a megacolon brought about by her mother's critical harangues. The patient could actually feel herself trying to push back her mother's words, which were experienced as piercing arrows or painful pinpricks in her abdomen. Somehow, the maternal relationship, instead of being nourishing and providing healthy levels of narcissism, had become painful and had provoked painful responses. It seemed as if her unconscious were saying, "I cannot take any more shit from my mother," and her colon refused to continue functioning. For her gastrointestinal tract to function harmoniously required an inner calm that her mother disrupted.

Her somatic symptoms were also aggravated when she had no relationship and when she felt lonely and isolated, a void because of a lack of engagement. This often occurred at work; her current job was boring and it did not keep her busy or challenge her. She needed excitement in order to feel alive.

I believe that the patient had problems being soothed, and that self-soothing mechanisms were not very well developed in her psyche. As I have described, the nurturing relationship can be divided into two components, the foreground of actual nurture and a soothing background. This patient's mother, apparently, could not soothe her daughter, an interaction that requires an ability to give, which is associated with an adequate amount of healthy narcissism and self-confidence. The mother was too needy to cater to the needs of her children, and this led to a state of narcissistic imbalance.

Such an imbalance, accompanied by a lack of empathy, was strikingly clear in an experimental interaction that was part of a research program, a longitudinal study of the mother–child interaction and the development of psychosomatic symptoms. A mother and her baby were filmed in a room with a one-way mirror. The child, a 4-month-old boy, was sleeping peacefully in a crib. This was an open-ended situation in which the mother knew she was being observed, but was given no particular instructions. She could do as she pleased. After a short period of time, the mother showed increasing signs of restlessness. She started pacing around the room indicating that she felt she had to do something. Knowing she was being filmed meant to her that she had to give a performance. She had to be in the narcissistic spotlight and in this context, it meant that she had to demonstrate her virtuosity as a mother.

Finally she picked up her infant son who had been sound asleep and started rocking him. She swung him in a jerky manner, our first spontaneous impression being that she was jerking him around. Naturally, he was jarred awake and started crying. To counter his crying she tried humming, but it sounded like a shrill wail resembling the keening sounds of relatives accompanying the dead. Her son, as would be expected, cried louder, which only caused the mother to strengthen her efforts. She kept up her wailing, rocked him harder, and started poking him with her fingers in the abdomen, making both the scene and noise intolerable. Finally, one of the attendants interrupted this chaotic crescendo when it became clear that the infant could not take any more soothing or, to use an oxymoron, disruptive soothing.

We had witnessed a negative feedback sequence in which the infant's vulnerability had reached a peak and the mother had failed in elevating her self-esteem as a mother. We observers felt we were looking at a highly traumatic interaction, a catastrophic disaster equivalent to watching someone being murdered, at least a psychic murder. We were impressed with how violently boundaries had been violated, but the lack of realistic motivation was just as appalling. The mother's motivation was based on the inability to enjoy the initially peaceful situation of her infant comfortably sleeping. She needed an interaction in which she could feel some narcissistic aggrandizement. Her failure to achieve it caused her to desperately increase her efforts.

Perhaps the infant's lack of defenses against the maternal assault was the most poignant and tragic factor in the mother–child interaction. We felt that his pain was reinforced by his helplessness. We were witnessing the vulnerability of an unformed psyche that was being torn to pieces by someone else's misguided vanity and low self-esteem.

The impact of what the child suffered was well illustrated at a meeting of the Illinois Psychiatric Society when the film was presented. After viewing it for about five minutes, the audience loudly protested to turn off the sound. They could not stand it any longer. This was an interesting phenomenon, because the audience was mainly composed of psychiatrists, psychologists, and social workers, persons who had considerable training and clinical experience. If they felt threatened and vulnerable in spite of their understanding, sophistication, and defenses, imagine how devastated a child with practically no defenses would feel.

My patient seems to have undergone similar experiences during her childhood, but most likely of lesser intensity. As an adult, she had defenses, but she was still sufficiently vulnerable that she had somatic reactions. These traumatic, narcissistically draining experiences had become enveloped in the repetition compulsion.

At an unconscious level, she must have sought relationships with narcissistically demanding persons because she had so many of them both in her love life and her employment. Her women friends were also demanding but not to the same extent as men. The latter were not as disconcerting because her investment was less. She was looking for commitments and marriage. Without these expectations, she could be more comfortable and relaxed.

Early in therapy she revealed how anxious and needy she felt. She needed her mother in spite of feeling exploited by her. It was the only mother she had, the only source of nurture she knew. Unconsciously she believed that she had to be taken advantage of if she were to have a relationship. Inasmuch as she had a partial awareness of this orientation, she was angry at the world and it showed in her facial expression. This caused her to feel further isolated, because the men who might have been suitable would be frightened away, whereas exploitive men sensed her vulnerability and pursued her for their own ends.

Although her psyche pushed her toward exploitive relationships, she viewed herself as a worthwhile person. She had an ego-ideal, or, better expressed, she had an ideal self representation. She wanted to be respected and valued, but the repetition compulsion interfered with her forming mutually rewarding relationships.

This patient presents clinicians with an interesting paradox, which is seen in many patients who have a paucity of narcissism and low self-esteem. Nurturing is a painful experience for patients who have characterological problems. In this case it is the background of the nurturing relationship, which is associated with soothing, although in other patients the main problem relates to the foreground, the absence of the nurturing product. As with most psychological phenomena, there are no absolutes. Both the background and foreground are always involved, but in any particular case clinicians determine the emphasis, that is, which part of the caregiving experience is most involved. These early life traumas and subsequent defective capacities to incorporate structure and esteem-promoting interactions lead to characterological problems. If the narcissistic balance is upset, then emotional progression is hindered and lacks, in many instances, compensatory defenses and adaptations.

NARCISSISTIC IMBALANCE AND FUSION

The next patient, unlike the patient just discussed, had very little if any narcissism. She demonstrated how narcissism contributes to the cohesion of the self representation. Inasmuch as her narcissistic level was low, she had identity problems and exhibited many of the features of an as-if personality as described by Deutsch (1942). Rather than being a true as-if, I believe she was a pseudo–as-if personality, meaning that her lack of an identity sense and her ability to absorb those of others by fusing with them was a manipulation and defensive maneuver. Perhaps they were examples of an extreme type of false self, that is, a complete adaptation to the external world at the expense of all individuality.

The patient, a middle-aged woman, described herself as an expert in humiliation. Prior to therapy, she accepted a humble status that was overtly inflicted on her by her husband. He had an odd way of humiliating her, which involved not recognizing her presence. He would criticize and ridicule her behavior and opinions by referring to her in the third person.

She was the older of two children, with a brother several years younger. She recalled being blamed by her mother for being forced to remain with her father, and having to live with her husband in the city, whereas she preferred remaining in her hometown. The patient's birth was responsible for the mother's unhappiness. The mother clearly indicated that she wished the patient had never been born. However, after the brother had been born, she doted on him and expected the patient to do the same.

This was not exactly a Cinderella-type situation. She felt her mother was a nurturing person and recalled being fed and rocked by her in a soothing fashion, but the mother often sang a song about the death of a little girl. This was, of course, a somewhat traumatic nurturing relationship but she was fed, and, to some extent, soothed, although the theme of a little girl's demise must have been somewhat disturbing.

She definitely played second fiddle to her brother, being pushed into the background and related to only when she was given some task relevant to his care. Her father occasionally would take a strap and chase her as if he were going to spank her. She had done nothing to provoke a beating, but she hid and ran and he was not able to catch her. The one time he did spank her, she did not know why. In retrospect the patient believes that her father was playing a game, that he liked to tease. She did not react with pleasure at his chasing her, as some children do when their father pretends to be a monster and pursues them as they run and squeal with delight. For the patient, the situation was dead serious. The patient accepted both her mother's and father's behavior as the norm.

The parents played a game in which the father stole his wife's wedding ring. He might hide it in his pocket. The mother finally found out that the ring was not lost and was annoyed with her husband. On one occasion, the mother gave the patient the ring and this caused the father to become angry at his daughter. She did not understand what kind of game they were playing but she felt she was being used as a pawn.

Affectionate acts were intertwined with moments of nonexistence. She recalled being given a box of candy by her father, and her mother would bake cookies and put them in the patient's suitcase when she returned to college after a vacation break. The patient even remembers receiving a Valentine's Day card from her.

The patient was nonassertive and compliant; she accepted whatever role was imposed on her. When the patient was a child and her brother was a baby, she had to pick up after him when he threw things around. It never occurred to the mother that the patient was a person in her own right with needs of her own.

At the age of 4 or even earlier, she was aware that the brother was the center of attention. She vied with him to please the father, who was described as somewhat of a tyrant, but she felt that her brother and she finally reached a point when she gave up. She recalled an episode when her father asked where his glasses were. The patient and her brother scurried to find them, but she found them first. Feeling resigned she handed them to her brother to return them to her father. The patient felt rejected and humiliated but she hid her feelings even from herself. She talked very little and was withdrawn.

As she grew older, she created the illusion that there was nothing unusual in her position in the family. She felt that was the way things were. There were differences in the way boys and girls were treated. Furthermore, her brother was charming and she was not, so he deserved favored treatment. She did not feel that there was any reason for her to feel jealous, because she believed he did not take anything tangible away from her. She could face the fact that he was getting the major amount of love the parents were capable of giving.

It took the patient many years of treatment before she became aware of feeling rejected and was, in fact, jealous. She realized finally that she did not deserve to be treated the way she was. Her narcissistic supplies were so low that she calmly accepted the inequities between herself and her brother.

She had two analyses and she discovered in the first therapy that she felt rejected by her parents. It was not until she was quite far along in her second analysis that she became aware of her jealous feelings toward her brother.

The confusion created in her infancy was connected to how she was nurtured, particularly by her mother but also by her father. There were good aspects to her relationship with her parents, but there was always a flaw that spoiled its self-enhancing potential. I refer back to the mother singing a lullaby about a dead girl while feeding her daughter. The patient cried when she heard the song, but only now does she realize that she was crying for herself. The father might have been teasing and playing with her when he chased her with a strap, but for her it was not a joke.

Still, the patient was able to reconcile herself to the family situation by accepting it. She received a modicum of good feelings that she did not want to spoil with the anger of frustration and rejection. She had to survive in the environment, which required that she split off her resentment and true self. The surface layer of the personality was mainly one of acquiescence and compliance, a false-self, as-if personality. But this was a surface layer hiding a true self, which is emerging in her current therapy. This makes her a pseudo–as-if personality.

Why did the patient not build more structured defenses rather than the blankness of a pseudo–as-if organization? Perhaps she did not receive sufficient narcissistic supplies to structure a self representation. She felt depleted and withdrawn but by presenting herself in an amorphous fashion, she was able to avoid conflict with her family. She could adapt to their needs.

The surface lack of structure, the false as-if self, could be used in the service of adaptation, which meant fusing and blending with external objects. As-if and pseudo–as-if characters have a heightened ability to fuse, in which they lose themselves in the fusion state. The patient several times referred to the fable in which the robin swallowed the worm. At first the worm was frightened and indignant, but as it was being devoured, it acknowledged that robins had to eat. The worm had incorporated the robin's viewpoint at the expense of its existence.

A robin is a much more complex structure and higher in the evolutionary scale than a worm. Similarly, when dealing with psychic structure, the looser the organization, the greater the capacity to fuse, although there are many types of fusion ranging from the psychopathological to states of healthy intimacy associated with commitment and creative accomplishment.

The concept of the self-object implies that the fusion state can lead to developmental progression, that it is a process in the interest of growth. This type of fusion is an example of secondary narcissism in which the narcissistic balance swings toward the child and away from the mother. During such an early stage of emotional development, the mother as a person in her own right is not recognized. She is merely a functional entity who nurtures and soothes, a maternal function, an introject that can be used but not acknowledged. Nevertheless, the mother who is operating at a higher level gains considerable satisfaction in her merger with her infant, which started during her pregnancy and was manifested in a state Winnicott (1956) called *primary maternal preoccupation*. Mother and infant are operating at different levels of psychic sophistication in the process of emotional maturation, and there are different distributions of narcissism.

There are apparent inequities of narcissistic supplies in fusion states that occur in psychopathology. The worm was destroyed as the robin was enhanced. A fusion state in which one person drains the other might be called emotional parasitism, but I doubt that many such relationships exist. Most object relations in which some degree of fusion occurs are based on a certain amount of mutuality and in that sense can be considered to be symbiotic. The levels of narcissism involved determine whether it is connected with psychopathology. The mother–child interaction described here was characterized by uneven levels, whereas equal levels of narcissism are characteristic of both psychopathology and so-called normal relationships. There can also be different levels of narcissism in psychopathological relationships, but these are short-lived and the involvement is not very deep.

There are mutually adaptive qualities in long-lasting relationships, particularly in those of married couples (Giovacchini 1958). I have reached the conclusion that the character structures of the partners were identical. At clinical seminars, therapists often hear that the patient had made a bad marital choice in that she unfortunately found herself with a schizophrenic husband. From the relationships I studied, it turned out if the husband was schizophrenic, so was the wife. This equivalence of psychopathology was especially true for couples in which one partner was an alcoholic.

These mutually adaptive or symbiotic relationships are often complementary, which means that if one partner is active, the other is passive, or there may be a sadistic spouse married to a masochist. In alcoholic couples, this complementarity is particularly striking. For example, the husband may be the problem drinker and the wife is the long-suffering spouse. If, as happens, the husband gets treatment and stops drinking, the wife very often may become a heavy, disruptive drinker. Both husband and wife are alcoholics, but at any given time, only one of them is an active drinker.

In this situation, the wife needs to be actively suffering, most likely because of the impact of the repetition compulsion as it reprises the infantile milieu. She may have lived in an alcoholic household and learned to adapt to it. The fact that she can become an alcoholic when the emotional balance is upset indicates that she has been able to identify with an alcoholic parent, probably an identification with the aggressor. The husband becomes, in the present, a character in the wife's infantile scenario and the same applies to him in that the wife represents an important person from his past.

Thus, in spite of different behaviors, marital partners are very much alike in terms of internal conflicts and character structure. They need each other to achieve cohesion of the self representation and a level of narcissism to maintain it. By allowing each other to construct the infantile environment in the present, they are able to use adaptations that served them in childhood. How congruent these adaptations are with the demands of current reality determines the extent of psychopathology.

This is a relativistic concept of psychopathology based primarily on adaptation rather than on absolute standards. During short periods of time, there have been rapid cultural shifts, as discussed in Chapter 1, that have affected at least the manifest forms of emotional disorders.

Persons involved in symbiotic relationships may be able to adapt to the surrounding world as they contain the disruptive elements of their personalities in the symbiotic fusion. Inasmuch as they spill over into external object relationships, they relate in a maladaptive fashion that brings them into the realm of psychopathology.

Symbiotic ties in marginal relationships create sufficient narcissistic supplies to enable those involved to adapt to the demands of reality and maintain a sufficient amount of self-esteem. In healthier mergers, the fusion state generates energy, as happens in a sexual union. Freud (1920) described this energy-creating sexuality at the unicellular level.

In psychopathological mergers, one of the partners deprecates the other in order to elevate his level of narcissism. It is a common clinical phenomenon where the patient (husband) needs to step on the wife in order to enhance himself. This often happens in reverse, that is, the victim is the husband while the wife seeks aggrandizement in the relationship. In either case, the patient, either the aggressor or the victim, constantly complains and often threatens to leave the marriage but seldom does. This indicates that they are both deriving narcissistic supplies from the relationship.

A supervisee reported that his patient, a woman therapist, constantly complained about her husband—that he continued smoking, in spite of being well aware of the health dangers, and that he drank too much and at social gatherings he embarrassed her by being loud, indiscreet, and garrulous. Vacations were a nightmare because he insisted on making all the arrangements, but he managed to get the most inconvenient flights and the most expensive but worst hotel arrangements. All of her sessions consisted only of a litany of complaints.

At first the therapist believed he could work with this material, viewing it as some defensive protective maneuver. As time went on, he believed that she was repeating a pattern in her family in which the mother constantly deprecated the father. To safeguard her position in the family fold, she could not do better than her mother, whom she thought of as a jealous, covetous person. She allowed herself to excel intellectually because neither of her parents felt that scholastic achievements were important for girls, but in the interpersonal, heterosexual realm success was dangerous.

The therapist waited for some signs of projection, which he believed would have taken the form of a father transference, but she never complained about the therapist. She respected his skills and held him in high esteem. In fact, she was proud that he was her therapist, and frequently she bragged to her colleagues about being in treatment with him.

She never developed negative transference feelings, but even if it were outside the transference the therapist felt it was important that he make an interpretation about her feelings toward her husband. He pointed out the repetitive aspects of the marital relationship, comparing it with her parents' situation, and added that in many ways she was like her husband and that she had fused with him. By complaining about him she was putting unacceptable parts of herself into him. She agreed with everything he said and complimented him for his perspicacity. Still nothing changed; she continued berating her husband.

This went on for seven years, and the therapist wondered whether he should give up (see Chapter 5). He became exasperated and even started counting the minutes before she would begin talking about her husband. On many occasions, there were no preambles; she started these sessions by immediately berating him.

Finally, I was contacted for consultation and supervision. I knew because of my own experience that the patient's pattern was a difficult one to break. I adhered to the belief that patients should verbalize whatever they pleased and this would continue as long as they needed to. It seemed that this patient would go on forever. The therapist emphasized the lack of transference, but he was referring to a specific father transference and identification with her mother.

It soon became apparent that the therapist was having a countertransference problem in that he did not realize that her positive feelings toward him were sufficiently intense to be an idealization, and in themselves constituted transference. When this was pointed out, he recognized that his narcissism interfered with his recognition that he was being idealized. He had assumed that her positive feelings were realistically based. He enjoyed her admiration, which bolstered his narcissism. If he regarded it as transference, then it would be a phenomenon that had to be analyzed and then she might stop giving him narcissistic supplies, or, at least, he would recognize its infantile sources and it would become, from the viewpoint of his vanity, meaningless.

Together, we explored what the infantile sources might be. This required that the therapist interrupt the patient's litany and encourage her to focus on early family relationships. He learned that she was actually ambivalent about her father. She remembered many affectionate moments with him, such as going to amusement parks and movies with him, just the two of them, her mother usually being indisposed at the time. Thus, we concluded that she did, indeed, have a father transference that permitted her to attack her husband. She split her feelings, projecting the affection she felt toward her father onto her therapist and the hateful feelings, which in part were the outcome of identifying with her mother, onto her husband. In this way, she could fuse with both loved and hated parts of her father and maintain narcissistic equilibrium.

She felt fairly independent from her mother. She had many academic achievements that far surpassed anything her mother had accomplished. In many ways she was similar to her father and husband concerning feelings and behavior she disliked. She also tended to drink too much and to be pushy and garrulous, once again indicating a similarity of character structure in symbiotic unions that are long lasting. She made up for the negative parts of her fusion by projecting the positive parts onto her analyst and then fusing with him. As she split her father into good and bad, she split her fusion in a similar fashion by distributing good and bad parts between the analyst and her husband. This, of course, is characteristic of a preambivalent state as Klein (1946) emphasized, a state in which good and bad feelings cannot be contained in the same objects. Prior to treatment, the patient was able to feel ambivalent about her father, but she let the negative part dominate. This was a safe position because her mother disapproved of any attempts to sexually compete and it supported the mother's negative stance toward her husband. The therapy led to the splitting of the father imago, a movement that might be considered regressive. Nevertheless, regression is an inevitable process if therapeutic resolution is to occur.

The therapist interpreted these various currents and the patient was impressed with his insights and astuteness. She totally accepted everything he said. The therapist felt he had his countertransference under control and was able to objectively analyze her feelings and behavior, but, as had happened before, nothing changed. She continued as usual and never made any mention of the interpretations she had been given. Three more years went by, making it a total of ten years of treatment. The therapist felt frustrated in that she was not changing in response to his interpretations. He decided to set a termination date with the hope that it would stimulate some movement. He finally confided his frustrations to her and set a date six months in the future. He timed it badly in that he made his announcement at the end of the session.

She started the next session in the usual manner, something the therapist had not expected. He interrupted her litany and asked her about her feelings regarding the edict he had given her. For the first time in a decade, she was angry. She resented his interruption and told him he had no business telling her how and what she should feel. This was her therapy and she would continue it as long as she felt she needed it.

When my supervisee told me about this incident, I immediately remembered a similar situation in which a patient showed the therapist a bloody handkerchief she held in front of her mouth. She was nearly dying of tuberculosis when she entered treatment but for many years while in therapy she was symptom free. When her analyst confronted her with the length of treatment, she responded by having a hemorrhage and afterward by reading him the riot act and telling him to get further therapy, which he did (see Chapter 5).

My supervisee's patient's response caused us to alter our viewpoints about the purpose of her therapy. The patient who had tuberculosis needed to be in treatment to remain alive. Could something similar have been going on with my supervisee's patient? We finally concluded that the treatment had provided the patient with a setting in which she could maintain a narcissistic balance because she was able to effectively split various transference constellations and, at the same time, fuse with her mother, husband, and therapist, the last of these through transference projections. She needed the treatment to support her various fusions and identifications, which contributed to the cohesion of the self representation. Furthermore, from a professional viewpoint, she upheld the belief that she was having a prestigious analysis.

Although the therapy was not lifesaving, as was true of the patient who coerced her therapist into continuing the treatment by showing him a bloody handkerchief, the patient needed to have a continuing relationship with her analyst for the preservation of her psychic life. Her treatment continues to this day and the patient is still married and doing exceptionally well in her professional life.

I have heard the objection that continuing this therapy is only perpetuating the neurosis and supporting a psychopathological adjustment. I believe this is more of a philosophical than a practical issue. Certainly the patient finds the therapy valuable even though many of her positive feelings are based on an idealizing transference. Her therapist, however, is well liked and respected in the professional community and he is still giving her interpretations. With the tuberculosis patient, very few clinicians looked askance at the prospect of interminable treatment. Perhaps the same value can be given to preserving psychic life. The patient indicated that she would feel lost without therapy. In Chapter 5, I will discuss these questions further, emphasizing countertransference factors rather than narcissism, although the two are intertwined.

It is possible that with some other therapist, the impasse might be broken. However, this is a moot question, because she made it emphatically clear that she would not even tolerate the idea of seeing anyone else. In her mind she needs the various relationships and attitudes that can only be constructed in a warm, nonjudgmental treatment relationship.

She demonstrates the importance of object relationships in producing emotional homeostasis even if they are somewhat based on psychopathology. It is interesting that in what appears to be a stalemate, the patient has visibly progressed in her daily life, and even her relationship with her husband, from her friends' perspective, seems to be harmonious. One of her friends is in treatment with me and occasionally mentions that the patient and her husband seem to be quite amiable with each other. Although the patient continues her litanies, she may have incorporated the interpretations and they may have led to changes in the external world rather than in her treatment. Her husband has had similar successes in his profession, per-

haps indicating that there may have been a parallel process further-
ing his maturation and aided by a symbiotic fusion with the patient.

Many narcissistic characters require a partner whom they view as
inferior in order to bolster their self-esteem, such as the husband of
the pseudo–as-if patient. This type of relationship, also symbiotic,
can be subtle, and its sadomasochistic qualities may be hidden. In
treatment, the patient reveals that the spouse is the receptacle of the
bad parts of the patient. Both projection and fusion are the psychic
mechanisms that characterize such object relationships. The following vignette is another example of this type of fusion.

> The patient, a middle-aged businessman, sought therapy shortly before
> his wife completed her treatment. She suffered from multiple phobias
> that kept her tied to the house. Many of her symptoms rendered her
> immobile, such as being unable to move more than fifty feet away
> from a toilet. She constantly reviled herself for being "such a baby"
> and felt sorry for her long-suffering husband.
>
> She admired him for being so patient and understanding, which only
> made her feel worse. He did blame her, however, for his not advancing
> in his career. Because of her infirmities, he was not able to be active
> socially within his business circle so that he could promote himself.
>
> In therapy he was not as noble toward his wife as he apparently
> seemed to be when with her. He complained about her and vehe-
> mently blamed her for his lack of advancement. He was also not pleased
> about her therapy, admitting that since she began treatment he was
> having increasing amounts of anxiety, which caused him to seek treat-
> ment himself. Actually she was improving and many of her symptoms
> disappeared. The patient did not understand why he should feel anx-
> ious, but he kept complaining about his wife's lack of progress. His
> material led to a dramatic denouement, which was highlighted in a
> surprising session.
>
> The patient, who was always punctual, did not appear at the specific
> time of his session. As I was wondering what happened to him, my
> telephone rang. As I expected, he had called me and I asked him where

he was. He told me he was in the lobby, but could not come up to see me. He added that the idea of coming up in the elevator precipitated intense amounts of anxiety. I went down to the lobby, took him by the arm and brought him to my office, which was on the twenty-third floor. (I can see Robert Langs frowning as he reads this.) He was silent and visibly anxious as the elevator went up.

Naturally, I was curious. He had no difficulty whatsoever getting to my consultation room the past year and a half. Why this unexpected and dramatic turn? The patient then revealed that far from being displeased with his wife's lack of progress in her treatment, it was the progress she made that disturbed him. Most of her phobias had disappeared and she had become mobile, no longer being tied to the house. The patient then became disturbed and he now experienced exactly the same phobias his wife had. He could not be too far away from a toilet and he certainly had a fear of heights, but he was able to repress his symptoms and hide behind those of his wife.

When he thought about his new "freedom," now being able to become socially active to pursue his career, he felt frozen and immobilized. The problem with the elevator to my office was because it had to go above the twenty-first floor, the number 21 symbolically representing maturity and adulthood. His unconscious was afraid of moving up to adult levels, something he could deny as he protected himself with his wife's immaturity.

This is another type of symbiotic fusion, a masking variety, and a disguised version of the narcissistic relationship in which one partner needs to demean the other partner. My patient did not denigrate his spouse. His attitude toward her was superficially benign, sympathetic, and tolerant, but I detected a subtle sneering quality when he described her symptoms, which was later acknowledged and understood as being his contempt for himself.

Prior to the marriage, the patient and his wife were both shy, timid, and reserved characters. Her condition worsened and she developed definitive symptoms as the years went by, whereas he showed a modicum of aggressivity. The latter was mainly confined to resenting the successes of his co-workers and his being passed over for advancement.

He finally understood the dynamics of the marital interaction and gradually revealed why he was afraid of success and petrified about growing up, but there was nothing particularly unusual about the further course of treatment. It suffices to mention that he overcame the twenty-first floor phobia immediately or that he was able to contain it to the extent that it did not hinder access to my office.

Clearly both the patient and his wife were very similar characters in that the spouse's symptoms covered up those of the patient, very much like the situation in which one partner becomes an alcoholic after the other one stops drinking. In that sense this relationship was also an example of a complementary symbiosis, but the enmeshment of personalities involved all areas of their lives, extending far beyond one activity, such as drinking. The similarities in many alcoholics may be just as profound but often this is not obvious.

There are also relationships in which the needs of both partners for each other are intense but not equal or at the same psychic level. The total personality is not involved, only a particular segment.

A highly creative scientist sought treatment because he knew something was wrong with his adjustment toward marriage. He had been married four times, each marriage ending in divorce.

I encouraged him to give me extensive descriptions of his former wives, hoping to find some common denominators in their personalities that might help explain his initial attraction to them. This search proved to be a difficult task in that there were very few similarities among them. Toward the end of the marriage, his last wife manifested schizophrenic symptoms, including delusions and persecutory auditory hallucinations. Another wife was a vivacious hysteric, quite irresponsible and immature, factors that led to divorce, but otherwise she was charming and sexually attractive. His first wife was covertly depressed when they married. After a year the depression intensified and she became suicidally preoccupied. After she was hospitalized several times, he was able to get a divorce. I did not get any definite impressions about his second wife. She seemed to be an ephemeral creature who was never there. There seemed to be both sociopathic and as-if qualities to her personality.

I was puzzled and dismayed because the data he presented seemed to shatter my theory about the equivalence of personalities of symbiotic relationships. My narcissistic investment in this theory was being threatened. To save my theory, I took note of the fact that none of these relationships was long lasting. In fact, two of his marriages were extremely short lived, lasting less than a year.

Otherwise, he felt rather good about himself and his life. He was born in a small rural community, but his life had been a series of successes, athletically and scholastically. In school he always found a mentor who was impressed by his superior intellectual skills and who encouraged him to pursue a professional career. He had scholarships throughout his training and finally acquired a faculty position at a prestigious university in which he was engaged in research that led to a professorial chair at another university.

By contrast, his childhood years had been turbulent. He never knew his father, who deserted his mother before he was born. He lived with his mother in a mountain cabin and believed that they were close to each other, but he was uneasy about the relationship. He attributed his uneasiness to her unpredictability. He never knew what to expect. For example, one minute she might be sitting on the outside porch affectionately petting the cat. Then without warning, she would go into a rage state, grab a shotgun, and cut the cat in half by shooting it.

Her mood states would often vacillate with him. She did not treat him as violently, but often during playing some board games with him, she would become angry or despondent and throw the board across the room, and he was never able to determine what had set her off.

He liked science because it is orderly and enables the investigator to make predictions. Events have causes that can be related to other events. Science assumes that nothing is haphazard, that there are laws that explain and predict phenomena. To the patient, his mother was an enigma, a riddle that puzzled and frightened him, an unknown quantity who could be dangerous. He could find security in a problem-solving setting.

His investment in science must have been related to the turbulent, unpredictable environment in which he was raised. He felt vulnerable, exposed, and unprotected. He had no father to act as a buffer between him and his volatile mother. Science permitted him to create an environment that he could control.

His relationship to his mother must also have been related to the choice and number of wives. They were certainly characterologically quite different from each other, but now I realized that they had a common denominator and that was unpredictability. Their behaviors were erratic and could not be anticipated. The patient had to solve the riddle of the unpredictable woman in order to master his inner anxiety, to feel that he was in control of the situation rather than being confronted with an overwhelming dilemma. Both his security and narcissism were involved. He had to master a problem, that is, he had to extract order from chaos.

Unlike the symbiotic relationship of the previous patient, this patient was not totally fused with his wives. The anxious part of his self representation that was disturbed by a woman's unpredictability merged with the unpredictable aspects of his wives' personalities. Inasmuch as it was only a partial fusion, and other layers of the personality were not involved, these marriages were short lived. On many occasions he was able to understand considerably his wives' psychodynamics and he succeeded in making them predictable. It is interesting that this understanding was often gained at the same time as he solved a problem in the laboratory. Since he did not need the wives after he gained the security and increased narcissism by mastering what he viewed as a riddle, there was no basis to support the existence of the marriage. Furthermore, their psychopathological behavior was intrusive and he was glad to get out of the marriage. He was sufficiently introspective, however, to realize that there was something askew inside himself responsible for such a poor track record.

He used his scientific orientation and method to understand and deal with his wives' seemingly chaotic behavior. Undoubtedly his relationship with his mother was instrumental in choosing science as a profession, which enabled him to construct a sense of mastery and heightened self-esteem. The solution of a problem leads to narcissistic enhancement, as occurs with any creative endeavor. His mentor's admiration also added to his feelings of self-worth.

I am not stating that his infantile background was the sole factor in making him a scientist or that his scientific achievements are the outcome of his psychopathology. Not everyone has the capacity to be a scientist. This patient has special talents, perhaps genetically determined, that would have caused him to pursue science as a career even if he had an entirely different background. I believe that he happened to use his constitutional endowments in the service of his personal neurosis. (I discuss creativity and narcissism in Chapter 7.) This does not mean that the neurosis augments his productivity. If anything, the personal factor would, to some extent, interfere with his creative capacity as evidenced by the fact that as he gained insights in his treatment and improved, his work became increasingly acknowledged.

He formed a special type of symbiosis in his first four marriages. He needed his wives for only one attribute, their unpredictability, rather than for their total character. These relationships are *symptom object relationships* in that the subject incorporates what might be called a symptom, a surface expression of the spouse's personality (Giovacchini 1958). The patient could not relate to the deeper elements of the wives' character structure and this accounted for the termination of the marriages when he was able to successfully transcend the symptom. I call relationships in which the symbiotic union is total *character object relationships*.

The pseudo–as-if patient whom I described earlier is an excellent example of a character object relationship since she incorporated her partner totally into her self representation. This happened in her first therapeutic encounter with her first therapist.

I have discussed fusion states as they occur in an object relationship, primarily a marriage. They also occur in other relationships, and frequently patients fuse with their therapists. This can be a delicate situation, which can become disastrous or can be a turning point in treatment that leads to therapeutic resolution. Regarding the former, either the patient or the therapist may feel depleted by the fusion, their narcissistic balance being upset. This, in my experience, occurs most frequently with therapists who feel intruded upon and exploited by their patients. Patients, usually paranoid patients, may have similar feelings about their therapists.

A successful fusion in therapy can be beneficial in that the therapist is well attuned to the patient's needs and the patient feels understood and protected, and in turn is sensitive to the therapist's moods and sense of therapeutic direction. Because they are not blocked or resisted, these fusions are successful, and they do not lead to stalemates in treatment and disruption.

The pseudo–as-if patient, at one stage of her life, used the feeling of deadness as a defense against the painful feeling of aliveness. Her reactions were similar to those of a patient described by Flarsheim (1975), a patient who was described as a fussy baby. The parents hired a nurse who was supposedly an expert on fussy babies. Her philosophy was simple and devoid of any scruples, to paraphrase Ogden Nash. When the baby showed any sign of discomfort or indicated that she had inner needs, the nurse would immediately respond, but not to the need. For example, if the baby was wet, the nurse would feed her; if the baby was hungry, the nurse would change her diapers. She would also put mittens on her hands so she could not suck her thumbs. At first, the child would scream even louder than usual, but finally she became quiet and was no longer a fussy baby. Needless to say, her subsequent character was schizoid.

Any need or desire was experienced as painful because it was always thwarted, causing her to feel painful frustration. Eventually, she recognized that it was a section of the external world that caused her pain, but, at first, she attributed it to something within herself. She became afraid of her feelings, and later she included the external world in her repertoire of what was perceived as dangerous.

What should be pleasurable, life sustaining, and a developmental impetus, that is, a good nurturing experience, was instead painful and dangerous. She must have felt helpless and vulnerable as inner needs produced disruptive responses. I have referred to this situation as *primal confusion*, a confusion based on paradoxical responses. Consequently, she could not even try to move into the external world, which in her experience only served to frustrate her.

This is quite the opposite of Winnicott's (1953) concept of the creation of the transitional space. There the infant from the adult's viewpoint says, "I am the source of my own nurture," because the mother is so perfectly attuned to her child's needs. With this poor little girl, her banner was inscribed, "I am the source of my own pain." In each case the external world is ignored. In the former case it is finally acknowledged because the child has developed a sense of aliveness that impels him to playfully explore the world and satisfy his curiosity. In the latter instance, the patient could not completely block out the external world because of the strength of its impingements. Rather than explore the environment, she had to withdraw from it and deaden her feelings and needs to alleviate the misery they caused.

The sense of aliveness, at first, is based on the perception of inner needs. Once internal requirements are gratified, that is, when homeostatic equilibrium and narcissistic balance are established, the infant develops curiosity and moves into the external world. Years ago, clinicians wrote about surplus energy (Alexander 1961). In terms of narcissism, there is sufficient self-love; probably the infant is too immature to experience love in the more sophisticated sense, and some attention can be pleasurably directed to exploring the mysteries of the immediate surroundings.

Thus, the interaction with the external world becomes part of the sense of aliveness as it is playfully explored. Here, again, there is a positive feedback sequence. As the child participates in various activities and interactions with caregivers that go beyond nurturing, there is a heightened pleasurable excitement that reinforces the sense of well-being. This contributes to the consolidation of the identity sense, which is cemented together with positive narcissism as well as the construction of ego boundaries that distinguish the self from the outer world.

Again, the concept of the transitional space is useful. It is the area in which the sense of aliveness is constructed, and as it incorporates the outer world into the self it also helps differentiate one from the other.

From the infant's attitude of "I am the source of my own nurture" develops the capacity to be comfortably dependent on external objects. First, healthy infants believe that their boundaries encompass the surrounding reality, and the external world goes along with this illusion. Then the child learns to enjoy and play with illusions that build up a feeling of mastery, creating self-confidence. As play is separated from reality, external objects are recognized in depth and are acknowledged as more than simply their functional modalities. They are gradually perceived as persons in their own right with their own space as they are extruded from the transitional space into the external world. The differentiation of the inner and outer worlds and the sense of aliveness are in direct proportion to one another as object relations continue to mature.

The patient who had been a fussy baby never fully created a transitional space in that she had no capacity for illusion and had never played. As a child she was diagnosed as autistic, and her attitude was concrete and mechanistic. The outer world was experienced as disruptive and she protected herself with a shield of deadness and schizoid withdrawal.

The same was true of the pseudo–as-if patient, who maintained object relations by fusing with external objects, and this was especially noteworthy in her first analysis. Her therapist was a depressed man who had a gloomy view about the future of psychoanalysis. He stated that psychoanalysis was dead and the only way to preserve it was to put it in a museum. He suggested that he should be stuffed, placed in a chair, and put in a display case. The patient replied that there is no such thing as a psychoanalyst without a patient. Therefore, she should also be stuffed, placed on a couch, and put in the same display case.

Patient and therapist would be bound to each other forever, a permanent fusion in the context of deadness, a deadness that contained a painful state of aliveness. Their narcissistic levels were low but constant because of the fusion.

The fussy baby patient, by contrast, could not fuse during her early years. Diagnosed as autistic, she spent most of her childhood in a residential treatment center. She was slowly pulled into the outer world by a dedicated therapist who was at her constant beck and call, catering to her needs as best he could, the antithesis of how the "expert" nurse had treated her.

The ordinary baby fuses with the nurturing source. The pseudo– as-if patient had a conflictful fusion in that she both desired and felt afraid of her mother. She enjoyed acceptance and feared rejection, an ambivalent attitude toward the caregiver. The fussy baby patient found nurturing so catastrophic that she had to block it out and withdraw from the caregiver, a primitive adaptation to intensely traumatic circumstances.

She was fixated at a primitive level of development in which object relationships are only minimally, if at all, established. She could not effectively fuse with anyone, so she did not construct transitional objects or transitional phenomena that would enable her to move into the outer world. It was the task of her therapist to act as a catalyst to bring her to the pathway that led to object relations and developmentally enhancing fusion states.

The first hurdles to be overcome dealt with inanimate objects, actually places and settings. After she was discharged from the residential treatment center, she could not go to the therapist's office. He had to go to her house, but this did not work out well. She remained silent and withdrawn in her home. The therapist had learned while he was treating her in the residential treatment center that she was similarly withdrawn when he saw her in one of its rooms, usually her bedroom. Even there, she would not even tolerate the idea of being seen in an office or one of the treatment rooms. If he took her for a walk, things would go much better, and she would make an occasional comment or observation.

The therapist concluded that he could not continue making house calls, that he had to get her out of the house, but she would not come to his office. Apparently it was a too highly constructed segment of the environment that she could not internalize or integrate. It also seemed that it was too abrupt a quantum leap from the uncomfortable but protected state of autistic withdrawal to a highly structured external world setting.

There had to be transitional in-between stages on the journey toward reconciliation with the external world and the establishment of object relationships. The therapist knew about another patient who had a similar problem and how it was handled. Based on what he had learned, he suggested that they meet in hotel lobbies and the patient acquiesced. Then they moved to park benches and finally they would have breakfast together in a cafeteria. There was a rationale to this sequence that had to do with the number of people in their background. The hotel lobby contained the most people and the park bench the time of day they were there had considerably fewer. The table they sat at in the cafeteria was in an isolated corner and had the least number of people.

Apparently, she was afraid of being completely alone with her therapist, who had come to represent the nurturing source. The background of people was viewed as protective, and as they diminished in number she became increasingly anxious. By gradually introducing her to different environments he was able to acclimatize her to increasingly dangerous settings, as might happen in conditioning or desensitizing a patient who is trying to overcome a phobia.

If she was so afraid of object relations, it is puzzling as to why she needed people surrounding her and how she could use them to protect her.

Her reactions regarding her need to have people around her developed while she was gradually being introduced to the various settings described. Prior to these experiences, while she was in the residential treatment center and later in her home, if not content, she at least preferred being alone. Many times, as expected, she found people to be dangerous and she needed to isolate herself. During the postresidential treatment, she sought to remain isolated at home but needed people around her when she was in the external world, at least physically.

Again, it is useful to think in terms of foreground and background, and this applies to object relationships in general as well as to the nurturing dyad. Winnicott (1958b) divided the mother into two components: the giver of nurture and the environmental mother. He was describing "the capacity to be alone in the presence of someone else" (p. 416) in which the child gained autonomy but still felt protected by the environmental mother in the background, acting as a holding environment might in a treatment relationship.

When dealing with severe psychopathology, it is important to determine whether the external object is in the foreground or background; depending on its position, the patient's reactions will vary as they did with the fussy baby patient. The therapist was becoming increasingly real to her, and at first this was frightening. As they met in these various public places, she relaxed somewhat and was able to talk about current activities, indicating that some of her psychic energy was no longer held in an autistic shell. When she finally was able to have sessions in her therapist's office, she was able to use him both as a foreground and a background figure.

In this treatment there was no repetition of the infantile past within the transference context. The therapist had succeeded in creating a series of transitional spaces, transitional in that they were way stations on the road to the establishment of object relations. This path moved out of the mantle of deadness as it achieved a state of relative aliveness for the patient. At the moment, the patient is fully employed and has a boyfriend, indicating a modicum of self-esteem and some narcissistic equilibrium.

❖ C H A P T E R 5 ❖

Narcissism and Countertransference

The efforts some therapists make to treat their patients are sometimes enormous and may seem either heroic or ridiculous. Clinging to the intrapsychic focus requires that all facets of the therapeutic relationship be explored, even why therapists want to or continue to treat severely disturbed patients. At the ground level, the therapist has to make a living, so finances become a prime motivation. In some instances, money is not involved, as when the therapist is a salaried employee and does not have to put up with the abuse patients may heap upon him. The patient may be so demanding and difficult that money alone cannot explain why some therapists stick to their task as long as their psychic endurance allows them to. Narcissism once again enters the picture and is involved in various ways as it becomes entwined with countertransference elements.

I have discussed countertransference in many different contexts (Giovacchini 1989). Usually I have focused on what parts of the analyst's personality are involved, such as the self representation and the ego-ideal. I carry those discussions further in this chapter.

Countertransference factors operate in all therapies, especially psychodynamically based ones that are aimed at achieving characterological changes. My emphasis, however, is on particular interactions the patient and therapist create that are the outcome of unique features of the patient's psychopathology. Every case presentation and vignette in this book has included a discussion of the role of countertransference, since it is the essence of any treatment interaction. I now further highlight its role as it becomes involved with narcissistic issues and specific clinical constellations that are commonly encountered and may be particularly difficult and irksome.

Whether these situations existed in the past is a problematic question. Perhaps they represent different manifestations of psychopathology associated with changing tides in the cultural milieu. Certainly, violence plays a significant role in the therapeutic interaction and has a notable impact on countertransference responses.

COUNTERTRANSFERENCE: BENIGN AND MALIGNANT

The therapist of the fussy baby patient described in Chapter 4 let his professional life become tremendously disrupted as he tried to provide a series of transitional settings so that his patient could eventually move into the external world, beginning with an attachment to him. Even this attachment was painful because the patient treated him as if he were a slave, a transitional object that had the status of a rag doll. I know that I would not have been capable of leaving the comfort of my office for the drabness of a cafeteria and letting myself be treated as an inanimate object. Both my physical and mental comfort would have been compromised, since I am a creature of habit and like the constancy of the therapeutic ambience I have created for myself.

Was this therapist heroic or a masochist? Knowing the therapist as well as I do, I doubt that his motives for treating his patient were based on masochistic needs. Even if they were, the treatment was an outstanding success, and he should be commended for his efforts.

Our task is to treat patients, with the goal of their achieving maximum autonomy. What they do in the real world is not our primary concern, nor do we have any special expertise to set them up in a particular vocational frame of reference. Clinicians try not to be judgmental, either about psychopathology or the patient's achievements. Still, it is hard to keep all of our narcissism in check and not to feel proud of a successful therapeutic outcome that is reflected in good object relationships and effective adaptations to the external world.

Undoubtedly strong countertransference factors were operating in the therapist of the fussy baby patient, but we would have to label them as benign, because the outcome was good. This is a relative judgment, however, because what if treatment had failed or, worse yet, led to intractable regression that required long terms of institutionalization or led to suicide? Clinicians hear of more failures than successes, and the type of outcome I have described is rare.

It is obvious that the therapist had a strong narcissistic investment in his patient that transcended his personal comfort and for which he was able to make sacrifices. Why he picked such a difficult, seemingly impossible patient must be related to particular elements of his infantile environment. At the beginning he had no choice, the patient was assigned to him, but later, after she was discharged from the residential treatment center, he chose on his own to continue her treatment. Whatever unconscious factors were operating, they did not interfere with his capacity as a therapist. He was able to maintain his therapeutic intent and had a rationale for what he was doing, and judging by the results it proved to be right. The therapist's need for narcissistic gratification can again be called benign because it seemed to enhance rather than hinder his therapeutic acumen. I am not, however, making the converse statement that if the therapy had been unsuccessful, the therapist's countertransference was malignant. I can envision many treatment situations in which the countertransference was benign, in that the therapist's narcissistic needs were in keeping with his professional ego-ideal, but the therapy failed. Perhaps the most negative thing that can be said about such therapists' attitudes was that they made an error in judgment by believing the patient could be treated with an intrapsychic approach.

I recall my own experiences in which I have been attacked for accepting patients for psychoanalysis who were considered unsuitable. The therapist just discussed never considered that he was psychoanalyzing his patient, but when she was finally able to come to his office, he made interpretations in the context of unconscious motivations. By contrast, I was advocating a psychoanalytic approach for the treatment of severely disturbed patients and some critics considered such strivings dangerous. In a milder fashion, I was called an ideologue and accused of being motivated by grandiosity that could not help invading the countertransference. Some of my colleagues viewed my attitudes as benign but misguided. Perhaps I had idealized psychoanalysis, which led me to the belief that the intrapsychic focus could be extended to patients suffering from structural problems and included some schizophrenics. Can a misguided idealization lead to a benign countertransference that can be useful for therapy? Would such optimism be compatible in the objective climate of psychoanalysis?

The latter question has been transposed into a critical declarative assertion that those of us who believed we were psychoanalyzing severely disturbed patients had strayed so far from the standards of psychoanalytic technique that our treatment could in no way be called psychoanalysis. Our narcissistic investment in a treatment method clouded our judgment about treatability, and our efforts would have to be counterproductive. This refers to the first question about benign countertransferences being useful in treatment.

I do not wish to dwell on the question of whether we are practicing psychoanalysis, since I intensively discussed it elsewhere (Giovacchini 1979, 1997). I have gradually reached the view that it does not matter whether it is or is not psychoanalysis. The label does not matter as long as clinicians understand the process and that working with intrapsychic processes, unconscious motivation, and transference projections are in the forefront. Countertransference is often the catalyst that makes the analysis of the transference possible and it is created by shifts in narcissistic equilibrium.

I grant that unwarranted enthusiasm and idealization may create countertransference responses of a "Walter Mitty" nature, in which the severity of the reality of the patient's condition is glossed over. These treatments are short lived because the patient's pain and misery are not addressed and the therapist does not choose to acknowledge them. He is blinded by the idealization of a method that bolsters professional self-esteem. This type of relationship eventually collapses because both patient and therapist become increasingly frustrated.

I would not call what is essentially a destructive idealization benign countertransference. On the contrary, it is malignant, and the criteria to make such a judgment are not just phenomenological, such as the failure of treatment. Rather, its malignant nature is related to the fact that the therapist's needs override those of the patient. The therapist's narcissism is first and foremost. It does not matter whether it is expressed by idealization, which in some instances would imply that the subject of idealization is the focus of narcissism. In these instances, the therapist is in a sense fused with a technique rather than with a person. But often psychoanalysis is equated with Freud or anthropomorphized. If the idealization is shared with colleagues and directed toward the founder of the school, whether it is psychoanalysis or one of its branches, there is collective as well as personal narcissism, as I discussed in Chapter 3 particularly as it pertained to Kohut and his disciples.

Narcissistic needs on the part of the therapist are always involved in any therapeutic encounter, but they have to be kept in bounds. In a way the enthusiastic therapist is similar to the satisfied baby. The contented baby whose needs have been met, maybe enthusiastically met, does not remain fixed at a particular developmental level just because it is a comfortable state of well-being. Somehow pleasure and enthusiasm are mixed together, and the child moves into the outer world to joyfully explore fascinating mysteries with a sense of aliveness. This description is somewhat adultomorphic but the infant's pleasure in explorations that involve the heightening of a sense of mastery and bewilderment is obvious.

The therapist who has faith in the intrapsychic focus and in his training can also explore hitherto uninvestigated areas of, if not the external world, then the clinical world. This means that these therapists will treat patients who previously were considered unsuitable. I have repeatedly observed that most patients seen today are these unsuitable cases, and inasmuch as behavioral and cognitive techniques that do not try to delve into their unconscious minds with the goal of releasing a developmental potential are not particularly effective, the intrapsychic approach is worth a try; in many instances treatment has been reasonably successful. The joy these therapists experience when involved with such a successful treatment could be compared to the infant's acquired sense of mastery as a result of the satisfaction of curiosity and playful exploration. In both instances, there is further progression on the developmental scale for the infant and for the therapist's professional development.

When I wrote that it is worth a try to treat patients with characterological problems, I intended to add: What is there to lose? To some extent, I have already answered this question from the critics' viewpoint. They allude to the dangers of being a wild analyst (Freud 1910), which pertains also to the selection of patients and ignoring the indications and contraindications Freud (1914a) wrote about.

When there is no hope left for the patient and everything else has failed, what is there to lose becomes a pertinent question. The question can be abused if the clinician is making a trade of a supposedly lesser evil for a greater one. This was the rationale about lobotomy and shock therapy, although many practitioners deny they have any deleterious effects, which I do not believe. However, pursuing psychotherapy by itself does not have any implicit risks even if the therapist made an unwise decision about taking the patient for treatment. The worst that can happen is that the treatment will be ineffective.

I have noted the objection that ill-advised treatment can produce malignant regression and even suicide. I have never had a patient in which the treatment has caused an intractable regression that resulted in the patient's being in a worse condition than he was in before he started treatment. The few occasions that were brought to my attention when this happened could be attributed to malignant countertransference and the therapist's anxiety. Ordinarily, treatment is simply terminated when it does not go well.

The narcissistic element is operative in malignant countertransference in a specific fashion that is different from the enthusiasm of the exploratory therapist. Usually the therapist is able to break through the patient's resistance to therapy by his enthusiasm for his treatment approach. In a sense, he talks the patient into treatment by raising expectations and creating hope. The therapist often takes on a managerial role as well as an analytic one and the boundaries between analysis and management are blurred. The book *Hollywood on the Couch* by Farber and Green 1993 reveals numerous examples of analysts who are enraptured by their celebrity patients and try to run their lives, even telling their patients' directors how to handle them. Their narcissism is markedly inflated by having famous patients, and they often identify with their patients rather than the reverse that usually happens. The idealized transference is experienced mainly by the therapist and the boundaries between patient and analyst are totally lost. These situations are travesties of therapy.

Unfortunately, many types of interactions have been included under the rubric of therapy, but they are social interactions in that the needs of the therapist are as prominent as those of the patient. I believe that therapeutic intent, as well as ego boundaries, is eliminated. Though these analysts may not be aware of it, they have relinquished their conceptual orientation and deal with these patients as if they were their children and in need of rescue. Needy patients may present themselves in such a fashion, but if therapists respond in the same frame of reference, their responses may be manifestations of a malignant countertransference, although to the outsider it may appear that they are sincerely trying to help a vulnerable, suffering person.

In their eagerness to be helpful, perhaps based on some unconscious need to rescue and to augment their narcissism, therapists may overtly or covertly promise more than they can deliver. They infuse hope in their patients, which in some instances can be helpful but at other times can be reckless. The distinction is not altogether clear, but hope should be supplied cautiously and not in overwhelming doses. The latter means that ego boundaries are not violated and the therapist maintains a professional stance.

Many recent films depict psychiatrists as "nice guys," perhaps dressing down and relating to their patients in an earthy fashion, sometimes becoming upset and revealing their weaknesses. There is little professional decorum, but if there were, it would be considered reactionary and pompous.

The reactions of certain segments of the professional community to dramatic, if not unorthodox, treatment relationships are interesting. The therapist who chose different settings other than his office was occasionally criticized for his ever-changing venues. By contrast, the following situation was highly praised, and the therapist was lauded for his efforts, even though they led to the patient's suicide.

The therapist, a well-respected child and adolescent psychiatrist and a psychoanalyst, decided to have an unruly 18-year-old son of a prominent wealthy business tycoon move into his house as he conducted treatment. He believed he could create a better holding environment in his house than could be constructed in a residential treatment center. Again, one has to question why he felt he could offer more than an institution such as Chestnut Lodge or the Menninger Clinic since money was not a problem.

Perhaps he was following in Winnicott's footsteps when he wrote about his experiences with a child that he had live with him. The therapist was a firm follower of Winnicott's ideas and he admired his clinical acumen. He prepared a schedule of organized activities for his patient and he had daily sessions with him. The therapist's attitude was sanguine and he reassured his patient as to how well the therapy was progressing.

It was a shocking surprise when a member of the household found the patient dead in the garage, where he had hanged himself. Friends and colleagues were sympathetic and tried to reassure the therapist that the patient committed suicide in spite of heroic efforts to save him.

I believe this vignette warrants careful examination. It seems that the therapist was, indeed, dedicated to the treatment, and he certainly went out of his way to provide a safe setting in which he conducted treatment. Still, the nagging question persists as to why he obliterated all boundaries by bringing the patient into his house, introducing him to his wife, and blending the professional relationship with a social, familial ambience. The therapist was a certified analyst and should have known that psychodynamically oriented treatment cannot survive without the establishment of professional boundaries. With this patient he abruptly changed both his professional and personal lifestyle. Why? If it were simply the patient's welfare that he had in mind, he could have persuaded the patient's father to send his son to the Menninger Clinic. If that were to occur, he would have lost his patient to another therapist, and he did not want that to happen. This therapist had to remain in charge and obviously he must have been more concerned with his narcissistic needs than with the patient's ultimate response to treatment.

Many factors beyond therapeutic intent and the enhancement of the professional ego-ideal were operating in this therapist's mind as he attempted to treat his adolescent patient. He was enthusiastic and eager and tried to get his patient to develop the same hope he professed.

Obviously the patient did not share or absorb this therapeutic attitude and he might have found the shattering of boundaries threatening. Ostensibly he was given everything and had a dedicated, devoted, and highly respected therapist. Yet he still felt angry and miserable. The therapist had created a world in which his needs would be omnipotently met and this still was not enough. If everything is not enough, what is left? Nothing worked, so he killed himself.

This is a somewhat different perspective from the belief that the patient killed himself in spite of the therapy. It would have to be amended to state that the patient killed himself *because* of the treatment. The obliteration of boundaries, the making of promises that could not be kept, that is, the therapist's reassurance that all would be well, and personal narcissistic ambitions could be considered as the source of a malignant countertransference that proved to be deadly.

In a sense, the therapist had tried to create a perfect setting for the patient that would have supplied what had been missing in childhood. The setting was supposed to create the state of infantile omnipotence Winnicott (1953) described as he was discussing the construction of the transitional space. I do not believe an infant feels omnipotent, because such a feeling is too structured and sophisticated for a 6-month-old mind, but it was something this adolescent could have been capable of feeling. The therapist was not aware that he was trying to create a transitional space, although he was a follower of Winnicott's ideas, but he tried to construct an optimal nurturing environment as would occur with a mother who was experiencing primary maternal preoccupation (Winnicott 1956).

For the infant the optimal nurturing setting leads to the formation of an illusion that he is the source of his own nurture and this is later elaborated into the enjoyment of illusion as illusion, and then to creative exploration and play. These beliefs and activities lead to developmental achievements, narcissistic enhancement, and the formation of meaningful object relationships. To try to construct such a setting later in life can be dangerous, as exemplified by the adolescent's suicide.

Effective therapy recapitulates the transitional phase, but this occurs in a transference–countertransference context under the propulsion of the repetition compulsion (see Chapter 6). This is, however, different from the deliberate re-creation of an infantile setting in external reality. In therapy, the contrast between the real world and some of its deprivations and the disappointing world of childhood serves as a backdrop for the maintenance of boundaries and reality testing. The construction of a developmental enhancing holding environment occurs spontaneously and usually slowly, and cannot be contrived and imposed upon the patient.

In hospitals and residential treatment centers in the past, the ward was tailored or was attempted to be geared to the patient's needs (Shur 1994). Perhaps this can be considered as an effort to construct an infantile environment to make up for the deficits of the past, which I have just judged to be dangerous.

The hospital or ward, however, is not part of an ordinary, everyday reality, and the therapeutic interaction was kept separate from the activities of the caregiving staff, whereas in the case just described the nurturing ambience and the therapeutic process were blended, a prime example of the blurring of boundaries. Furthermore, the inpatient ambience does not really attempt to undo past traumas. Rather, it is designed to support the treatment process, and in the ideal setting, although there is communication between therapist and staff, the therapist does not get involved in administrative decisions. Often a consultant reviews controversies and countertransference difficulties when there are divisive feelings between the ward personnel and the aims of the therapy.

This is, for the most part, a moot discussion, because with a few rare exceptions, psychiatric wards are little more than detention settings designed to control behavior. They rely almost totally on drugs, make no attempt to understand patients, and therapy practically never exists.

The adolescent patient could not profit from the optimal setting the therapist tried to create because he was not able to integrate it into his ego. Children who seek entrance into the external world through the portals of the transitional phase are already well integrated and balanced, an equilibrium that will later be experienced as self-esteem and confidence, a state of positive narcissism. This means that they have been well taken care of and loved since birth and they enter the transitional phase with a healthy ego.

I asked Winnicott if the child's illusion of being the source of his own nurture required an ego that had a good capacity to endopsychically register nurturing experiences that were skillfully created by the good, nonintrusive mother. He agreed that it did, and the mother's response to the infant's "gesture" without intruding herself leads to a smooth incorporation of her response to her child's needs. The gesture is, of course, the child's signal of neediness, an awareness the mother had and not the child.

I postulated that this would lead to the formation of a well-structured nurturing matrix that becomes the fount of narcissism. During infantile stages, this narcissism may appear to be grandiose, as Freud (1914a) described it as "His Majesty, the Baby." Perhaps this is more an adultomorphic construction and projection rather than the child's orientation, but the capacity to play that develops during the transitional phase is later associated with illusion and fantasies of power that amuse rather than threaten.

The nurturing matrix, actually an introject consisting of positive reflections of desire, needs, and their satisfaction, can be understood in the context of privation and deprivation, again Winnicott's (1963) concepts. Privation is a condition in which the infant does not know what it means to be gratified, as was the situation with the fussy baby patient. Needs are always painful because they were never satisfied, and therefore the ego could not construct a nurturing matrix.

Deprivation, by contrast, indicates that the ego contains a nurturing matrix, not necessarily a well-integrated one, but sufficiently functional to know what it means to be gratified. It has experienced satisfaction of needs, which serves as a backdrop that causes the ego to recognize when needs are not met. It has to have felt satisfaction in order to know when it is being frustrated.

It is doubtful that there are persons who have a total absence of a nurturing matrix. It would be difficult to understand how anyone would survive without having any concept about the satisfaction of basic needs. All children have to be fed in order to live, but feeding by itself can, in instances of severe psychopathology, be so joyless and mechanical that the experience is not internalized and does not form a nurturing matrix. Perhaps there is a minimal amount of incorporation that is required for survival.

Spitz (1945, 1946, 1965) described situations of cold, mechanical feeding and total lack of object contact, and the children did not survive. Briefly, Spitz wrote about an anonymous orphanage in which the children were in cribs kept in cubicles that had walls that were higher than their eye levels. They were fed on a precise schedule but never spoken to, touched, or held. These children probably had no internal security, physically and psychologically, in that they came close to having a complete lack of a nurturing matrix. Physically, they most likely did not develop a functional immune system, since these children were wiped out by a measles epidemic. I also conjecture that narcissism, recognition of the self, and a sense of values were totally nonexistent for this group of children.

If it had been possible to treat one of these children, it probably would have been folly to think in terms of a treatment based on psychodynamic working through and the intrapsychic focus. There would not have been a psyche to scrutinize and undoubtedly no capacity to introject that might lead to some narcissistic input.

To impose a treatment procedure that is eons beyond the patient's psychic capacity is unrealistic and destructive. Only a therapist who can develop a malignant countertransference would be capable of such a gross misjudgment. The severity of privation and the depth of fixation and developmental arrest of the children Spitz discusses are so primitive that it is immediately recognizable how impossible it is to approach them from a psychological perspective. They are fixated at a prementational level, and in these cases there is no psyche.

If treatment at a psychological level is impossible, then what could have been done for these subhuman creatures? Could they have been placed in a benign custodial environment that would attempt to make up for the severe lack of love and attention, the absence of narcissistic supplies, and the cumulative and murderous traumas of their everyday lives? It might be argued as postulated for the adolescent patient that even in a benign environment, they may not have survived because they lacked the psychic structures to adapt to it.

I recall an 8-year-old girl who had been shackled in a closet for many years. She was as small as a 4-year-old and her body was covered with hair. She crouched and looked more like a monkey than a little girl. To augment her appearance as an animal, she did not talk but grunted.

She was placed on a child psychiatry unit where she was given tender, loving care. In less than three months she died of inanition and a failure to thrive. Apparently without a nurturing matrix, she could not progress to psychological levels of adaptation and relating, even in a benevolent setting that tried to make up for the outrageous treatment she had received.

The nurses and residents on the ward felt extreme compassion for the patient, but they admitted it was difficult to become genuinely attached to her. She lacked all human attributes and they found it incongruous to look upon her as a pet. It is hard to classify their feelings as countertransference, since there was no transference from the patient to counter. Still, the ward personnel's feelings were partly determined by their backgrounds, and these infantile phenomena would account for some transference implications in their reactions.

There have been other patients who have been prementationally fixated and toward whom therapists have had positive countertransference feelings that were benign. I believe that the adolescent patient's therapist had a positive countertransference but it was nevertheless malignant because his therapeutic intent was overridden by his narcissistic needs. Positive countertransference can be malignant, but I do not believe the converse is ever true, that is, that negative countertransference can be benign.

COUNTERTRANSFERENCE, THE SELF REPRESENTATION, AND THE PROFESSIONAL EGO-IDEAL

All ego systems contribute to the psyche's narcissistic reservoir and, in turn, narcissism energizes their operations. If there is a loss or a threat to this narcissistic balance, the ego reacts in a negative fashion and during therapy produces countertransference responses. As has become increasingly recognized, the therapeutic process is based on the recognition of transference–countertransference interactions. What elements of the therapist's personality are involved are as important as those of the patient's that are being explored.

In the movie *Good Will Hunting*, which is not a master exposition of the treatment process, the main character succeeds in getting himself rejected from therapy by six psychiatrists. This young man, an intellectual genius, was also a genius at finding prospective therapists' sensitivities and then exploiting them. This may have been a compensatory destructive retaliation for the abuse and cruelty of his infantile environment and an attempt to bolster his narcissism by demonstrating that he is in control. The psychiatrists who represent authority figures are reduced to helplessness and are ineffectual in dealing with him.

Therapists go to unusual lengths to preserve the therapeutic relationship for a variety of reasons, some of which are not in the patient's best interest, as I discussed above. There were occasions, especially in the treatment of the fussy baby patient, when the therapist felt imposed upon and resented that he had to make such intense efforts to hold the relationship together, but he plodded ahead, and although he might have thought about ending the treatment, he did not really want to. The situations I am about to describe involved stronger negative reactions. The therapist's fundamental narcissism was encroached upon and the ensuing discomfort led to strong desires to terminate the treatment. These treatment encounters became even more disruptive when the therapist had to doubt himself and the objective truth he thought he had discovered, a dilemma that should not bother postmodernists and intersubjectivists since according to them there is no objective truth.

The patient, a professional artistic woman in her middle thirties, had seen at least a dozen therapists before she called me for an appointment. Apparently, after a week or two, they all became exasperated with her. Two of these upset therapists recommended that she see me because I had the reputation of being good with difficult patients. To this day, I do not know whether these therapists were my friends or my enemies.

Her background, as expected, had been highly traumatic. She described her mother as a helpless, angry woman who had fits of catatonic stupor requiring periodic hospitalization. According to the patient, her father was kind and seemingly caring but mostly unavailable. He was a highly skilled professional and very much in demand by government agencies, so most of his work was highly classified. The patient knew very little about his professional activities except that he was acclaimed and a celebrity in his area, but he was as much a secret to her as was his work.

Although the patient felt unprotected from her mother's periodic angry onslaughts, she idealized her father. She admired his brilliance and how he was highly respected, but lamented that she did not get much for herself from his fame except for financial security; materialistically, she could have whatever she wanted.

As a child, she was able to draw other children around her because she had many toys, a swimming pool, elaborate playrooms, and all the things that attract children. The patient felt she was buying her friends as she had bought everything else. She believed her friends were sycophants who cared not for her, but for her possessions.

Her teachers were ambivalent about her. Her intelligence was noteworthy. In fact, there was no one else in either elementary or high school who even approached her intellectually. She had a straight A average, which continued in college and graduate school, although at these higher levels the competition was tougher, but she was still considered head and shoulders superior to her peers. She was not gracious about her innate talents and both mentors and colleagues were uneasy in her presence, except those who were totally subservient to her, who praised her incessantly because they derived some narcissistic gratification from being friends of such a bright person. They treated her as a celebrity and eventually she became one because of her outstanding accomplishments in her work.

In general, however, she was disliked. There was a certain ruthless quality in her interpersonal relationships and even in her approach to a difficult technical problem. She would tear into the problem with apparently boundless energy, usually solving it quickly. She was admired and resented, partly because of envy, but mainly because she was grandstanding. Her grandiosity, however, was devoid of any deference to a superior. She was, in her mind, simply demonstrating how superior she was and in a particular context she had the upper hand, but by emphasizing her supposedly infinite professional capabilities she created only reactive resentment.

The patient also used her intelligence for self-scrutiny. She knew that she antagonized people and was considered obnoxious. To some extent she did not care, but she was sad about the thought that she was liked not for herself but only for how she could be used, even though her material rewards were great.

Over the years her sadness increased and the narcissistic gratification she received from her creativity became less and less satisfying. She had had a series of short-lived relationships, but these lovers, too, used her to enhance themselves. Her narcissism was diminished as theirs was enhanced.

She finally decided to seek therapy because she was feeling her isolation and loneliness more and more keenly. As would be expected, she was ambivalent about embarking on such a venture, because she believed that, to some extent, she would have to give up some control and this would make her feel vulnerable to her therapist. She envisioned that he would be in the spotlight and this would take some of it away from her. Again she viewed the therapeutic relationship as she did any relationship, as a narcissistic struggle.

As in the movie *Good Will Hunting*, she manipulated her therapists into rejecting her. She succeeded in convincing them that she was smarter than they were and that their theories and beliefs were false. They clung to their conceptual systems because of their character defects and inadequacies and because they had no creativity of their own. Depending on their age, she assailed them for their idols, Freud or some later analyst, because basically they knew nothing and their compensatory attitudes caused them to behave like misguided pompous asses. Apparently, her talents also extended to a capacity for pounding and hammering her barbs with such energy and intensity that she succeeded in breaking down their protective barriers and penetrating their reservoirs of self-esteem and narcissistic supplies. She could pay whatever fee they wanted, but they would have nothing to do with her.

The patient told me about her experiences with these therapists, which were confirmed by one of the therapists who gave her my name. He told me how devastated he felt by her behavior toward him, but part of him was intrigued and he suspected that she might have been able to accept him as a therapist. Nevertheless, after some inner struggle he decided not to become involved. He was further discouraged because recently she had started drinking heavily and he did not want to deal with a beginning alcoholic. This would only make the prognosis worse.

Eventually, she called me. I offered her several appointment times, but they were not suitable. She asked for evening hours, but I told her that my day ended at a certain time and I would not extend it.

Then she asked about Sunday morning, to which I replied, "Are you serious?" I was slightly surprised when she chuckled, but, at the moment, I felt a little lighter in view of what was proving to be heavy and tedious, but this feeling did not last long.

She then started telling me about an uncle who was the most knowledgeable person in the world about psychoanalysis and after years of psychological research he reached the conclusion that the whole conceptual system was fraudulent, that it was not a science. She waited for a response but I did not give one. Obviously my silence created some discomfort and I finally broke it by getting back to the question of whether she wanted an appointment. However, she would not let go of her compulsion to have a sophomoric discussion of the scientific validity of psychoanalysis. I simply replied that science was just a viewpoint, a method of observation that could be applied to all aspects of the world, including the mind. With finality I added that if her schedule became more flexible, she could call me and I would be glad to arrange an appointment, and I bade her good-bye.

Immediately, I wondered why I had made myself available. I clearly felt her conversation as intrusive and I was irritated at what I experienced as carping. Her history of having defeated so many therapists made her even less appealing because I could see myself as another scalp on her belt. For the moment, I felt relieved and did not expect her to call back.

As would happen so often with this patient, I was wrong. She called back several days later and somewhat cheerfully stated that she had given considerable thought to what I had said about science being a method. Prior to her call I wondered if I had any desire whatsoever to treat her and I concluded that a part of me found her intriguing. This was obviously an extremely bright, creative woman and to have succeeded where everyone else had failed would be a considerable narcissistic achievement. As I listened to her during this second telephone call, the negative side of my ambivalence increased even though she was praising me for an observation that seemed obvious, especially to her because she was quite sophisticated about scientific matters. After some wrangling she accepted an appointment during the noon hour, which she did not keep.

I thought that was the end of it and decided not to pursue the matter further. To my surprise, I received a call from one of the psychiatrists who referred her to me. She had called and told him that I was being difficult and making it hard for her to see me. She asked him to call me and intervene on her behalf. Throughout the conversation she kept referring to me by my last name without the doctor. She would let it roll over her tongue, apparently enjoying prolonging its various syllables. I told him that she had broken the appointment that I had given her. He then wondered whether she was drunk at the time of her call.

She called about a dozen times to schedule an appointment. I found her somewhat exasperating, especially as she tried to engage me in conversations about psychoanalysis, but I must confess part of me was flattered that she sought me out, whereas, as far as I knew, she had no further contact with the previous psychiatrists she had seen. She pursued me but had never seen me, and those she had seen she did not pursue.

I had the feeling she could only value me at a distance, which is what I finally told her. She immediately stopped bantering and made an appointment that I could fit in my schedule. I felt that possibly I had broken through some defensive barrier, but, again, I wondered why I had done something that enabled her to see me. It seemed that I, too, was most comfortable when there was distance between us.

When I finally saw her, there was nothing particularly unusual in her behavior and demeanor. She gave me relevant material and was almost deferential in her manner. She had read some of my writings and by her responses indicated that she was in resonance with my ideas. For the moment I forgot about all the calls and the broken appointment and conjectured that maybe I would be able to treat her.

In retrospect and because of the course of her treatment, I wonder why I felt so sanguine after I first saw her and ignored the difficulties in setting up an appointment. I believe I was attracted by her intelligence, was somewhat influenced by her celebrity status, and felt moderately inflated, that is, narcissistically enhanced, by her interest in my work. Her calling me by my last name indicated to me that she fondly respected me and felt that I was as adept as she was. My professional ego-ideal was pleased, which made me vulnerable and a victim of her later sadistic manipulations.

I was impressed by the keenness of her observations and the extent of her sensitivities and intuitiveness as she made observations about everyday experiences as well as broader issues. Most of the time I was in agreement with her, and she seemed pleased, but I could sense that she did not particularly want my input. On occasion, she would allude to my beliefs when she recognized that her evaluations were similar to mine.

She became extremely interested in my writings and read practically everything I wrote. Not only did she read them but she appeared to understand them, as was evidenced by what I considered to be intelligent discussions and appraisals. I know that at many levels I was pleased, but I was disquieted and perhaps feeling some guilt because of the attention I was getting. I also felt that therapy should proceed in a different direction.

There was also something unpleasant about what she was talking about, but it took some time before I became fully aware of it. I noted that as she talked about her opinions, she was mainly talking about herself and though she had mastery of the material, she was more interested in putting on a show. It was a spectacular narcissistic display, and this took considerably away from its appeal within an interpersonal context. Patients do not have to bring in appealing material, but the analyst's reactions, their countertransference nuances, if they are not attuned to the associative flow, have special significance and affect the treatment process. I derived the feeling that this woman had no feelings about anyone except herself.

At first I was not aware of what I now call her complete narcissistic containment, probably because she was able to give me, or more correctly, I was able to receive, some narcissistic supplies in the professional arena. I finally realized that what enhancement I was feeling was primarily due to my introjections rather than her projections.

Of course, introjective processes are always operating in tandem with projections, but there can be an unevenness in which one is dominant over the other. Basically, the intent to praise me was superficial and she was more interested in my mirroring, as Kohut would have stated. She had cleverly picked a topic that she knew I would find attractive.

As I understood more about her motivations, I found her insights about my writings and those of others increasingly tedious, and she became more open about the expression of her narcissism. She candidly confessed that she did not care about anyone else's feelings because she did not value anyone. She had some friends she kept because it was convenient, but she did not feel any bond with them. She told me about leaving a prestigious girls' school because they forced her to take gym and she did not want to work up a sweat or shower at that time of day because it would get her hair wet. This leaving caused her considerable inconvenience since she would have inevitably been given a scholarship to a highly acclaimed university, whereas now she would have had to take a competitive examination. She won a scholarship, but from a financial viewpoint it did not matter; it was simply a question of vanity and another opportunity to assert her superiority.

Gradually she switched away from discussing my writings but indicated that she accepted my point of view and implicitly indicated that I knew more about psychoanalysis than her scholarly uncle. However, she continued giving outrageous examples of her unrelenting narcissism. She boasted about not having any patience and that she looked at many pedestrian transactions as being impositions. She would fly into rage states, for example, if she could not find a parking space in her office parking lot, even though there were no assigned spaces.

One day, because of a telephone call, I had kept her waiting a few minutes, which I intended making up at the end of the session. She stormed into the consultation room and angrily proclaimed that she was quitting therapy and that I was "fired." I commented that she had a short fuse, realizing that I was trying less to be therapeutic and more concerned with expressing my reactive anger. I did not examine whether my anger was justified, and in view of her onslaught I remained relatively calm. Actually, I did not want to take a therapeutic stance because it would have made me feel defensive and demeaned. I did not want to be the victim of her childish tantrums, although I still kept in mind that I was dealing with serious narcissistic pathology that had to be understood, but I did not feel this was the moment. My professional self representation was undoubtedly challenged and affronted, and perhaps I should have been able to understand her explosion as the outcome of an insecure, vulnerable person who was reacting to the damage inflicted on her by a psychotic mother.

In retrospect, I believe that to have adopted a strictly professional stance, which means keeping the intrapsychic focus and not reacting to content, would have put me in the victim position. This is an interesting example of what I have previously described as the psychoanalytic paradox (Giovacchini 1979, 1984, Giovacchini and Boyer 1983).

Sometimes the analytic setting unwittingly has similarities to the infantile environment. Though neutrality has been justifiably eliminated in favor of objectivity, even an objective attitude may strike some patients as uncaring and rejecting. Many patients have been raised in an environment that has rejected them, usually emotionally rather than physically. The low decibel atmosphere of the treatment relationship, on the surface, is similar to that of childhood.

Furthermore, she would shut me out as she usually did, and then accuse me of using the intrapsychic approach as a defense, which, to some extent, was true. She responded by stating that she was not upset just because I had been late. As she was driving to her appointment, she was questioning the value of the treatment and had already been debating whether she should continue.

I did not reply and made no attempt to participate in the decision as to whether she should remain in treatment. She must have sensed that a part of me would feel relieved if she left, so she decided to stay. Her rationalization was that since she was seeing me in my home office she had no parking problems.

Close to the end of the first year of treatment, she had frequent dreams of my being inept. She would dream that I was infirm and confined to a wheelchair. In other dreams I would be blind or deaf. During her sessions, she now reviled me for being useless and unable to relate to her needs. I learned to understand how the psychiatrists she saw before me must have felt.

I could understand why she had to render me useless. She had to get rid of the psychotic, infirm mother by projecting her into me. The father was also put into me, because in spite of being brilliant and somewhat of a celebrity in his own right, he was not able or he did not care to protect her from what she felt to be a maternal onslaught.

To survive, she had to get rid of these malignant introjects, which meant destroying me, more specifically my professional self representation. She did not leave treatment because she needed someone to revile. On the other hand, by making me ineffectual, she was repeating childhood traumas, which threatened to expose her vulnerability, an inevitable dilemma. All she could do was strengthen her narcissistic defenses, which were often manifested by frustration, intolerance, and temper tantrums.

Knowing all this, I wondered why I kept finding her to be my most difficult patient. She should not have been a real threat to my professional self representation, especially since I had been able to piece together a plausible formulation. Eventually, I concluded that I had absorbed more of her father than I thought. It seemed that he did not want to get emotionally involved with his daughter and that basically he did not care for her welfare, and I was having the same feelings, but there were other factors operating.

Ordinarily, I find it discomforting when patients are unstable about their dedication to continuing treatment. Often their vacillations are the products of a concrete, mechanistic orientation, and in general such patients are poor candidates for in-depth treatment. After the outburst I have just described, when she demonstrated the intensity of her infantile rage, I became inured to her threats, and did not particularly care whether she terminated. This should have been a liberating feeling.

I should have felt comfortable knowing that I understood what was going on. My professional self representation was not compromised and knowing how vital it was for her to consider me incompetent permitted me to establish a professional equilibrium that could have been therapeutically effective. Still, I was bothered.

In spite of my insights, I was not satisfied with my professional performance. I continued feeling that I was not fulfilling the requirements of my professional ego-ideal, and as I thought further about it I concluded that I was not. This was accompanied by the feeling of unease that I had when I contemplated the coming session. I felt she was a burden as she pounded me with my ineptness.

I really felt inept and I finally realized why. The patient was not permitting me to function as a good therapist and she boxed me into a corner. As she complained that I was not meeting her needs, I had to acknowledge to myself that I was not because I did not know what they were. Most of the time I did not know what she was talking about and I found it very hard to listen to her. For long periods of time, her language was pedantic and convoluted as she ventured into lofty, esoteric topics.

During one session, I became a stenographer and tried to write down verbatim what she said. As I read it later, I found out that I could not make any sense of what I wrote. It lacked coherence and meaning, but it was not a word salad. She was rambling and never completed a thought before she moved onto the next one. She was also circumstantial as there were series of modifying and qualifying clauses, disconnected from a topic. Her content and flight of ideas were somewhat hypomanic, but her tone and affect were not. She gave the appearance of being rational but she was not understandable.

True, she was correct when she insisted that I did not understand her. I did not and for a long time my professional self representation felt assailed because I thought I was not a competent therapist. I did not know that she was forcing me into such a position, that she was making me an incompetent therapist because she could not be understood.

This insight led to further dilemmas. If I interpreted that she was the source of my ineptness, she would have accused me of being defensive and paranoid, that I was covering up for my inadequacies by blaming her rather than admitting I was inadequate. If there was something in our relationship that was causing some inhibition of my capabilities, then I should look within myself to uncover whatever neurotic difficulties I have and not let them impede the course of therapy. She gave me considerable material to convince me these would be her responses.

On occasion, she assailed me for having personal problems that accounted for my obtuseness. It was ironic that she used the intrapsychic focus against me. How could I understand her if I did not explore my unconscious processes, indicating that I disdained intrapsychic exploration? If I attempted to analyze her, I was defending myself against analyzing myself. This was another way she rendered me useless. If I tried to use my main therapeutic tool, interpretation, she would devastate me by making counterinterpretations. That is why I did not immediately confront her with her lack of coherence, because I was afraid interpretations would assume the qualities of name-calling and accusations.

By this time she was no longer talking about my works, because she now recognized that I was misguided and this had to apply to my writings. The natural inclination would have been to inquire why she continued seeing me if she got nothing out of the relationship. It was a question I wanted to ask, but I did not. I know there would have been no therapeutic import to such a query. It would have been a retort and a challenge.

Besides, I believed she was getting a good deal out of treatment but she could not admit it. At the same time, she was also suffering. Even if she could not express herself, she still felt very needy and she was intensely frustrated. In her own way, she had also boxed herself into a corner. She felt helpless, vulnerable, and in need of nurture and soothing, but she could not avail herself of a potentially helpful experience because she could not internalize or give the proper signals to indicate that she was in distress.

A narcissistically defended pugnacious personality cannot sufficiently relax to reveal a basic vulnerability that requires nurturing and emotional sustenance. If someone knew how to relate to her she would not be able to integrate it because such an experience would not be in synchrony with her ego's orientation. She did not have a nurturing matrix sufficiently structured so that it would incorporate helpful and protective experiences.

Her frustration, in some respects, was similar to mine. I could not get through to her, because this would mean that she would have to relax narcissistic defenses and expose her vulnerability. Though she never tried, she basically felt that she could not get through to me. She never learned to communicate needs, to make the "spontaneous gesture" Winnicott (1960a,b, 1967, 1971) wrote about because there was no one there to meet it.

We both exhibited parallel ego defects, although mine were not intrinsic to my character structure. Rather, they were a reaction to her personality organization. Within the treatment process, our egos' executive systems were deficient. She did not have the adaptive equipment to reach out and be nurtured and I could not respond because I did not know how.

In childhood, she had had no opportunity to gradually develop a mutually enhancing interaction in which she could increasingly clearly communicate her inner needs and her caregiver could become a more and more skillful participant in a satisfying and rewarding relationship. She did not acquire the techniques necessary to achieve comfortable dependency and I had no signal to which I could react.

To survive, she had to achieve a minimal capacity to make her needs known, and the surrounding world had to respond to some degree. She had nannies who were reasonably competent, so she was able to maintain some contact with the surrounding world beyond her narcissistic exploitations. This enabled her to recognize situations that might have some nurturing potential. Nevertheless, she would manipulate these experiences so that they worked against the possibility of close contact. I believe that something similar happened with the therapists she had previously defeated.

For example, during one session, she was particularly sullen. She had attended a lecture given by a psychologist and she liked it very much. She did not know whether she believed he would be an interactive, exciting therapist. She felt, however, that during his lecture he had been talking to her, something she accused me of seldom doing. If I said something she felt it had to be dragged out of me. She said she was seriously thinking of calling him and becoming his patient.

I knew this psychologist quite well. In fact, he had been a student of mine for several years. He had never had a private practice so there was no possibility of her becoming his patient. This was especially interesting because my patient already knew that he was an academician and she could recognize that much of his lecture dealt with ideas that were similar to mine.

What impressed me was that she could, in her mind, conjure an interactive therapeutic relationship, but she would not allow it to happen in actuality. I was being reprimanded for not giving her what she felt she needed, but if I tried to respond she would not let me, or if I did manage to interject what I thought was a meaningful comment, she would either ignore it or not recognize what I was trying to do.

I was becoming increasingly aware of inner tension and annoyance at her narcissism especially as it continued being directed at diminishing me as it impinged upon my professional self-respect. I found myself taking an adversarial stance, and this did not improve my therapeutic outlook.

Many times I considered responding to her challenges and suggesting that maybe she was right and perhaps we should consider terminating treatment. Here, narcissism came to my aid; it did not permit me to make what could be a self-destructive confrontation as far as the continuation of the therapy was concerned. It would have been a counterproductive and an antitherapeutic action. I knew that it would have gone against my concepts of good therapeutic responses. It would have been defensive and vindictive.

As I reflected on our interaction I had the amusing thought that to be a good analyst, I had to go along with the patient's need to view me as a bad one. I had to accept being a bad analyst so that the therapy could survive, an interesting paradox that compromised my narcissism.

If therapy is eventually successful, then clinicians would think that narcissism served a useful function, and although there may have been many painful moments for the therapist that could have masochistic elements, they were able to be brought into the service of the treatment. However, if the treatment failed, as is so often the case, then narcissism would be viewed as a hindrance and something that the patient and therapist may need to work through. Thus, narcissism is a relative issue and has to be explored in a wide context and often retrospectively.

The influence of narcissism on the therapeutic process always asserts itself in the framework of transference–countertransference transactions. In these instances a character trait intrudes itself in the patient–therapist interaction and may work in two ways—either to terminate the treatment or to preserve it. It is possible that either outcome may have been due to psychopathological reasons.

Still, it behooves therapists to be aware of and keep track of their responses. I can envision instances in which refusing to give up may lead to disastrous consequences, and eventually to the patient leaving feeling bitter and often developing a paranoid delusion about the treatment experience. Rather than treatment being an insight-provoking process, it could degenerate into an adversarial contest in which the patient feels vulnerable and exposed and interpretations are often attacks and impingements, in Winnicott's (1952) sense, that lead to chaos and disruption.

Regarding my patient, the therapy continued and I believed this was possible because of a sensory distortion I had, a distortion that I have made from time to time. As she lay on the couch, which she frequently protested, I imagined she adopted a fetal position, while actually she was simply lying straight. Instead, I conjured a picture of her being on her side, her arms around her drawn knees, the profile of her face having lost its sharp features and replaced by the more amorphous features of an infant. This was first a momentary perception but it modulated my feelings about the usual attacking narcissistic material that inevitably followed.

Although I had been aware of the helpless little girl that was behind her hostile, arrogant facade, my distorted observation drove home how she desperately clung to her talents and creativity to hold herself together. Her attacks turned into feeble rubber darts and I felt a slight sense of shame that I should have taken such umbrage at her attempts to bring me down, as if I were defending myself against the attacks of a weak infant.

This was a sharp contrast to my previous feelings and the way others, in general, felt about her. Again, I had to wonder about the extent of my contributions, that is, how much my attitude colored and intensified the harshness of her statements and the tyranny of her narcissism. Was this a tug-of-war we had both created where we each pulled harder as our interaction became increasingly intense?

I know that at a phenomenological level she was outrageous, but after my "vision" I experienced her in an entirely different fashion. I no longer felt uneasy about the role of bad therapist she had assigned me. I realized that was what she had to do. I knew this for a long time but after having seen her vulnerability at a primary process level within myself, an actual distortion of reality as I conjured an infant, this vision became integrated into my memory system and was at the disposal of my professional ego-ideal. This led to a narcissistic balance that gave me an entirely different viewpoint about the treatment, and this viewpoint, though it was never verbalized, dramatically changed the therapeutic ambience.

I no longer felt the impact of her words and I began to realize that this patient did not live in the same world most of us live in. She was truly an alien in an alien land and could exist only because she was completely cut apart from her surroundings. She could produce and what she gave the world was valued as a supercomputer can be valued. Unfortunately, her attunement to the world was also similar to that of a robot, as she did not have the feelings or sensitivities that characterize most of us.

I can now realize that when she shut me out or ignored what I said, there were other factors operating besides the maintenance and invulnerability of her narcissism. Part of her had no idea what I was talking about, because even though we had the same vocabulary, we were speaking different languages. We came from different planets and could not communicate with each other. This realization caused me to feel compassion rather than resentment.

My change in attitude had an impact on the treatment that was silently communicated because I did not verbalize my feelings and reactions. I mention reactions because I had relaxed and did not feel tense as I had felt in the past, and I actually looked forward to her sessions. She stopped attacking me and accepted that I was probably right about her narcissism, but she did not care. She understood that according to other people's standards she was selfish, had no patience, and was disliked, but this all seemed meaningless. She had no intention of changing. In fact, she could not even conceive of what change meant. It was, as she stated, incomprehensible.

In spite of her lack of understanding, or because of it, she started feeling sad. She felt the same loneliness that impelled her to seek treatment, only now it was worse.

I no longer felt challenged and apparently she needed to challenge. She had to have someone react to her onslaughts, but now she was punching in a vacuum. There was no longer an adversary to subdue, so that she could feel victorious. She could not continue depleting me of my narcissism to add to her huge coffers. If she had no one to fight with, she was forced to face her basic vulnerabilities and her state of pathetic loneliness.

Whenever she addressed me by name, which seldom occurred, she still let my last name melodiously roll on her tongue. I had the feeling now that she was talking to me more as a veteran who had returned from battles that we fought together than as a competitor.

As her material became increasingly mild and nonthreatening, she had less to say until she reached a state where she believed she had nothing to say. She commented that she had "run dry."

In what seemed to be an uncharacteristic fashion, she started complaining about herself. She questioned the reality of her perceptions and said that what she felt was devoid of meaning so it could not be put into words. That is why she often felt blank during sessions.

She also recognized that we were having a language problem in that most of the time she literally did not understand what I was saying. I recognized more than ever at this time that her inability to take in helpful experiences was because she had no inner template to help achieve an endopsychic registration, but this lack caused her to feel empty—another painful state, which, at least in therapy, she could no longer fill up with narcissistic enhancement.

On occasion, I would make an interpretation that she found helpful for the moment but it would quickly vanish. This was different from the destruction of potentially good internal objects as described by Klein (1946). She simply was not able to hold them and make them part of herself; they were not even felt as intrusions. My interventions, although given in my language, could sometimes partially be attached to her mode of comprehension so that they could enter the intrapsychic sphere, though this happened only on rare occasions and toward the end of therapy. They could be allowed a certain entry and then they would be divested of meaning, and their self-enhancing potential would be mitigated.

Another patient described a similar situation in which he also found it painful to be nurtured for a variety of reasons that are not particularly relevant. His mother was good intentioned but naive, and during his childhood would give him frequent enemas, which he dreaded. He would run and hide, making her chase and corner him to give him an enema. She felt that he had to be clean inside and she also gave him weekly laxatives.

What was supposed to be good for him was painful, disruptive, and intrusive. This created a dilemma different from what many patients who have been abused during childhood have experienced. In their cases, they were sadistically and brutally assaulted and any introjective process is felt as dangerous because it was intended to be dangerous. Their reaction is to employ splitting defenses (Grotstein 1981, Ogden 1982) and their narcissistic supplies are often nonexistent or minimal. The patient who was subjected to enemas had problems with his self-worth, but these were due to intrapsychic conflicts about self-esteem rather than reactions to massive trauma that threatened to totally disrupt ego integration and the stability of the self representation.

The principal difference between the woman I have been discussing, the young man with the well-intentioned mother, and savagely abused patients is related to the diffusiveness of the self representation. In the last instance, it is precariously balanced and further disrupted by splitting defenses, whereas in the former instances there were conflicts about the identity sense that involved narcissism but not to the extent that the self representation would be in danger of crumbling.

Both these patients were very much concerned about their creativity. The woman used her talents to feel secure and maintain the illusion that she could get support from the external world. By contrast, the young man felt that he could not let himself be helped. He believed that others liked and wanted to relate to him. He conceded that his friends and colleagues wanted to support him from an emotional viewpoint, but he would not let external objects' ministrations work intrapsychically for his benefit. He had to render them sterile, because otherwise his introjections would be too rich or toxic. The noxious substances within him had to be eliminated by enemas or laxatives, and the acts of intake and expulsion were confused with each other. He was invaded in order to establish internal harmony and equilibrium rather than being fed in a soothing and nourishing fashion.

Introjective-projective processes were not in synchrony and did not lead to psychic stability or creative accomplishment. He was convinced, however, that his caregivers wanted to help him, but he experienced what they gave him as dangerous. He blamed himself for this attitude and felt considerable guilt. He also despaired because he knew that this type of confusion would lead to an inhibition of creative activity and hinder the generation of ideas. His "insides" might be clean but they were also sterile and nonproductive.

He had a fantasy in which he was fed intravenously rather than being allowed to eat normally. Ordinary food would become noxious and poisonous, which he recognized as irrational fantasy. He believed this was derived from his mother's compulsion about intestinal cleanliness.

To be safe, he had to sacrifice the pleasures of eating, and for a brief period of time shortly before starting treatment he had been anorexic. He resented not being able to have access to oral satisfaction. More important, he was upset about his lack of creativity, an activity he felt to be liberating and held in high esteem. His inability to function creatively was a significant blow to his narcissism.

The narcissistic woman wanted to believe that she could build up self-esteem by relating to the outer world, and in a sense this was not entirely an illusion. It was what might be called a half-illusion, in that she could receive positive response for her creative accomplishments, but it was not positive feedback. It was not an interaction because she did not have the capacity to relate to the world other than in her robot-like capacity to produce at the materialistic level. The development of healthy narcissism depends on a mutually enhancing interaction that fosters creative activity and self-esteem in a positive feedback sequence.

She was able to give in a constrictive fashion and what she could take in was also limited. The latter incapacity became strikingly clear after the covert and overt adversarial qualities of the treatment interaction were no longer operative. Her attacks were not toxic, and she was no longer able to make them the central focus of her material. She was mute or mostly silent for many of her sessions, insisting that she had nothing to say. She stated that when she arrived at my office all of her thoughts disappeared and she felt empty inside. This feeling frightened her, but she did not think of terminating her treatment. She voiced some sentiments that approached the expression of gratitude, but her ability to make affective responses was limited. Previously it had been nonexistent.

I felt we had developed a language that enabled us to marginally communicate with each other. It was not a rich or expressive language, but at times I could make myself understood if I latched onto some phrase or clause that she was vocalizing. Since she started the train of thought, she could bring it from the motor sphere into the sensory sphere and partially internalize my contribution as a coda. I had to sneak in but it made some form of communication possible.

I expressed my thoughts but stated them only in her words, especially her nouns. This type of interaction was somewhat effective in that it caused her to feel that someone in this world could understand her, or would at least try to learn about the disruptive qualities of her loneliness, a reaction to her feeling isolated in an alien world. But it was not enough. She continued to come to her sessions with a sense of dread and she said practically nothing.

It became clear that although our relationship was much more civilized, it had lost its spark. She sadly said that she wanted to stop treatment. She knew that I had done my best to help her and felt that I had in many ways succeeded, but, for the time being this was as far as we could go. We had not reached an impasse. We had just reached the limits of how far our psyches could reach out to each other. She expected that she would call me in the future, but she never did. I hear about her occasionally, and know she is doing well professionally.

I had to reconcile myself to my limitations as a therapist for her. I still felt a narcissistic urge not to give up, but I also had to respect her acquiescence about the limitations of our relationship. I had to remain content in knowing that for ten years I was a significant part of her life. This had to be enough to satisfy my narcissism.

The considerable detail I have gone into in describing the course of this patient's treatment emphasizes that my subjective responses and narcissistic involvement are countertransference reactions that are inextricably woven into the fabric of the treatment process. The study of subjective responses as elements of the countertransference includes the exploration of the contribution of narcissism. In the past, transference and countertransference enactments have been discussed in a more superficial fashion, mainly in the context of the repetition compulsion. This is a salient approach, but to round out our understanding of the entire therapeutic arena, the therapist's and the patient's narcissism are in the forefront.

Patients can use the therapist's approach and stance against the treatment, producing special types of countertransference reactions. They may reverse the treatment flow by probing the analyst's unconscious and defenses. Again the professional self representation is involved but in a special fashion. It is not the therapist's competence or content of interpretations that is challenged. It is the professional modus operandi that is called into question. The philosophy of the treatment interaction and the validity of the intrapsychic focus are challenged by turning them against the analyst.

There are patients who will not let the therapist function as a therapist, and this can totally disrupt the clinician's clinical style. The undermining of the treatment can occur subtly and it may take some time before the patient's sabotaging of therapy becomes apparent. Usually, the analyst feels some uncomfortable countertransference feelings and suspects that something is wrong.

A middle-aged architect apparently had no problems free-associating. He talked freely and covered many topics. He frequently spoke about his work and I found it quite interesting. Still, I developed feelings of uneasiness, which I could not at first understand.

I gradually felt that I had nothing I could get hold of. I could not focus on any material I could analyze. The patient covered many topics, but only on the surface. There was nothing reflective or anything that led to self-inquiry. It was as if I were listening to a newscaster and I could not find an entry where I could make an interpretation. The material was phenomenological rather than free-associative, and it also had an obsessional and pressure-like quality that Freud (1909b) described.

The one definite feeling I had was of being shut out, but I did not feel that I was being attacked. For the patient, there seemed to be something wrong about the methodology of treatment. He insisted that he was free-associating and that he was simply telling me what came to mind, yet I could not understand what he said as the derivatives of unconscious processes.

I finally told him how I experienced our interaction. I tried not to blame him and emphasized that I was simply making an observation. I wondered how his method of speaking was perhaps interfering with the unfolding of the treatment process. I was also curious as to how he developed such an adaptive or defensive mechanism, although I was not at all certain as to what he was doing. All I knew was that I felt paralyzed as an analyst, but this feeling was quite different from my responses when I was being openly attacked and demeaned.

I suspected I was having some countertransference difficulties that caused me to experience some narcissistic imbalance. In other words, I was entertaining the possibility that issues of my own might have been involved in my response. However, I was not particularly dismayed and felt that many therapists would have similar responses to mine. I tested this hypothesis by presenting this patient to colleagues at a clinical seminar and they also felt a sense of frustration.

The patient acknowledged what I said, but he again repeated that he felt he was free-associating. He said that if I believed he was not free-associating, then what was he doing and how could he get on the right track. I must admit that I found these to be difficult questions and did not immediately know how to answer. I was able to gain some time on the second question when I gave a rather standard and trite lecture on free-association and its purpose. Then I was able to make some comments as to how a patient can achieve the capacity to speak freely with just a minimal selection and inhibition of thoughts. I used some of Freud's metaphors in his papers on technique.

From then on the patient narrowed his range of discourse. He limited his remarks to questioning many psychoanalytic concepts, especially as they related to technique. He wanted to know, for example, what was the purpose of making the unconscious conscious and how do we know that dreams have meaning? He was voicing the opinions of those neurologists who believe that dreams are the products of degenerative processes, as I mentioned in Chapter 1.

He was not being argumentative or challenging. He was discussing in a calm matter what he believed were interesting ideas. He was particularly interested in discussing the curative process. How does insight lead to cure? This question plagues most analysts, because the working-through process, despite all that has been written about it, is poorly understood. In my own way, I tried to answer his questions and I hoped I had put the matter to rest.

I was not entirely satisfied with my responses, because at times I felt I was being trite and formulaic. There is a tendency to take the answers to such questions for granted, perhaps covering up our imprecise understanding. Being forced to put such ideas into words could be clarifying but there was a part of me that experienced him as an inquisitor, and I felt a slight sense of annoyance.

Undoubtedly, he was being somewhat sadistic and intrusive, but these were low-keyed feelings and attitudes. I felt that he respected me and even admired the way I responded to his questions. I also asked myself why I continued responding and concluded that if I withheld from him, I would indeed be creating an adversarial atmosphere. The iatrogenically created, reactive hostility would have obscured the real anger that was located in his infantile milieu.

I wondered further about my reactions and two elements stood out. One: I was becoming increasingly annoyed as he continued talking about analysis rather than doing analysis, but my annoyance was controlled and not particularly disruptive. Two: I asked myself why I did not point out that he was forcing me into a meta-analysis, and thereby not getting into his feelings and problems.

I hesitated in making such an interpretation, essentially an interpretation of resistance, because my motives might not have been in the best interest of the therapy. They could have been interpreted as the outcome of annoyance, a response that must have some negative countertransference elements, and the patient would feel that I was blaming and criticizing him.

Regarding my motives, it was clear to me that I wanted him to change his material, that is, to stop indulging in meta-analysis. Interpretations are not designed to be prohibitions even though they often are. They are supposed to enable patients to get in touch with hidden or split-off parts of the self and to enhance autonomy. I did not believe my interpretations or confrontations would have achieved that purpose. I would have been covertly telling him to change the course of his narrative.

At first, I felt that my annoyance was the outcome of frustration about a treatment that did not seem to be going anywhere. I could feel justified about not being comfortable about a therapeutic relationship that had reached an impasse. I soon realized that much more was involved. I was disturbed because the patient was not allowing me to do my job.

Unlike some of the previous patients I have discussed, he was not attacking me personally or demeaning me for being incompetent. On the contrary, he praised me and was satisfied with his progress in treatment. He was praising me, however, for being a good teacher and not a good therapist. Although he was not assaulting my professional self representation he was paralyzing my professional modus operandi.

He told me I knew a good deal and was conversant with my profession but he would not allow me to practice it according to the standards of my professional ego-ideal. This latter juncture was where my countertransference entered the picture and my self-esteem was compromised. Being aware of my internal status prevented me from being active and intervening. I decided that he be allowed to choose whatever he wanted to talk about. At least he could have autonomy within the therapeutic setting.

It might be somewhat of a stretch of the imagination to believe that letting the patient be autonomous in treatment and permitting what was essentially a stalemate to go on without interruption was analytically feasible. I believe that fostering autonomy and viewing the patient's material as adaptive are essential factors for the analytic interaction. This set me somewhat at ease regarding my modus operandi and professional ego-ideal.

After many months, I felt we were running out of material. A course in psychoanalytic technique has to have an end point. True, the topic is virtually inexhaustible, but there are limits to the number of questions that can be asked and the answers that can be given. There was a spontaneous winding down and for a while he was silent.

From time to time, I had attempted to relate to him at an analytic level in spite of my reservations about looking at the motives behind his questioning rather than responding to their content. As I feared, he accused me of being defensive. My dilemma could now be pithily stated. The patient had put me in the position that if I tried to function as a therapist I was being defensive and acting out some untoward countertransference feelings.

After the silent period, which I did not interrupt, he started talking about his childhood. He humorously asked me if I liked this subject better. Knowing he would expect and insist on a response, I replied that I felt more comfortable with this material than with silence and what I had called meta-analysis.

To regain my professional stance and to restore my narcissistic equilibrium, I wanted to learn how functionally paralyzing me served him as an infantile adaptation. Perhaps this was the wrong tack and his probing behavior might have been a character trait without any specific antecedents in the infantile milieu. It could be related to a concretely oriented, mechanistic psyche rather than a reenactment of an infantile relationship.

I learned that his behavior in treatment was a reactive adaptive pattern to his infantile insecurities. His father was a celebrity, a famous athlete who had a large fan club. As a child the patient was given considerable attention by many women who adored his father. The patient soon recognized that he was being used as a pawn who was a reflection of his father's glory. He looked upon his father as an omnipotent person who could do no wrong. He admired him but he was ambivalent. Underneath he was extremely envious and harbored a deep resentment.

Outwardly the patient was passive and compliant but his anger manifested itself in a curmudgeon-like attitude. He was highly critical of conservative politics, the current president, and other movements that leaned toward the right, but he could not commit himself to the left either. He railed against current fads and made himself the oddball of the group. Still, he was invited to many social events because of his famous father and this only increased his resentment.

Because of his name, or so he believed, he was able to secure a position in a large architectural firm. Apparently he had sufficient talent to hold his own, but was still in the shadow of greatness. His mentor, who liked the patient, was very famous and could at times be unpleasant. Again, the patient was in a position where he both admired and resented a personage.

I believe the first time he gave full vent to his resentment, although it was disguised, was when he became my inquisitor. Later in treatment he expressed his gratitude for my letting him express the negative elements of his ambivalence. He needed to render me helpless, to stop me from functioning as an analyst and make me a servant to his questions, in order to gain narcissistic supplies by taking them away from me within the context of a father transference.

The positive elements of his ambivalence were expressed by the respect he felt for my knowledge and the relevant answers I gave him.

Although I experienced his meta-analyzing as tedious it had its lighter moments, which helped alleviate my negative countertransference and reestablished some of my lost narcissism. He had given me the opportunity to be somewhat exhibitionistic in my replies as I tried to be cogent and precise. I was also able, on occasion, to make a humorous remark that amused him. For example, he once asked me to define character. I hesitated and told him this was a difficult question. It was a word we took for granted but it would be hard to give a precise definition. I then went into a rather lengthy discourse beginning by pointing out that it referred to the architecture of the personality and explained how various ego subsystems were formed and had unique elements that became part of the self representation that led to autonomy and the creation of a specific style. This was a style created by the ego's executive system and determined how the psyche related to the outer world.

I went into considerable detail and after I finished I said, "Well, that's it. How did I make out?" I added that I did not know whether I could answer his question, but I just started talking and was curious to see where I would go. I finally thanked him for the opportunity he had given me to sharpen my wits and that I enjoyed the exercise, which I did. The patient laughed and assured me that I had done very well. I silently conjectured that I had given a good performance and I was pleased with myself. Though this was far from an optimal analytic response and would not have been accepted as a professional modality, it was narcissistically gratifying, and humor helped create a positive bond between the two of us, which served the treatment well.

The father transference became increasingly strong, and within its context he was able to exact revenge by attacking me with his questions. As a child, he was not able to directly express his anger because he felt small and weak. His rebellion became imbued in a passive stance, but with me he was openly aggressive. Rather than displaying athletic prowess, he was using his intellect as a weapon, but he was grateful that I did not succumb or try to get rid of him.

In many social relationships, he believed that after an initial acceptance, he was eventually shunned. This caused him to feel bitter, an attitude that became a character trait. His morose style and sarcasm led to his feeling lonely and isolated. His social life was the direct antithesis of his father's mode of relating. His father is outgoing, friendly, and sociable, and has a wide circle of friends. The patient was not aware of the extent of his resentment toward his father and the intensity of his passive withdrawal.

My mock expression of gratitude when he asked me to define character changed the nature of our interaction. It became lighter and relaxed. I did not feel as much under fire, and he gradually stopped challenging me. On occasion, he would tell me a joke, and I often replied with a wry or witty comment. Our interactions were no longer grim and often contained humorous elements. The countertransference, in a manner of speaking, mellowed.

The patient is still in treatment. I experienced the initial stages of therapy as problematic, but I believe we had reached an impasse that produced countertransference difficulties, but because of a humorous trend they were transcended.

In contrast to other patients I have presented, I did not feel that my professional self representation had been directly attacked. It was challenged but not denigrated. I felt functionally paralyzed but not demeaned. I was struggling to maintain an analytic setting, but I believed the role he had forced on me was that of a teacher. He was interfering with my professional stance, an uncomfortable situation, but nowhere near as devastating as when the patient attempts to destroy the therapist's professional self representation.

There are many facets to the professional modus operandi, which is a facet of the professional self representation. It is a special type of identity sense, which, like any psychic element, can be viewed in terms of a structural hierarchy (see Chapter 3).The identity sense or self representation encompasses many psychic levels. A particularly important aspect is its mode of functioning, and in the clinical arena this would refer to how the therapist conducts treatment. Erikson (1956, 1959) might have called this element of the identity sense the operational sense of identity.

It is quite understandable how the professional identity is involved with the ego-ideal, which functions as a psychic agency that evaluates the level of performance. In turn, it is a barometer of self-esteem, which supplies the narcissistic pool. Any doubts about the quality of the therapeutic performance are a threat to internal harmony and narcissistic balance that are manifested in untoward countertransference responses. Disturbances created by the ego-ideal cause countertransference reactions that warn the therapist that something may have gone awry in the treatment process. These feelings usually consist of a pervasive paralysis and often a sense of humiliation and guilt because we are not living up to our standards.

It could be rationalized that what I was doing by answering my patient's questions could be thought of as a feasible treatment response. This formulation would be supported by the fact that eventually we got on a more conventional analytic track, but this is risky reasoning. In therapy, I am not certain that the end justifies the means. There is no certitude that the means will eventually lead to therapeutic resolution, and it may be drastically harmful.

This professional modus operandi has a wide range and varies from patient to patient. Therapists have to adapt their therapeutic style to the patient's psychopathology. They have to exercise a wide degree of flexibility but there are limits beyond which they cannot go. This usually means that they have to establish some boundaries to keep the relationship professional. However, what might be an acceptable professional modus operandi for some patients could be completely inappropriate and intrusive for others.

Clinicians have to be careful about how much of the personal aspects of their countertransference feelings they reveal to their patients. In general, the continuous focus should be on the patient, and extraneous factors such as the therapist's conflicts should be excluded. However, focusing on the patient's problems sometimes blends with countertransference reactions that are in resonance with those problems. Furthermore, the therapist's personal orientation may be similar to that of a significant person in the patient's early environment, and perhaps in a crucial moment of treatment it can cause a reenactment of the repetition compulsion.

As I discussed in the preface, many of the clinical phenomena I have been describing in some ways resemble each other. What I am about to present is another example of difficulties with the professional orientation but it has a different and subtle twist that I believe should be acknowledged and emphasized. Countertransference interactions frequently involve areas of the therapist's personality related to the professional self representation. This is practically self-evident because the difficulties experienced occur within the framework of the treatment process. Nevertheless, there are a variety of problems stemming from the therapeutic interaction that are unique and memorable, and they warrant discussion because they are commonly encountered but often not recognized. Frequently, the countertransference causes the therapist to bury them, and this could be therapeutically disastrous.

When pointing out similarities, it should also be noted that each patient is unique and the therapeutic interaction will also have distinctive features. Therefore, it is risky to generalize, and although there are certain general technical principles, there is considerable leeway as to how therapists may respond to their patients. Still, they have to be based on understanding and remain within reasonable bounds.

The professional modus operandi cannot transgress ethical standards, but it must not be rigid. It has to accommodate the patient's needs and not stay fixed to standards that are believed to be professionally correct but that in some instances are obsolete and antitherapeutic. Sometimes standard rules and therapeutic procedures get mixed up.

I recall a challenging period of treatment of an elderly married man whom I have seen for many years. Throughout his life, he was extremely disorganized and totally inept, and had difficulties in conducting his daily life. He had been able to graduate from high school, but educationally he could go no further. A job was out of the question, since he could hardly get through a day. Frequently he had to be driven to sessions or he would get lost on his way to my office. He lived and was taken care of in the home of his wealthy parents.

I first saw him in his late thirties after he had been in various forms of treatment, including shock therapy. He had been institutionalized several times after being diagnosed as schizophrenic, although there were no gross distortions of reality testing or evidence of delusions or hallucinations.

During the early months of treatment, he spoke in a rapid, hypomanic fashion that was hardly comprehensible because he mumbled and ran words together, and if I wrote down what he said, the content did not make sense. On occasion he would get so painfully excited during a session that he had to get up and walk out, sometimes only five minutes after the session had started. He seemed to be in a state of perpetual agitation.

Because he was hard to understand, I was uncertain about his description of his childhood. Apparently, he had been both psychically and sexually abused by both his parents. Later in therapy, when he became coherent, I learned that there was considerable trauma in early childhood. His parents both protected him from each other, but they also attacked him. As some children do not know what it is to be nurtured, he did not know or he was confused as to what being protected meant. I was able to understand many of his symptoms and disrupted behavior as manifestations of an utter state of vulnerability. He was frightened most of the time and in a state of utter terror.

Despite the severity of his symptoms, he gradually became calmer and gained control of his feelings. Over the years, he slowly became self-sufficient and was able to work on a full-time basis. In fact, he made some wise investments that enabled him to move out of the house, support himself, and finally marry and have several children. He was a testament to the power of the analytic process.

He is still in treatment and views it as an essential ingredient of his life—the way a diabetic needs his insulin. I will return to the question of the length of therapy later, since some clinicians have been critical of interminable treatments, and their professional self representations view the therapeutic process as having a beginning, a middle, and an end, as exemplified by the three levels of clinical seminars given by the Chicago Institute of Psychoanalysis when I was a candidate.

I will skip the main body of the treatment because it is not relevant to the interaction. I wish to discuss how various aspects of the professional modus operandi clashed with each other and how my treatment approach became inconsistent. I found that I was questioning traditional technical values and challenging cherished beliefs.

In this case, unlike other cases, he was not attacking me or my treatment style. He reassured me that he held my analytic skills in high regard, but there were certain attitudes I displayed that he felt were at odds with my therapeutic integrity. He felt his complaints were reasonable in the context of therapy, whereas initially I felt he was trying to destroy boundaries.

We both agreed he had come a long way to be able to assert himself in such a coherent fashion about a complex topic that previously would have been outside the capacity of his comprehension. He praised me, himself, and the treatment for being able to recognize and become involved in a technical dilemma. He even attributed my asserting my position as due to his improvement, which was true. In the past, his vulnerability would have prevented me from asserting myself and revealing my feelings.

The beginning of our clash occurred when the patient started ruminating about the length of treatment and his dependence on me. Though he had no intention of discontinuing therapy, he was expressing the negative side of his ambivalence about remaining in analysis for the rest of his life. As he had felt toward his parents he admitted feeling vulnerable toward me, but to a much lesser extent. He also credited the treatment for protecting him as his parents claimed they did, but he was no longer confused about their roles. He now saw them only as predators.

Several times he asked me why he was so angry at me when I had helped him so much. He resented how long it had taken him to achieve what he had and to be as assertive as he was being by criticizing me. I replied that perhaps he found being gratified painful, and then without any deliberation I said that this might be the same reaction to the gratitude a child might have toward his parents. I added that being grateful to the mother for bringing one into the world could after a while become tedious. I did not at the time see why any of these little comments were relevant and I wondered why I said them.

To my surprise, my comments had a strong impact. He felt that having to be grateful to his parents constituted a major trauma. It tore at the core of his being because it presented him with a powerful paradox. To be attacked was bad enough, but to have to be grateful for being nearly destroyed was outrageous. He was facing murderous protection, an oxymoron. Oxymorons are often cogent and pithy summaries of the operations of severe psychopathological processes. These feelings had worked themselves into the transference and he was overpowered by his feelings.

He was silent for a few seconds, an unusual phenomenon because he usually filled up all his time with words. He then told me he had to make some silent deliberations and he would stop talking. Apparently, I did not hear him or I unconsciously decided not to let him be silent.

After thirty seconds of silence, I cleared my throat, a signal or, for the patient, a command that he should stop suppressing his thoughts and continue talking. He immediately showed his annoyance and attacked me for depriving him of his autonomy. Together we were trying to create a treatment setting that emphasized autonomy and my not letting him be silent contradicted such an endeavor. He had also read case histories, some of them mine, where being nonintrusive and letting the patient decide whether he would talk or not talk became the central pillar of the treatment process. (I discuss the silent patient later in this chapter.) The patient insisted that my prodding him to free-associate was an antitherapeutic breach, and he wanted to know what personal factors caused me to violate principles that I said I valued; according to the patient, something had gone wrong with my countertransference.

I was momentarily confused, because at first I did not understand his accusation that I had caused a breach in the analytic setting by asking him to free-associate. This did not seem at odds with my professional modus operandi, since I indicate by gesture or words that I want to hear what patients have on their minds. I had never asked him to tell me because I never had to. If anything, it was usually hard to get him to stop talking so I could get a word in edgewise.

Later, I realized that I should tailor my mode of relating to the patient's needs, and that one style may work for some patients and not for others.

I had what might be called a professional regression to a classical stance. I had been taught that the essence of the intrapsychic focus is free association. Patients impeding this process are resisting, and resistances have to be overcome as soon as possible. This is what candidates at psychoanalytic institutes were taught, and in my personal analysis my analyst would not allow me to be silent. These attitudes are responsible for the adversarial qualities of classical analyses, and for some reason I reverted back to what I consider anachronisms.

When the patient started probing into my personal life, I found myself resisting, but I recognized that my resistance had to be related to my infantile milieu and not motivated by the best interests of the therapeutic interaction. I could not pass it off as my not wanting to dump on the patient or my intent to be nonintrusive. I had already intruded on the patient's right to be silent, which I equated with standard classical analytic technique.

When the patient demanded to know about my personal motivations for my intrusion, I replied that I did not know what they were, but if I did I was not inclined to discuss them and added the rationalization, which I did not then understand to be a rationalization, that I did not want to burden him with my personal life or problems.

My reply was far from satisfactory, and he kept insisting on knowing the reasons for my intervention, which at the moment simply appeared to be the trivial clearing of my throat. I believed he was making a mountain out of a molehill and I felt I was being badgered. I was somewhat impressed, however, when he quoted me as writing that in some treatment settings the therapist has to create an environment where the patient can comfortably withdraw.

He stated that he wanted to be silent for at least two reasons. He was tired of repeating the same things over and over. He wanted to grow up and cut the umbilical cord, which would mean that he did not need to have someone around to listen to him. He was angry because he felt that he could not leave me. He had felt a similar anger at being unable to leave his parents' house, at being inextricably bound to them and trapped.

Because of the treatment he was able to leave them but he could not end his treatment. When in a humorous mood he compared himself to Woody Allen. This series of events was introduced by a discussion of gratitude. The therapy had succeeded in getting him out of the house and he felt he had to be grateful for this accomplishment. This was, however, a reflection of his parents' obligating him to feel grateful for having, in essence, made him into a recluse and prisoner, and this made him feel further anger.

The second reason for his silence was an active need to keep things to himself. His parents would not allow him to have his own thoughts, and now he was defending himself against my constant presence, which had been escalated to an intrusion by my refusal to respond to his question.

This patient confused me about my professional stance, but he was not asking me to do anything that would have threatened it. I violated my technical style by regressing to the classic position. Why this happened was not clear at the time. Revealing my personal contributions would under certain circumstances not have been objectionable to my professional ego-ideal. I rationalized not doing so because of being considerate of the patient, but I knew even then there were important reasons for my reluctance to explore my psyche in terms of my past rather than our relationship. In any case, as I have acknowledged, I could not think of any personal reasons and I did not feel my narcissism would have been threatened if I discovered some.

After several sessions and several parapraxes on both our parts, we reached some interesting conclusions. The parapraxes consisted of selective forgetting. During the session immediately following my classical approach, he forgot that he had wanted to know my motives, but I had not. I, in turn, forgot our discussion about gratitude and that children might feel angry at their parents for having brought them into the world and raised them. We both forgot the reasons he wanted to be silent, such as his desire not to reveal himself to his parents and to preserve his privacy and autonomy. Being unable to build a shield against their intrusiveness and having to feel a strong sense of obligation and gratitude only added to intense feelings of vulnerability and helplessness.

We concluded that there were several factors at work that confused me and made me feel constricted in my therapeutic approach. The first reason that occurred to me was phenomenological. I did not think of him as a patient who could tolerate silence and this certainly was true for the earlier years of treatment. I did not recognize that he had changed in this regard, a fact that later dismayed me because my lack of recognition may have been associated with the interminable quality of the treatment. He had complained about being chained to his parents, and my failure to appreciate the extent of his improvement might have been due to my need to keep him in treatment.

Nevertheless, he had no intention of leaving therapy because he felt it was vital to his being able to function in everyday life. He had compared himself to an electric device shaped like a bug that would wander around in a random fashion. However, it would not stray too far away from an electric socket to which it would periodically attach itself to energize its batteries. He felt the same way about his therapy. He had to periodically immerse himself in the therapeutic process to gain a sense of cohesion and vitality. I was able to accept the role of a therapist who created a setting in which the patient could feel replenished (see next section).

I also concluded that some of my countertransference feelings were a direct response to the transference. The patient was angry at his parents because they were constantly intruding. They would not let him alone with his own thoughts without demanding that he reveal them. I also felt his anger and then identified with his parents. This was also a reaction to the parental imagos he had projected onto me.

In addition, I identified with the patient when I was unable and unwilling to reveal myself to him. I was more interested in preserving my autonomy than in not wanting to burden him with my discomforts, an attitude that became part of my modus operandi. Undoubtedly, my childhood experiences may have contributed to my withholding and my insistence that he continue free-associating. To some degree, I must have felt a similar type of intrusion from my parents.

I finally interpreted to the patient that in demanding that I reveal myself, he was doing to me what had been done to him. This was a reaction to my having identified with his parents. He completely accepted this interpretation but he still wanted to know something about my personal motivations, outside of the treatment, that had contributed to my prohibition of silence. After all the discussion we had, I saw no reason for withholding and had now been able to recall certain childhood instances in which my parents uncovered feelings that I did not want to reveal. Within the context of our discussions, it no longer mattered to either of us whether I answered his question.

This patient once again illustrates how subtle and complex the therapeutic interaction can be. The treatment process also emphasizes that within a certain frame, the professional modus operandi has a certain amount of flexibility. It cannot be shackled by any hard and fast rule.

Personal disclosures react as foreign bodies and in general should not be revealed. They should be used to gain insights about the transference–countertransference interaction. My patient demonstrated that personal withholding on the therapist's part had special meaning as it resonated with his own experiences in which he tried to protect himself from his parents. These are special dynamics that have to be taken into account as the therapist relates to the patient and defines the professional modus operandi.

The therapist cannot equate maintaining a narcissistic balance with rigidly adhering to defined and accepted standards. Standards vary according to the conceptual school that constructs them, and feeling secure and gaining self-esteem within an established system helps maintain the narcissistic reservoir.

COUNTERTRANSFERENCE AND INTERMINABLE THERAPY: TECHNICAL AND SUPEREGO PROBLEMS

Freud wrote of the length of analysis in terms of months. During the revisionist period of the Chicago Institute for Psychoanalysis, therapists tried to practice brief therapy but many of these clinicians did not consider what they were doing to be psychoanalysis. At best, it was a modified version involving the introduction of parameters that became part of the treatment, in contrast to Eissler's (1953) recommendation that parameters be eliminated as soon as possible.

For a while the Chicago Institute's practice of brief therapy became a dominant concern. I recall some fellow candidates having completed their analyses from nine months to a little over a year, but as far as I know they all had at least a second course of treatment.

Regarding so-called training analyses, psychoanalytic institutes require a certain number of sessions. I believe the Chicago Institute at the time I was there required four hundred analytic sessions at a minimum of four times a week. The length of such analyses with a minimum of four hundred sessions would be somewhat over two years and today a two year-course of treatment would be considered brief.

After a colleague and I had been in practice for five years, we discussed how many of our patients had completed their treatment. We were disturbed because only a very small percentage had reached a conclusive resolution of their problems. Some had left treatment because it did not seem to work or they had to move away for various reasons. Still, most patients remained with us and did not especially complain about the length of treatment.

Naturally, we wondered whether we were doing something, most likely unconsciously motivated, that prolonged treatment.

The first thought that came to mind involved financial factors. Pragmatically, this was not feasible, because in those days when psychoanalysis had reached its apogee (see Chapter 1), patients were plentiful. Some practitioners even had waiting lists, but I did not believe it was right to keep patients waiting to start treatment, especially in a city such as Chicago in which there was a good supply of analysts. Still, most of us had and could get all the patients we wanted, a utopian situation for many clinicians and in sharp contrast to the current environment that the struggling young practitioner encounters.

Perhaps we were overly fond of our patients, and we had problems involving separation. That might have been true in some instances, and we did have patients whom we particularly enjoyed working with. But there were other patients who were hardly likable, but who would have been resentful if we suggested discontinuation of therapy. Having weighed all factors, we could not reach any conclusion about why therapy took much longer than we had been taught to believe. If our ego-ideals had standards other than those we were following about the length of treatment, then our narcissism and self-esteem were being threatened.

Consequently, we asked one of our mentors, a senior analyst with many years of clinical experience, what he thought about the length of analysis. To our dismay, he replied that five years was the maximum amount of time he would give any patient. After that, they were on their own. This was particularly vexing, because we had been practicing for five years and we still had with us most of the patients who began treatment when we started practice. Our narcissism was further involved, because we felt that it was our lack of skill and experience that accounted for our inability to "cure" our patients more rapidly.

We both took our mentor's pronouncement seriously, but my colleague was impelled to do something about it, whereas I took the more passive position of doing nothing. I just could not see myself telling so many patients that we had to conclude treatment because of the edict of another clinician.

I reviewed my formulations and had to acknowledge that certain important inner conflicts had not been resolved. In my confusion I asked myself whether they would ever be resolved, but since a teacher I respected had set time limits to treatment, I could not accuse myself of being impatient. I remembered a session with a supervisor who asked me, after a year of being in practice, what I believed was the most important attitude a therapist could bring to clinical work. I spontaneously replied, "Patience," and she complimented me for what she believed was the highest technical virtue. Now I wondered if patience could be carried too far.

My colleague also reviewed his caseload and focused on a patient who had made remarkable progress during the five years she had been in therapy. In fact, she credited the treatment with saving her life. Prior to starting analysis, she was dying of tuberculosis. She had spent two years in a municipal tuberculosis sanatorium and had had extensive thoracic surgery, but her disease progressed and she was dying. This occurred during the golden era of psychoanalysis (see Chapter 1), so one of her psychologically minded physicians recommended psychoanalysis. This seemed to be a preposterous suggestion, but since the patient was dying, any straw in the wind was worth a try.

This was an aggrandizement of psychoanalysis, but most of the analysts at that time would not accept her for treatment. They were not up to the challenge. Apparently their narcissism was not sufficiently strong to enable them to face a life-and-death situation.

Patients were plentiful and young therapists could relatively easily fill their consultation hours. As might be expected, they usually got the hardest patients to treat, whereas the so-called transference neuroses went to the senior analysts. I believe this is another factor that caused the young Turks to move away from classical concepts and techniques. Narcissism again enters the picture because they did not want to feel demeaned by treating patients senior analysts would not accept. Patients were also demeaned by this selective attitude and some older clinicians felt that many patients were not worthy of treatment. The younger practitioners, to maintain self-esteem, had to elevate their patients to a position that made them worthy of them.

My colleague was also reluctant to treat a dying patient, but his narcissism was not so powerful that the patient had to meet elitists' standards. He tried to ignore that he was dealing with a dying patient and decided to treat her as he would any patient. He tried to adopt such an attitude in order not to feel narcissistically challenged or to become upset and anxious.

She was not a pleasant patient and not psychologically minded. He found her tedious because she did not bring in much material he could analyze nor did she seem to respond to his sparse interpretations, but as far as could be determined she was cured of her tuberculosis. Physically, she was completely well by the end of the first year of treatment.

Was this a miracle? Was it due to therapy or simply an unexplained remission that sometimes but rarely happens? It was difficult to make connections between the therapeutic process and her recovery, but it was also hard to ignore that the disappearance of tuberculosis took place in the context of therapy. At the time we had no answers, but since then, I have encountered situations in which serious illnesses disappear once the patient achieves a degree of psychological mindedness that usually means he is able to get in touch with his unconscious (Giovacchini 1986, 1997).

This patient, at the beginning of treatment, was both moribund and concretely oriented. As the years went by, she had become interested in psychological processes and had been able to develop some insights, but she was a demanding patient who had an imperious, peremptory demeanor. Her therapist was gratified because of her recovery, but he had many ambivalent feelings about her. He wanted to take credit for saving her life, but he did not really believe that he should count her as a display in his narcissistic showcase.

After considerable deliberation, he decided he should broach the subject of termination with her. When he told me later about what he had done he used the word *termination*, a term we had both assiduously avoided because of its destructive connotations. I believe my colleague's use of the word *termination* indicated he had considerable foreboding about what he was about to do.

Despite the therapist's ambivalence, he confronted her with the prospect that they think about making some plans for ending the treatment. He added that he enjoyed working with her and that she had improved sufficiently so that they could consider that they had reached their goal. The patient said nothing and because it was the end of the session she quietly left.

The next session she made a dramatic entrance. Rather than lying on the couch as she usually did, she stood in front of her therapist, drawn to her full height and holding a white handkerchief in front of her mouth. For about a minute, she glared at him, and then she slowly withdrew the handkerchief from her mouth. It was soaked with blood.

My colleague reported that she had read him the riot act. She was extremely angry that he had brought the subject up. She added that this was her analysis and he could not deprive her of it. She would determine when and if it would end. She might expect him to see her through her death and if he had any problems with that, he should seek further analysis, which, incidentally, he did.

I was impressed by the drama and power of this confrontation. The patient was demonstrating how vital the treatment was for her. It was life-sustaining in that when she contemplated that she would no longer have it, her lungs started bleeding again; the old hemoptosis returned.

It was her treatment, a fundamental support system, and no one was going to take it away from her. The treatment, as a material possession, had become integrated into her personality. In many ways, it had become an adjunctive ego that made it possible for her to cope with the world as well as her body.

The usual arguments about limiting the length of treatment, which often caused pangs in my superego, seemed pale when applied to this woman. I am referring particularly to the admonishment that lengthy therapies infantilize patients and make them intractably dependent. In view of this patient's bleeding lungs, dependence does not seem to be much of an issue.

I have compared these lengthy analyses to chronic illnesses, such as diabetes and hypertension, that require medication for the rest of the patient's life. These patients are as dependent as those suffering from emotional disorders; they are dependent on their medications. Is it a significant argument to emphasize that there is a difference between dependency on a drug and dedication to a process? I have heard that therapists are dedicated to a process. Should patients not be allowed to do the same if they feel such a need? With medications, the internist understands how the life-sustaining drug operates and how it maintains physiological harmony. These etiological connections are harder to make with emotionally disturbed patients.

The patient I mentioned who described himself as an electric bug is relevant to this discussion. It will be recalled that this bug wandered around but never too far from a socket to which he could plug in so that he would never become enervated. The electric charge can be compared to psychic energy or narcissistic supplies, and as long as this socket was available and reachable, the patient-bug could explore the surrounding world and live in it.

Insulin is given to diabetics because the insulin-producing cells of the pancreas are not functioning normally. It is a replacement therapy. Other drugs reestablish a chemical or a metabolic balance because various organs are not operating properly or producing the required hormones. Clinicians can draw analogies for patients suffering from character disorders. These are conditions that have defects in psychic structures that lead to various types of psychic imbalance that determine the clinical picture. Many such patients are rigid, and their approach to life is concrete and mechanistic. They seem to have no unconscious, or they are unable to get in touch with it.

Apparently being able to get in touch with the unconscious can be energizing and liberating. In some cases, like insulin, it can be life-saving, as it may have been for the tuberculosis patient who indicated she could not live unless the treatment process was available to her psyche. The treatment was a venue in which her psyche could get in touch with other parts of her self, especially the unconscious, that otherwise were separated from the main psychic stream. The isolated psyche, in extreme instances, could be functionally inoperative as well as life threatening.

The patient who told me about the electric bug viewed treatment as vitalizing and supplying him with both energy and insight that enabled him to be self-sufficient and maintain a serviceable level of self-esteem.

It is well known that dreamless sleep is not refreshing. In dreams, the psyche is dipping down into the unconscious and this seems to be necessary if the psyche is to function in a coherent and synthesized fashion and with a sufficient level of energy for the ego's executive system. Therapies that stress the intrapsychic focus may act in a similar fashion to dreams. Dreaming can never be terminated, and perhaps in some instances the same can be said about the treatment process.

I believe that the lack of psychic replenishment not only may be a factor in patients with characterological problems, but also may be involved in the production of some somatic or different psychosomatic disorders.

The following case demonstrates the energizing restorative elements of the treatment process. This patient's treatment abruptly ended with the death of his therapist, so he is not an example of treatment without an end, but it is clear that if his therapist were still alive he would have continued therapy. This is another example in which treatment was a lifesaving situation.

The patient, a middle-aged professional man, was the husband of one of my patients. His wife was very distressed because, in spite of the best medical treatment, he was dying of regional enteritis. He had lost over fifty pounds and was listless, apathetic, and emaciated. I thought of the woman with tuberculosis and I made a similar recommendation, that is, that he see a therapist. As I had anticipated, my patient thought this recommendation was preposterous, but when I explained my reasoning and the context in which I made it, she enthusiastically related it to her husband, who unexpectedly thought it was a good idea.

His therapist found him to be tedious because of his concrete mechanistic orientation and his fixation on his inflamed bowel. He talked about it only from an organic perspective and totally blamed his body, his genes, and noxious elements of the environment, but never considered that his mind might have possibly made a contribution. This was a responsibility he could not conceive of, indicating a total lack of psychological mindedness. The therapist despaired at the prospect of being able to get him into treatment, and after the first interview he did not believe the patient would return. Nevertheless, he suggested a four-time-a week schedule and he was surprised that the patient calmly accepted the appointments given to him.

At the next appointment the therapist explained free association to him and suggested that he lie on the couch. Again, he did not protest but the therapist did not believe the patient understood what he said about the treatment process, free association, and the role of the unconscious. The patient lay down on the couch and in a less than a minute he was sound asleep and he slept through the rest of the session.

Initially the therapist was so taken by surprise that he did not know what to do, so he did nothing, although this was very difficult. He awakened him at the end of the session and he was certain that this was the last time he was going to see him. It was another surprise when the patient appeared promptly for the next session and seemed eager to be there. In a few minutes he was again fast asleep.

This continued for about six months, in which the only discourse consisted of an initial greeting and the announcement of the end of the session. At about this time, upon being awakened, the patient commented on how refreshed he felt, and that the couch was the only place he could sleep without the influence of sedatives. Shortly later, he added that this was the first time he could remember dreaming, and from then on he free-associated to his dreams.

He no longer slept and he displayed, again for the first time as far as anyone could judge, a degree of psychological mindedness that stood in sharp contrast to his previous concrete orientation that was fixated on surface phenomena. He had also gained all the weight he had lost and had no evidence of regional enteritis. His bowel has been well for close to thirty years so this was not simply a remission, as a prominent gastroenterologist stated.

The treatment continued in a more traditional fashion for at least a dozen years, until his therapist died and the patient did not choose to continue with someone else. I have heard that he is getting along well both physically and emotionally.

This is a striking demonstration of the energizing and restorative qualities of the psychoanalytic process. The organism has to rest by sleeping to replace the energy it has lost through the experience of daily living. The objection could be made that it was his sleeping and not the therapy, for what was happening could hardly be called therapy, that was responsible for his improvement. This argument was made at a seminar where this patient was presented, but this is an extremely feeble objection. He could not sleep without sedatives or feel refreshed except in the therapist's office.

Obviously, there was something about the relationship that made this possible, because it could not happen anywhere else. At the least, the therapist had succeeded in creating a holding environment in which the patient could feel a modicum of security and trust that allowed him to relax sufficiently so he could sleep. Apparently he felt safe in the therapeutic setting.

After he stopped sleeping, he found that periodically free-associating, something that could not have occurred prior to therapy, added a verve to living and lifted his depression. He found the workings of his mind interesting and marveled at the subtleties of the unconscious.

Discovering what had been hidden or split off permitted him to find dimensions to his mind that he never suspected he had. He found therapy exciting. Finding that he had an inner life was fundamental to his existence, and this journey of discovery occurred in the context of treatment. The fact that he stayed well was not only a testimony to the treatment but would seem to indicate that therapy need not be interminable.

His wife, whom I saw once or twice a year for several years after we completed treatment, told me that her husband would have needed to continue treatment on an indefinite basis if his therapist had lived. She believed he survived because he had been able to internalize the nourishing aspects of his treatment. She had read some of my writings, and concluded that her husband had been able to survive because he had constructed an analytic introject. I had described an analytic introject as an endopsychic registration of the therapeutic interaction containing its nurturing and soothing aspects as well as its focus on self-scrutiny.

What his wife described reminded me of the mourning process (Freud 1917). He was able to assimilate bit by bit the good aspects of the treatment interaction and transform the object relations quality of his treatment into an introject that became assimilated as a character trait. Instead of turning to treatment for narcissistic supplies and energy, he could now rely on inner resources that were the products of successful treatment. I believe the analytic introject is similar to the nurturing matrix I described earlier, the former being the product of analytic treatment and the latter a developmental achievement associated with the construction of the transitional space.

Perhaps interminable treatment is the outcome of a structural deficiency in which the patient cannot construct an analytic introject. Understandably, this inability would be associated with severe psychopathology and could be related to patients who had overwhelming trauma during early developmental phases. Those are the patients Winnicott (1963) described as suffering from privation, patients who do not know what it means to be gratified.

I believe if clinicians are aware of such structural deficiencies, their countertransference response may be less harsh and their attitudes about interminable treatment more charitable. I would speculate that my mentor's rule about five years being the longest he would treat a patient may have been partially based on his lack of understanding of structural factors and the developmental role of object relations. He was fixated on the classic psychodynamic position.

COUNTERTRANSFERENCE AND THE SILENT PATIENT

In the previous section, I discussed clinical situations in which patients were silent or slept through a part of their treatment. This might have puzzled the therapist but it did not create any special problems, though colleagues were critical that the therapist allowed this situation to continue unchecked.

Silent patients are especially vexing for many therapists. This may be partially due to an adherence to the classical position in which silence would have been considered a resistance, and Freud admonished patients to give up their resistances as quickly as possible. Therapists' difficulties with silence may have been the outcome of a misguided technical dictum.

The therapist may have constructed in his ego-ideal a model of how treatment should be conducted, one in which the patient talks and the analyst listens. Any deviation from this type of interaction would upset the therapist's narcissistic balance, since the process would not be proceeding as it should be. This is a selfish viewpoint, because only the therapist's needs are recognized, even if they refer to the ego-ideal. In this situation the patient's characterological orientation is ignored.

Again this is an example of a narcissistic adherence to a conceptual system, which, in this instance, refers to rigid technical rules. The methodological essence of psychoanalysis is free association, what Freud called the fundamental rule, and letting the patient be silent would be a violation of this rule. Many analysts say that a treatment without free association is not psychoanalysis.

More is involved than simply definition in determining the analyst's feelings about nonassociating patients. The principles of the intrapsychic focus could still be adhered to even if the patient is allowed to be silent. Therapy based on the exploration of the psyche is not focused on the elimination of symptoms. Rather, it is concerned with discovering the unconscious and the achievement of maximum autonomy. The therapeutic setting has to be devoted to the fostering of autonomy, and therapists' nonjudgmental and receptive attitudes are just as important as their interpretations. Being receptive often means accepting the patient's right to fall asleep or to be silent.

Silence has to be understood in terms of its dynamics. It can have many meanings. It may be a resistance, as Freud wrote, often an unconscious resistance, because the patient is struggling with intrapsychic conflicts based on the need to repress forbidden sexual impulses. This has been the classical position and rarely do clinicians find patients who are having such struggles. To get access to the unconscious, Freud believed that the therapist had to confront patients with their resistance and exhort them to overcome it. This would be tantamount to forbidding what might have been a significant defensive stance.

In a more pervasive manner, silence may be a characterological trait, a manifestation of a general need to withdraw. In extreme cases, the infantile world may have been traumatically abusive, and these patients protect themselves by using schizoid defenses that are characterized by silence. Inasmuch as the current world has been structured in a similar fashion to the infantile world, these patients find withdrawal a mode of survival, and within the therapy it is manifested by silence.

Withdrawal and the accompanying silence are found in various psychopathological states, particularly the narcissistic neuroses, depression, and schizophrenia, as Freud (1914a) described. It is difficult to understand how a defensive adaptation can be prohibited. Still, it must be acknowledged that therapy depends on communication and language.

Silence can also have positive features. The patient discussed in the previous section wanted to be silent because he was trying to establish his autonomy in the midst of his parents' intrusions that were demanding he reveal and thereby expose himself, a state of helpless vulnerability. Winnicott (1958b) wrote about the capacity to be silent in the presence of someone else as an achievement along the path of emotional development and psychic maturation.

If therapists were able to make such distinctions about the meaning of silence, their attitudes might soften and their narcissism would not be threatened. There might not be any untoward countertransference reactions. With the silent patient, therapists have countertransference problems because they have expectations of their patients. They expect them to talk, as well as to make progress and get well. This creates a paradoxical situation, because the therapeutic ambition is a hindrance to progress. These very sensitive, thin-skinned patients react even to the therapist's benign and compassionate hopes for success as intrusive assaults in the same way they experience the traumatic impingements of childhood.

Besides being a stereotypic picture of the analytic interaction, countertransference problems arise when therapists feel they have been put in the position of sitting around and doing nothing. Doing nothing is often the hardest thing to do, and clinicians frequently find their silent patients intolerable; usually the therapy ends before it begins.

One of the most difficult and frustrating patients I have ever seen was a young man in his early twenties. His childhood was an unbelievable nightmare, a chamber of horrors, in which he was frequently sexually and physically abused. It was hard to understand how, in view of the overwhelming traumas he suffered, he was able to survive outside an institution.

Early in life, it was recognized that he was of superior intelligence; on an I.Q. examination he tested at the genius level. Because of his extraordinary intelligence he was able to find a lucrative position in a protected setting, which means that he was left pretty much to himself and did not have to engage in an interpersonal context.

He sought treatment because he was in a constant state of terror. At times his speech was accelerated to the extent that he stuttered because he had to slow down the rapid stream of words. He often had a slight tremor and perspired easily.

Most patients with such severely traumatic backgrounds are concretely oriented and have little or no concept of intrapsychic processes. By contrast, this patient was psychologically minded and regarded mental phenomena with the same interest and logic that he applied to his work. I suspect the enormous attention and admiration he received at school had some remedial effects on the damage that was being inflicted on him by the infantile environment. Still, he was overwhelmed and incapable of sustaining interpersonal contact, as evidenced by his pervasive and constant anxiety. He was able, however, to give me a history and already knew about free association and the use of the couch. During the second session, without being asked, he lay down on the couch and completed the narrative of his life. I wondered what areas he would pursue after he completed the recitation of a formal, well-organized history.

As I expected, he gave me a litany of complaints both of the past and the present. Regarding the present, he felt that he was not appreciated enough, that the value of his work was not recognized, and that he could not relate to people. He felt shy, always afraid, lamented his lack of social skills, and was tortured by feelings of inadequacy. He bitterly lamented his awkwardness with women and his lack of a sex life.

He continued in this fashion for several weeks and then he stopped speaking. I prompted him to keep talking and for a while he would respond, but after a few minutes he would lapse back into silence. Several months went by in which his sessions were punctuated with long periods of silence.

In the classical tradition, I interpreted his silence as the resistance to the unconscious. He seemed to explode and, at the same time, his anxiety titer seemed to rise considerably. The back of his neck turned beet red and he was visibly perspiring. In an angry, loud voice he asked me how I dared to presume to know what his unconscious was doing. He called me arrogant, smug, and pretentious in that I could pretend to know what was going on at the deepest levels of his personality. My intervention was inappropriate and uncalled for and an assault on his integrity. I was taken aback by this tirade and felt that I had inadvertently struck a paranoid chord.

He continued his criticism by attacking me for prompting him to speak. Was I not astute enough to realize how frightened and vulnerable he felt? Just walking across the street was sheer agony. Every step he took, every person he encountered, caused unbearable pain. Life was simply a huge torture chamber. Did I not understand that he was totally exposed, that he had no skin? He felt his whole body was on fire and a cool breeze felt like a hot, consuming flame. I had no right to tell him what to do, because anything I commanded felt as if he were hit by a lightning bolt.

I must confess that although I was aware of the violence he had endured, I had lost sight of how seriously damaged he was.

I gathered that my following the fundamental rule of treatment, that is, that the patient free-associates, represented the assaultive infantile environment for this vulnerable, exposed patient. I decided that I would not impinge, as Winnicott would say, any further and not say anything or make any sign that I expected him to talk. I also felt inhibited about making an interpretation because I suspected that he would view it as an assault rather than an attempt to promote insight.

Furthermore, the material he brought me consisted, in essence, of attacks on himself and there was not much that I could do with it. On occasion, I would ask why he had to tear himself down, indicating that perhaps it gave him a sense of control in that he would beat others to the punch. He scornfully rejected what I offered and viewed his debased condition as a reality rather than a defensive adaptation. I believe, however, that I was correct, or at least partially correct, because I thought that he was pushing me away in order to protect himself when he angrily rejected my interpretation.

I decided not to interrupt his silence, which quickly followed the renunciation of my interpretation, and so I remained silent myself. For me this was an uncomfortable situation because I did not feel it had any therapeutic potential.

It was not unexpected when he attacked me for rejecting him and not giving him anything. What was the point of treatment unless I was able to help him? I found myself between the Scylla and Charybdis of talking and not talking. If I remained silent and unobtrusive, he viewed me as cold and rejecting, and if I tried to provide him with insight, I was attacking him and undermining whatever minimal self-esteem he had.

I had hoped that letting him be silent would give him some sense of mastery and control and that he would begin to feel a modicum of security in the setting I was trying to create. Instead, his tension mounted, as was easily discernible by the flushed color of his skin and his perspiration. I also felt tense, partially because I did not think, as he complained, that anything was being accomplished. I am certain we each contributed to the discomfort of our relationship in a negative feedback fashion.

After about six months, he decided there was not much point in continuing the treatment. I must say I was relieved, although I regretted that I could not offer him any relief for his constant tension. I was particularly disappointed because he had a fine mind and positive attributes. We left on friendly terms and I wondered further about the limitations of the psychoanalytic method.

I have described patients who were so brutalized that they had very few, if any, human features, either physically or mentally. It would have been ludicrous to consider any type of therapy within an interpersonal context. I have mentioned the little girl who had been chained in a closet for the first eight years of her life. She was very short, had hair all over her body, and walked, grunted and looked like a monkey (Giovacchini 1979).

In contrast, my patient was quite human, extraordinarily bright, and capable of thinking at the psychological level, but he was unable to use his capacity for insight to help himself or to let me help him. The nature of his problems trapped us in a no-win situation.

I suspect that his need to be silent and his inability to allow me to enter his inner world, because for him it represented a reproduction of the assaultive infantile milieu, created an impossible situation that we could not resolve. This was frustrating to both of us, because, in spite of his angry attacks, he showed a capacity to understand what was going on between us. This made our relationship especially poignant.

I seriously considered that there may have been something about my personality and unconscious countertransference responses that was blocking the resolution of the impasse we had created. I even considered that this impasse might have been an aspect of the repetition compulsion I have discussed happening with other patients suffering from severe forms of psychopathology (Giovacchini and Boyer 1975, 1983), but that somehow I was participating as some significant, perhaps traumatizing, person of the infantile environment. He knew the difference between reality and fantasy at an intellectual level but he could not apply this discrimination to himself.

With these thoughts in mind, after we discussed discontinuing therapy, I suggested that maybe there might be others who were better suited to treat him. I even brought forth the idea that since my childhood had been so different from his I might not have been able to sufficiently identify with his plight. I do not believe this to be generally true, but in a case as severe as his it might have been a factor that determined our failure. He sadly disagreed with me, replying that he had been too badly damaged to be able to stand the pressure and intrusions of the analytic process.

This patient could be an example of someone who could not be treated by the psychoanalytic method. If I am an ideologue, as I have been called, this could have created grandiose countertransference feelings associated with narcissism that prevented me from concluding that this patient could not be treated psychoanalytically. From the beginning I was aware that the prognosis was poor, but it is always difficult, if not impossible, to predict whether treatment will be successful. There are too many unforeseen variables that will obscure our vision as to the unfolding of the transference and the future course of treatment. His intelligence and psychological perspicacity were favorable signs that made him appear as an interesting patient, but for me he was untreatable.

I believe that my experience with this patient once again emphasizes that judgments about treatability cannot be made on the basis
of standard clichés, such as ego strength, a good sense of reality, and
even psychological mindedness. This patient had a unique characterological constellation that paralyzed my therapeutic activity. From
the treatment viewpoint, he would not let me do anything. He would
not let me be silent, but he would attack me when I talked. In turn
he wanted to be silent, but he would not let me accept his silence. I
felt there was no way I could turn. He had me completely tied up, a
state that probably exemplified how he felt as a helpless and vulnerable child in a world he could not control, but he would not let me
share this insight with him.

Silence can be destructive or it can be productive in that it sets the
developmental process once more in motion. Under these circumstances, the therapist has to create a setting in which the patient can
be comfortably silent. To some therapists the creation of such a setting means that they are doing nothing, which is an uncomfortable
state, so they attempt to get their patients to talk in order to feel they
are doing something productive. In many cases, exhortations to make
patients talk can be unproductive.

From a technical viewpoint, clinicians can ask how they can determine when silence is in the service of the therapy and when it
represents a withdrawal from treatment, requiring that therapists
encourage their patients to talk despite their anxiety. There are no
specific signs and rules. Clinicians have to make formulations and also
rely on their countertransference responses. Patients will give cues
as to the adaptive or nonadaptive meaning of their behavior.

An adolescent boy had been unable to remain in school because of
his disruptive behavior. His parents placed him in several private
schools, both residential and nonresidential. In a coed school, he would
make crude sexual suggestions to the girls, which was experienced
as harassment. He was also loud, asked irrelevant questions, and in
general was such a nuisance that the teacher had to have security
remove him from the classroom. In a military school he attended he

made the same remarks to boys, and on occasion they would beat him up.

He had seen several psychiatrists who refused to see him a second time. He would either be disruptive by making silly, incoherent remarks, similar to hebephrenic patients, or move aimlessly around the room threatening to knock furniture over. If he sat still, he remained mute, which was viewed by the observer as a deliberate refusal to talk. The therapists were especially disturbed by his silence, which they interpreted as the expression of hostile, rebellious, and even sociopathic feelings. They recommended institutionalization rather than outpatient treatment.

The parents were in a quandary because of their disappointing experiences with boarding schools. For reasons of their own, they preferred keeping him at home, so they continued their quest to find a therapist, but the patient had become increasingly resistive to the idea of seeing anyone. They finally found a woman therapist whom I had, on occasion, supervised and who was devoted to Winnicott's ideas.

The father had to practically drag his son to the therapist's office. The boy scowled at the therapist as he entered the office and belligerently told her that he did not want to be there. His language was foul as he degraded the whole of the mental health field. He vowed that he had said all he was going to say. The therapist calmly replied that she wondered how the patient managed to force others to bring him to her office. As long as he was there, they might as well try to see what could be done to make him comfortable. The therapist added that the patient should decide whether he wanted to talk or not to talk. Either decision might prove to be valuable. The patient was puzzled, and he was especially bewildered by the remark that the patient had forced others to bring him to her office. I am reminded of the patient described in Chapter 1 who believed that he forced a judge to "sentence" him to treatment. This patient screamed in protest that he was the one who had been forced and that his father had to literally drag him to the waiting room.

The therapist said, "So be it," and added that the important fact was that he was there and that was all that mattered. The patient again insisted that he would not talk, whereupon she suggested that he lie down on the couch and he could be silent and relaxed. He did not have to talk if he did not want to. To the analyst's surprise he lay down on the couch, supine and stiff.

The patient gave the therapist practically no information about his background. She would have preferred learning about his life from him directly, but for the moment, this did not seem possible. She wondered particularly what his defiant refusal to speak, that is, to reveal himself, meant. Was he protecting himself from an assault, as was the situation with the patient I just described? She felt that withdrawal was a factor, but his immediate compliance with her suggestion that he lie on the couch made her dubious, and it was not in keeping with his belligerence in general. She suspected that there was a more basic need involved in his need to be silent.

The therapist had extensive reports from school personnel and social workers, which shed considerable light on his behavior. The patient could not tolerate being around his father, who had a macho orientation; the father did not connect with his son. He might drag him to an analyst's office because he was demonstrating how powerful and dominant he was, but when his son had been hospitalized, the father showed no interest and did not once visit him. The patient had two short psychiatric hospitalizations when his behavior got completely out of hand and he could not be contained. The patient later reported that he never felt anything toward his father except resentment because he abandoned him and exposed him and his sibling to their crazy mother. The father did not protect the patient, perhaps because he wanted the mother to direct her feelings toward her son rather than toward him. The patient felt he was being used as a shield.

Outwardly, the mother appeared shy and timid, even mousy. Her neighbors knew her as a quiet person who loved her two children (the patient and a two-year-older sister), and animals. She supported animal rights movements to a fanatical degree, as she gleefully threw acid on fur coats whose owners were unfortunate enough to be her and her companions' targets. What seemed on the surface to be benign and calm sat on seething cauldrons.

These polarities were also reflected in her house, a modest but comfortable middle-class dwelling. It was well kept on the outside, freshly painted and with a trimmed, well-kept lawn. On the inside, however, the furniture upholstery was ripped, the carpets were stained, and the kitchen and bathrooms were dirty. She had innumerable pets—cats, dogs, parrots, and on occasion a squirrel and a monkey. They were allowed to run around loose and they created mayhem.

As was learned later in therapy the patient felt he lived in a noisy jungle. Internally, he was disrupted by uncontrollable agitation. He seemed to have internalized the chaotic infantile milieu. He was unable to cope with the world because he was in a constant state of panic. His clownish behavior was an expression of that panic as well as a defense against it. At times, he could not talk or eat.

Unlike the patient I just described, he did not feel he had a thin skin, but this was a matter of emphasis. It was the internal world that he could not control. Inner excitement got out of hand, and he could not modulate his feelings. This often caused him to go into rage states, and on one occasion he grabbed an axe and chopped down his mother's bedroom door. This behavior led to his first hospitalization. Rather than withdraw, as my patient did, he attacked the world, although his silence was often a defiant withdrawal. He was still afraid of the external world, but so much had become internalized at such primitive levels that he was overwhelmed and often rendered functionally paralyzed because of prementational agitation.

The social worker's reports were interesting, especially those describing the patient's neonatal life and his early nurturing experiences. The mother had very strong positive feelings about her second pregnancy. She was indifferent about her older child, a daughter, but expressed an intense eagerness to have a boy.

During her son's babyhood, she was constantly by his side, even when he slept. As she fed him, she smothered him with kisses and this continued through adolescence when he pushed her away. Nevertheless, there were still many occasions when she gave him passionate kisses.

I would assume that there was little psychological content, a prementational state, to the early disruption caused by her intense ministrations, a caricature of what Winnicott (1956) conceptualized as primary maternal preoccupation. I call it prementational because the patient did not as yet have the capacity to link feelings with outer experiences. He had not yet discriminated the inner world from the outer world. At the most, he must have suffered from a primeval confusion.

Prementational agitation throughout the course of emotional development became attached to the mother's provocative behavior, which was often erotic. On several occasions during his early adolescence, she displayed herself nude to him. Afterward, as might be expected, he became wild and went on destructive rampages.

The patient showed less reluctance to come to his second appointment, although he made a token protest. He walked in front of the therapist, whereupon she motioned him to the couch. This time, in contrast to the previous session, he was relaxed as he lay down.

Similar to the patient who had regional enteritis, the patient remained silent for several months, but in this instance both patient and therapist did not even make the usual amenities. She had given him his schedule after the first session, so there was nothing regarding his appointments that had to be discussed.

In spite of what might appear to be a bizarre wordless arrangement, something seemed to be going on in this silent interaction. For example, the patient's position on the couch changed. At first he held himself stiff and rigid. The next session he was still straight and flat on his back, but he was no longer as tense. He had loosened up considerably and the atmosphere in the office felt much less adversarial. After about two weeks, he lay on his side and finally assumed the fetal position. After several months he started to talk, but his volume was so low that he was hardly audible. The therapist, when she could understand what he was saying, responded in the same low volume tone.

This patient had many similarities to the other silent or sleeping patients I have discussed, but he also had unique features that made other therapists dismiss him out of hand. Therapists feel uncomfortable with these types of patients and therefore are reluctant to treat them. Their reluctance is often a reaction to the patients' defiance, but analysts are also aware of the defensive qualities of rebellion.

As provocative as this patient's behavior was, it represented an attempt to gain relief from intense internal pain. Unfortunately, it misfired, and the environment resisted his attempts to have him externalize his agitation.

His therapist, on the other hand, did not react to his provocativeness when he was defiant and would not provide a history. She assumed that even though it was destructive and self-defeating, his behavior represented an adaptive attempt. At first, similar to the last patient described, his silence was protective; it represented his need to withdraw from an assaultive environment, which, to a large measure, was the product of his projections. I believe that the therapist's telling him to be comfortable by lying on the couch unconsciously conveyed to him that there was a possibility that his needs would be met and that his plight would be understood. In any case, the therapist would not be oppositional by forcing him to enter a traditional treatment setting.

The patient's angry rejection was manifested by a silent, passive, hostile stance. This was another form of attack. Still, within the context of silence, his orientation toward therapy changed. As he relaxed on the couch and finally lay there in the fetal position, he was still withdrawing, but not violently. The therapist had been able to construct a friendly and safe setting in which he could comfortably withdraw. This again brings us back to Winnicott's (1958b) concept of the capacity to be alone in the presence of someone else. By tailoring her therapeutic approach to his conflicts, the therapist was able to achieve for the patient what he had been seeking. He was trying to get relief from his internal agitation.

In therapy he would have been inclined to do this by projecting it into the treatment setting, but for him to accomplish this the therapist would have to participate. She would have to feel uncomfortable about absorbing his inner disruptions, and this might have happened if she tried to get him to talk. By trying to break down the patient's defenses, she would have constructed a warlike atmosphere that required the patient to reinforce his defenses and further withdraw.

Instead, she intuitively permitted him to withdraw from the treatment by suggesting he be comfortable on the couch. Literally, she was indicating that they could both be comfortable with his withdrawal and this meant that she recognized his needs. She was not fighting silence with silence as often happens in psychoanalytic sessions that have turned into encounters. Even though many classical analysts would not even consider that what transpired with this patient was psychoanalytic treatment, sticking to the rules, which here means getting the patient to talk, would create a struggle that would cause the treatment edifice to collapse.

The knowledge that he could remain silent without a struggle enabled him to regress to a nondisruptive infantile state, something that he had never experienced. He was obviously comfortable as he lay on the couch in the fetal position. He felt soothed for the first time in an environment that was entirely different from the infantile milieu. The therapy had constructed a holding environment that was physically as well as psychologically quiet.

The patient's defensive provocative behavior was noisy. Silence is the opposite of noise, and though initially he was withdrawing, he was constructing an atmosphere in treatment that stood in sharp contrast to this noisy behavior and the internal noise that was so disruptive.

In this connection, it is extremely interesting that when he first started speaking, he spoke so softly that he was practically inaudible. His therapist instinctively replied in a similar fashion. The fact that they could communicate in a low-decibel fashion proved to be more important than the content of their communication. There was a definite soothing quality to their interaction, and later, they were able to speak at a normal auditory level.

It was a very long treatment, and the patient managed to finish high school. Despite his problems with his father, who finally divorced his wife, he ended up living with him and he went to work in his company. His job was somewhat of a sinecure, but he was able to move out on his own, support himself, and get married. Two or three times a year he sees his therapist because he feels relaxed after seeing her.

Apparently the therapist had high levels of self-esteem and felt secure about her narcissistic reservoir. She did not have to rely on the standard therapeutic model that required a talking patient. Such rigid formulas protect and provide security for therapists who cling to them and follow rules without questioning how they might apply to a particular patient. This therapist did not exactly know why she immediately suggested the couch and why she responded in an almost inaudible voice. Concerning the former, she confessed that she did not know what else to do, and regarding her responses, that she had to be in synchrony with his early attempts at communication.

Some analysts conduct treatment with a cookbook approach. Symbols in dreams are interpreted as if they have universal meanings and the patient is expected to follow certain rules, such as lying on the couch and free-associating. In turn, certain associations have standard meanings and often the analyst is correct when he uses such traditional approaches.

In this book, I have been exploring when these approaches do not work, and when the patient's uniqueness, special needs, and quandaries are not understood. Nevertheless, they can be put in an analytic perspective and what has been perceived as working against fundamental procedures can be the vehicle for an intrapsychically oriented therapy and the construction of an analytic setting that, in many ways, is similar to the one that is accepted by classical analysts. This requires therapists to be flexible and to be able to tolerate not being in command or not understanding what is going on. This is similar to the creative person's capacity to tolerate ambiguity, to be able to sustain a state of informed ignorance. Not having a formulaic system of rules to lean on or being involved in a clinical relationship where these rules only create havoc can be disquieting and narcissistically threatening.

In the case just discussed, the therapist admitted that she had no purposive design when she made her recommendations and later responded at the same volume level as the patient. She knew that she was not threatened by him and she felt calm. The only feeling she could recall was a poignant fondness for him, because she sensed how miserable he felt as he was trying to make others feel miserable. She viewed her quiet response as being almost reflexive. She just felt that she could not speak louder than he did, whether or not they could understand each other.

I find it interesting that this therapist was not antagonized by the patient, and an oppositional atmosphere was not created. The therapist did not know exactly what was happening, but she sensed that the patient was suffering from inner painful feelings that must have been reflections of experiences he had in the world. She did not feel demeaned by him as some other therapists felt, perhaps because their supplies of self-esteem might not have been as ample as hers. Her attitude was nonjudgmental.

I can envision other therapists also responding with low volume, but causing disruption rather than a progressive experience. They may be simply imitating the patient's mode of communication and involved in their response, there may be a tinge of mockery or sarcasm, which, in this case, would have been totally disruptive. The affect involved in dialogue is just as important as the meaning of the exchange.

The therapist, in a sense, had conditioned her patient to be able to gradually tolerate increased levels of sound. Of course, more than auditory stimuli were involved. Internal disruption had to be soothed for the patient to be able to tolerate ordinary levels of sensation as stimuli impinge upon the psyche. Not only was she a protective shield, a *reizschutz* as Freud (1920) described, but she acclimatized him to the stimulus level of an ordinary interaction. Later his inability to contain excitement became a prominent theme in their discussions. They had established an equilibrium between the two of them, an equilibrium that he had never before experienced.

COUNTERTRANSFERENCE AND THE SUPEREGO

As is true of most parts of the psyche, the superego has many faces. It is intimately involved with the ego-ideal as well as determining behavior and attitudes about the external world. The patients I have just discussed also had impact on the therapists' superego, as the therapists had to rethink their attitudes about therapeutic approaches that had become deeply ingrained during their training.

The superego interferes with the therapist's capacity to remain nonjudgmental, an attitude that has been the essence of the psychoanalytic perspective, and the external world has breached what for many of us has become a sacrament—our rigid unwavering adherence to confidentiality. Both of these factors can operate simultaneously, and in many instances there are no solutions to the problems we confront.

An anxious colleague asked for an emergency consultation. The previous evening a patient told him that she had drowned her baby in the bathtub. He did not know whether this was true, but he was inclined to believe her. The law required that he report this incident to the police but he was ambivalent about doing so for several reasons. First, it would have constituted a breach of confidentiality, and although he was legally bound to reveal this crime to the authorities, part of him felt he was violating ethical principles dictated by his professional superego. I did not help him out of his dilemma when I added that he would undoubtedly lose the patient if he reported her. He would be acting more like a policeman than a therapist. In view of the difficulties she had created, he did not mind losing a patient, but his conscience dictated that he do whatever he could to preserve the therapy.

There was not much counsel I could give him. My choice was narrowed down to two factors. I could tell him to obey the law as any good citizen would advise, or I could tell him to maintain his therapeutic perspective and not breach confidentiality. I also added that the latter recommendation included that he treat what she told him as material. We were both dismayed, however, as to how a clinician could treat a murder as material.

There were certain details about this woman's history that made me feel frightened and manipulated. In retrospect and with hindsight, had she been my patient I might have confronted her with my suspicions that she was trying to entrap me, but I cannot really be certain as to what I would have actually done. In any case, my colleague chose to call the police. In fact, she had not murdered her baby, and there was no longer any therapy. Her therapist felt both relief and guilt.

There are no happy endings to problems that contain conflicts of interest, forcing decisions that will inevitably cause damage. My colleague's problems had been intensified because this was not a new patient. He had known her well and he felt guilty about having made what he considered a bad decision. Within the context of self-condemnation, it did not matter whether she was being delusional or manipulative. He had stepped out of the therapeutic role and the results were disastrous.

In many such incidents, the therapist's hands are tied. The law has to be obeyed or he will lose his license and perhaps even face prosecution for criminal charges. His dedication to therapeutic activity has become irrelevant and the preservation of treatment is of little if any concern.

The situation is somewhat similar with managed care. Here, too, there is a conflict between maintaining confidentiality and maintaining a therapeutic stance. Instead of the therapist being legally jeopardized if he does not breach confidentiality, the insurance company will peremptorily terminate the treatment, so the clinician is once again faced with an impossible quandary. There is no reason to give information about patients except to supply insurance companies with the opportunity to save money by rationalizations that justify their decisions to terminate treatment. There are no clinical enigmas hidden in these controversies with insurance companies. The solution to these mendaciously created problems lies outside the clinical arena.

Superego countertransference problems also arise when there is no ostensible conflict with the external world for the preservation of treatment. The therapist's standards can be at odds with the patient's moral orientation and behavior, and this can lead to therapeutic impasses.

In a gross, almost comical fashion, Kardiner (1977) discusses a situation in which a Mafia hit man consulted him because his conscience interfered with his efficient functioning as a murderer for hire. These are extreme situations and I doubt if they are ordinarily encountered in the average analyst's office. If such persons seek therapy, it seems unlikely that there is much hope for success. I imagine that the negative transference might be particularly difficult to endure.

In an intrapsychically oriented treatment, the aim of therapy does not directly involve how the patient relates to the outer world. Behavioral change is not a goal. Of course, clinicians hope that their patients make satisfactory and happy adjustments to their milieu and gain the capacity to love and to form intimate object relations. But their primary concern is with internal changes involving the acquisition of psychic structure and the enhancement of autonomy and mastery of inner impulses.

If the patient's mode of relating to the external world is at odds with the therapist's superego, and even if there is no particular conflict with the law or with reality in general, treatment may still be extremely difficult or even impossible. This situation occurs when a therapist is treating a fellow professional or is conducting a so-called didactic analysis with a candidate in training at a psychoanalytic institute.

When I was in training, training analysts had to report their patients' status periodically to a committee. As far as I know, this outrageous practice has stopped because it is an obvious breach of confidentiality, and the analyst assumes tremendous powers over the patient's career and future, which would make analysis impossible.

Even outside the training context, therapists may have problems in accepting what their younger colleagues are practicing or the fact that they want to practice in-depth therapy. They may feel that the younger colleagues do not have the aptitude or the moral fiber to conduct a therapy that requires sensitivity, intuitive skills, and probity. I know of several instances in which senior therapists encouraged a younger colleague seen in training analysis not to pursue training and to change professions. In at least one of these instances it was clear to me that the therapist's narcissistic orientation interfered with therapeutic intent and caused him to commit not only a serious therapeutic error but also a grave moral travesty. He told the colleague that he had neither the talent nor the emotional maturity to become an analyst. He did nothing actively, but somehow his opinion seeped through the admissions committee of the local institute, and this young man was denied admission, a disappointment that he never recovered from.

The senior analyst was highly respected, but he also had many enemies. He idealized psychoanalysis and viewed it as a field that could only admit the elite, similar to the knights of the Round Table. In his opinion, this patient did not belong to this exalted group. This proved to be an unfortunate experience, because his former patient continued having an illustrious clinical and teaching career without the official certification stamp, something that does not seem to be of any particular importance now.

No doubt the negative attitude the senior analyst conveyed to his patient was based mainly on his own projections, which he acted out in the treatment interaction. He was judgmental, critical, and ma-nipulative. He stepped outside the therapeutic role and tried to man-age the patient's life instead of analyzing him. This is about as badly as a therapist could behave, most likely a consequence of a tyranni-cal superego and intense narcissistic needs.

There are situations, however, where the patient, although not breaking any laws, is conducting his professional and perhaps his personal life in an obviously immoral fashion. The therapist may be particularly offended by professional transgressions because they are offensive to the professional aspects of his superego. The situation becomes even more complicated if the patient is sexually harassing his own patients, which I believe is a reportable offense.

I have already discussed the intrinsic incompatibility of being both a policeman and a therapist. This is just as true when sexual trans-gressions are concerned. Therapists can operate only in one frame of reference if the patient's behavior, especially when prescribed by law, demands that the therapist assume another role that does not approve of the patient's behavior. Then the therapist can no longer retain the role of therapist. These therapists have to overcome their narcissistic investment in the treatment or overcome their professional arrogance sufficiently so that they can relinquish their position as therapist.

I believe that sociopaths are so hard or impossible to treat by the psychoanalytic method because they create the same superego tensions and countertransference problems I have just described. There may be some exceptions in which the patient's sociopathy might not have had much impact, because the areas in which the patient acts out are not familiar to the therapist. I recall a patient who was notorious for his shady dealings in trading commodities, but his therapist would not have been able to recognize a shady deal if it was under his nose, so when his patient bragged about his misdemeanors, his analyst remained unperturbed. The therapist was a moral, ethical person but his principles were attached to certain subjects and experiences and did not include the area in which his patient transgressed.

This is why it is easy to understand why sensitive clinicians are distressed when confronted with the professional transgressions of colleagues or students who are patients. This is at least conceivably another example that demonstrates that treatability is not determined solely by the type or extent of psychopathology. Internally, superego and narcissistic elements within the therapist make a therapeutic interaction impossible. In the outer world, managed care programs and laws requiring therapists to report certain criminal events also work in a therapeutically destructive fashion.

This discussion raises the whimsical question as to the nature of the therapeutic interaction if both therapist and patient are sociopaths. In this instance, it would mean that the therapist's superego is sufficiently unformed that it does not recognize or does not care about either moral or professional transgressions. The greatest involvement these therapists would have with their patients would consist of identifying with them.

It is difficult to envision how such relationships would lead to constructive changes. The patient may feel supported by the treatment process and experience his aberrant behavior as justified.

Based on our understanding of the treatment frame and the various transference–countertransference reactions that are compatible with the intrapsychic exploration of the mind, it would seem unlikely that there have been many therapeutic encounters in which both participants are sociopaths. The intrapsychic focus requires a certain amount of openness and honesty that is lacking in both therapists and patients who do not have the self-scrutinizing regulatory functions of the superego. I believe, however, that this type of parallelism exists in more psychoanalytic relationships than we suspect. In actuality these dyads consist of a self-serving symbiosis in which the participants are taking a paranoid stance against the world.

The transference–countertransference axis represents the interaction around which therapeutic activity revolves. Various facets of the therapists' and patients' personalities are intertwined and are understood in terms of the infantile past. For the patient this understanding is eventually made explicit.

CHAPTER 6

Structural and Dynamic Aspects of the Therapeutic Process

Formulations about the therapeutic process are dependent on clinicians' concepts about psychopathology. Freud wrote primarily about the neuroses, and, from a macroscopic viewpoint, his theories about the dynamics of emotional disturbances and how they are handled in the therapeutic relationship are fairly simple. They are mainly described in energic terms, and the role of psychic structure is for the most part ignored (Giovacchini 1984).

In essence, he viewed the neurotic patient as suffering from an intrapsychic conflict caused by sexual feelings that were not acceptable to the superego because of their incestuous nature. The central core of psychopathology was based on repression, which banished forbidden feelings from consciousness. Repression was the consequence of various defense mechanisms, which, when expressed in feelings or behavior, constituted symptoms.

The aim of treatment was to overcome repression, thereby enabling what had been repressed to enter consciousness. These feelings would be expressed in terms of transference, which means that the therapist represents significant persons of the infantile past. Somehow this sequence, which in essence consists of making the unconscious conscious, leads to therapeutic resolution.

Actually Breuer preceded Freud in demonstrating that the unconscious had tremendous power and could create painful and constricting symptoms, both mental and somatic (Breuer and Freud 1895). He hypnotized his famous patient, Anna O. (a.k.a. Bertha Pappenheim), and recovered traumatic memories that were then abreacted, meaning that as the memories were brought to consciousness, they were experienced with the same frightening affect that caused them to be repressed. The process was known as catharsis and led to symptom removal.

This is a simple linear description of the treatment process. Contemporary concepts about psychopathology go far beyond intrapsychic conflict, and include structural and developmental factors that emphasize that object relations and the infantile world are complicated in the production of emotional illness. The treatment process is quite complex and involves many variables.

Revelations about previously repressed material do not have the powerful curative effects that Freud and Breuer anticipated. Patients often badger therapists because now that they have insight, they do not feel any better, a confrontation that makes many therapists uncomfortable because they are not able to respond to this complaint. Simply making the unconscious conscious is not enough.

Freud (1914c) wrote about a process he called working through, which is associated with the recovery of lost memories rather than having them dissipated in behavior that has been labeled acting out.

Later Freud (1920) wrote about the repetition compulsion, which refers to repetitive patterns of infantile behavior designed to achieve mastery and overcome feelings of helpless vulnerability. He gives the example of his grandson who threw a spool of thread out of his field of vision, but hung onto the thread. This was a symbolic reenactment of banishing his father and then having him return. He controls his father's coming and going, a mastery that he did not have in real life.

Within the transference context, meaning that the therapist is part of the scenario of the repetition compulsion, the repetition compulsion is reenacted and interpreted. The patient becomes aware of the fact that he can maintain mastery and control without the complex ritual and self-destructive behavior that often characterizes the repetition compulsion.

Freud viewed the treatment relationship as unilateral and one-way. The material flows from the patient to the analyst; the analyst processes what he receives and then conveys to the patient the meaning of his associations. Supposedly, this occurs because of the therapist's neutrality; an attitude of noninvolvement facilitates the production of transference feelings and fantasies. It is the analyst's noninvolvement that permits the therapist to assess how the patient's orientation is affected by unconscious processes and how his image has been distorted by unconscious transference projections. According to Freud (1910) if the therapist responded personally, then he would lose his objectivity and not be able to make accurate observations. He would, instead, make prejudicial judgments.

Thus, for Freud and many of his early adherents, countertransference had to be resolved and eliminated as quickly as possible. It only obliterated analytic vision. This is almost the complete antithesis of what many therapists currently advocate.

The operations of the therapist's mind were ignored. It was simply a telephone that unscrambled messages, a particularly mechanistic description that would be more appropriate today than in Freud's time.

THE SELF-OBSERVING FUNCTION
AND PSYCHIC STRUCTURE

I believe that Sterba (1934) was the first clinician to bring psychic structure to formulations about the therapeutic process. He postulated that while doing therapy, therapists are able to construct a self-observing function. He first stressed that patients also had to develop such a function in order to be able to benefit from interpretations. The patient has to be able to look at the self in an objective, detached fashion, with a neutrality about his mind and its operations similar to that of the therapist. The patient introjects the analyst's self-observing function, and patient and therapist form a cooperative collusion as they explore the mysteries of the mind; interpretations are integrated by the patient.

It is a remarkable coincidence that in the same volume of the *International Journal of Psycho-Analysis* in which Sterba published his paper, there is another, similar article, written by Strachey (1934), that extends the discussion of the self-observing function. Strachey discussed the mutative factors that are the outcome of interpretative interactions. Though Sterba and Strachey do not go so far as to say that in therapy there have to be some structural changes and accretions in order to make the therapeutic interaction a potentially helpful experience, they imply that psychic structuralization is as important as psychodynamic regulation in a progressive treatment relationship.

Sterba felt that his ideas initially were not well received. He was straying from classical formulations that placed a heavy emphasis on instinctual factors, and although ego functions had been a subject of psychoanalytic scrutiny as to their defensive and adaptive roles (A. Freud 1936, Hartmann 1939), they were generally left in the background when the treatment relationship was examined.

In fact, the dynamics of treatment were not often examined, not because it was a taboo subject, but because it was an area that clinicians reluctantly entered, and that reluctance continues today. I believe it is our lack of knowledge about the dynamics that upsets our narcissistic pretensions. It is hard to admit that we do not know how therapy works in spite of the many books that have been written about it. Critics of psychoanalysis are screaming that it does not work, and in many instances, they are undermining our faith in a process that has been idealized, almost as a religion, by some practitioners.

All religions have their mysteries and the therapeutic process, that is, the curative factors operating in an insight-directed treatment designed to achieve character changes, are still pretty much a mystery. When the process seems to work, as I discussed in Chapter 4 with the two analyses of Mrs. A., clinicians are still mystified.

Some analysts were able to turn a lack of knowledge to a narcissistic advantage. They made a clinical discipline into a cult with its secrets and rituals, which they zealously guarded. Unless the therapist had the seal of approval from an accredited institute, the young practitioner could not use psychoanalytic technique. For example, in a particular residency program a resident would be fired if he had a patient lie on the couch. It is ironic that today many residency programs do not teach psychotherapy.

Sterba and Strachey were trying to explain the therapeutic process in terms of interactions between the therapist and patient as well as scrutinizing modes of psychic functioning dependent on structural accretions. The self-observing function is acquired at higher levels of integration of psychic structure. Some patients may have reached such levels in the course of their emotional maturation. Supposedly, such patients would be good candidates for analytic treatment.

The current patient population is somewhat concretely and materialistically oriented, and presumably it would not have a well-developed self-observing function. Somehow it has to be acquired through the treatment relation, and it would be the outcome of a smoothly progressive treatment process. In many instances, the patient acquires a psychological orientation by identifying or fusing with the therapist. Some apparently successful treatments are based on such fusions, and they have been pejoratively referred to as transference cures. I do not believe clinicians should be so dogmatic or critical of transference cures because all structural changes and expansions of the psyche involve some degree of identification or fusion.

I recall patients who were very primitively fixated at the beginning of treatment who sought therapy because they felt dependent and helpless. They needed someone to lean on in order to survive in a world that they found inordinately complex and incomprehensible. Therapy often can furnish support, but it may go further than just maintenance. Taking in the therapeutic values and learning from the treatment how to deal with problems are frequently accompanied by higher levels of ego integration and the acquisition of the self-observing function.

FACTITIOUS THERAPEUTIC SETTINGS AND GOALS

Years ago, Alexander and French (1946) wrote about the corrective emotional experience as it occurred in an artificial setting created by the therapist to offset the effects of the infantile traumatic environment. Many patients lived their lives fearing and defending themselves from expectations of traumatic assaults, which, in some instances, were actually experienced as they created settings through the repetition compulsion that echoed the cruelties of childhood. As is often the case, the best example comes from the literature, in this case

Victor Hugo's *Les Misérables*. The hero of the novel, Jean Valjean, is apprehended by the police because he is caught with the silver of a friendly priest who gave him dinner; Jean pays for the priest's kindness by stealing his silver. The police drag him to the priest's house to expose his crime. Unexpectedly, at least unexpectedly for Jean Valjean, the priest looks at him with some surprise and exclaims, "But Jean, you forgot the candlesticks." This is such a moving confrontation that it changes the course of the ex-convict's life, and he becomes a productive, upright citizen.

Alexander proposed that therapists create a similar scenario, but not many analysts have the talent of Victor Hugo. Some of the clinical examples the authors give are complex and seem contrived. Furthermore, the function of insight is underplayed and the therapeutic relationship is converted into a psychodrama.

Basically, the therapist is assuming a role much in the same way the self psychologists attempt to make up for some of the deficits of childhood. These therapists intrude themselves into the transference rather than letting it develop spontaneously, and then try to convince their patients that their fears and expectations are unfounded, as demonstrated by the analyst's benign response.

The reactions to these ideas were diverse. Locally, in Chicago, as might be expected, there was considerable enthusiasm for what was felt to be an innovative therapeutic maneuver. Alexander's strength of character and charisma helped make his contributions acceptable. In other quarters, particularly in New York, they were rejected and condemned. The principal objection was that Alexander was not practicing psychoanalysis because he was role playing, an argument that has been frequently used by psychoanalysts.

As psychoanalysis was understood when Alexander published his ideas, his detractors were correct. The transference was not spontaneous and the therapist became an actor rather than remaining an impartial analyst dealing with intrapsychic conflicts directly, instead of their behavioral manifestations. Both patient and therapist were, in a sense, acting out. When this occurs in the treatment setting it is called acting in. Freud's (1911–1914) concept of the therapeutic process involved the curtailing of acting out to the reproduction of memories that were the basis of such behavior. What Alexander proposed was the direct opposite of what Freud called working through, although Alexander believed that his corrective emotional experience would lead to therapeutic resolutions, but not much in the way of analysis seems to be involved.

The corrective emotional experience is very seldom mentioned today when treatment strategies are discussed, and in some circles it is a pejorative term. The question remains as to what the aims of therapy are. Jean Valjean became a respected citizen although his life was hard because of his persecution. It would seem that Alexander was thinking in terms of behavioral change and the removal of symptoms, similar to Freud's thinking when he was dealing with hysterical phenomena. This therapeutic model belongs in the purview of the medical model, which strives to heal the patient.

Still, in medicine many patients do not get well. Most chronic illnesses are not curable, although they can be managed. In psychotherapy can the treatment rid the patient of symptoms without any fundamental characterological changes? Most therapists would doubt that this could happen and the majority of treatments do not lead to vast characterological accretions and superior adaptations to the external milieu.

Classical psychoanalysts strayed from such goals as symptom alleviation in favor of character changes. In fact, they have gone even further by asserting that it does not matter whether patients feel better, such as by overcoming a depression or being free of anxiety. What is important is that patients understand what is going on within their psyches and that they have achieved greater autonomy, which determines how they choose to relate to their surroundings, and that they have mastered their impulses rather than being their victims. It would be difficult to understand how this could be achieved through a series of corrective emotional experiences.

The changing patient population, at least in terms of patients' overt attitudes, requires that therapists reexamine their therapeutic goals and ambitions. Concerning the latter, we have to loosen our narcissism from therapeutic ambition and heed patients' needs. Freud sought to relieve patients of their symptoms, but early in his career he stated that the purpose of therapy was to convert neurotic misery into common everyday unhappiness (Breuer and Freud 1895). Even then he was thinking in terms of character change rather than simply dealing with symptom constellations by interpreting the underlying conflictful impulses that are responsible for their impetus.

Although Alexander's controversial corrective emotional experience is passé, there have been changes in our therapeutic attitudes and techniques that have some similarities to what Alexander proposed. It has become apparent that the treatment of patients with extremely traumatic backgrounds will require more than just verbal interchange. The talking cure will not suffice for patients suffering from severe character disorders. Anna O., the first patient who claimed her treatment could be referred to as the talking cure was, herself, suffering from severe psychopathology rather than an hysterical psychoneurosis.

In the treatment of some of the patients I have already discussed, the therapeutic impact was the product of two factors. To be effective the impact has to be acquired in a particular transference constellation that echoes the repetition compulsion, which belongs in a treatment model that is quite different from the unilateral patient-receiving and doctor-prescribing model. Analysts are also active participants, and countertransference once again enters the picture. Therapists then face getting caught in the trap of narcissistic ensnarement.

The problems surrounding the aim of therapy are extraordinarily complex because they are intimately related to therapeutic technique and the worn-out question of what constitutes analytic technique. Nowhere is this better illustrated than in Freud's treatment of the Rat Man (Freud 1909b), which is thoroughly discussed by Lipton (1977).

The sequence of events is rather simple. The Rat Man, at the beginning of a session, announced that he was hungry. Freud responded to his patient's need by bringing him something to eat. Following this episode, the patient had several dreams in which he was exhibiting his grandiosity and omnipotence.

Freud's behavior toward the Rat Man has become the subject of many controversial arguments. Some therapists insist that Freud committed a technical blunder in that he stepped out of his role as an impartial analyst, that he had, instead, become a caregiver and was attempting to satisfy his patient's infantile needs. This would interfere with the natural course of the analysis and disturb the spontaneous development of the transference, a thesis supported by the dreams the Rat Man had after he had been fed. Freud had introduced an *unnecessary parameter*, a term that Eissler (1953) coined.

Lipton disagreed. He argued, in essence, that there were two Freuds, the analyst and the personal Freud. It was the personal Freud who fed the Rat Man, not the analyst Freud. He made the strong point that Freud did not have any therapeutic intent when he brought his patient food. He was responding as a typical Viennese who would find it unthinkable not to offer a guest food, especially if he asked for it. This would have been similar, in the days when practically everyone was smoking, to the analyst's offering the patient a cigarette if he was pulling one out of the pack for himself, especially if the patient was sitting up. Freud was simply illustrating a particular dimension of his personality that was independent of his functioning as a therapist, and Lipton insisted that this would not have a deleterious effect on the course of the treatment.

Lipton was able to separate the professional from the personal. Today the situation is much more complicated, because this Cartesian dichotomy no longer exists. The personal and the professional are blended, as is emphasized by the formulation of a transference–countertransference axis, and most of the so-called new schools emphasize the therapist's personality as something that cannot be discounted when discussing the therapeutic process.

Clinicians might ask whether Freud's interjection of his Viennese heritage had an adverse affect on the treatment of the Rat Man. As far as anyone can tell, it did not. If one remains in the classical perspective, how much of the therapist's personality can be brought into the treatment without being disruptive?

This question has been discussed in the context of countertransference, which has become both part of the treatment process and is also connected to the goals of therapy. This is far removed from the classical position, inasmuch as the personality of the therapist is intricately involved with the treatment process.

Lipton's argument recedes into the background as clinicians leave the classical approach behind. He stresses that Freud's feeding the Rat Man had no therapeutic intent, and that is why he had not committed a treatment blunder in terms of technical factors. What Freud had done might have been a boundary violation, but since he was totally in tune with Viennese customs and culture, his behavior was not inappropriate.

On the other hand, distinctions between personal factors and therapeutic intent are no longer as definite or as clear-cut as they had been, and oddly enough this represents a strengthening or extension of the intrapsychic focus. Even customary reactions have to be scrutinized in terms of unconscious motivation rather than being set aside and making them exempt as noncontributions or irrelevant factors to the therapeutic interaction. Every action or utterance by the therapist has some significance and will have an effect on the treatment process. How detrimental they might be would depend on how much of the therapist's idiosyncratic infantile conflicts are involved in his behavior, and apparently Freud's reaction was in tune with his reality rather than an expression of the traumatic elements of his infantile past.

As personal involvement and therapeutic intent are no longer as sharply separated, the aims and technique of treatment are more closely drawn together, and the former, to a large measure, determines the latter. This correspondence often creates paradoxes.

For example, clinicians might intuitively believe that the greater expectations a therapist might have about the results of therapy, the more thorough the working-through process and the greater access the patient would have to the deeper levels of the personality. Therapeutic ambition in most of these instances would consist of a complete reworking of the personality, but this refers mainly to behavioral changes without any particular acquisition of insight. The therapist's personality is often involved in vicarious entanglements with the patient's achievements and frequently gains a Pygmalion type of narcissistic triumph (see Chapter 7). Such expectations, rather than achieving deep characterological changes and accretions of psychic structure associated with developmental progression, result only in superficial modifications of adaptive techniques that are based on vulnerable identifications with the therapist.

This discussion of obliterating the distinctions between personal factors, ranging from supplying satisfaction of infantile wishes to therapeutic ambition and therapeutic intent, highlights that treatment in the context of the intrapsychic focus is a highly complex phenomenon. It involves considerably more than a didactic exercise, in which the patient's material is converted into interpretations that are incorporated by the patient and resolve internal psychodynamic conflicts.

To restate and summarize the current position of most therapists conducting in-depth therapy and psychoanalysis, the treatment process goes way beyond verbal interpretations in the context of transference. As countertransference has gained greater prominence in our understanding of the dynamics of the treatment process, the pedantic quality of classical therapy no longer exists. Many courses of therapy can be turbulent, consisting of a series of experiences that recapitulate traumatic experiences of the infantile past. A variety of primitive psychic mechanisms are called into play, such as fusion, which often leads to intense regressions. The weathering of the negative transference can also be a difficult and stormy task.

Fusion is an early form of object relations that is extensively used during the transitional phase of development.

The therapeutic setting consists of a fabric of experiences that eventually repairs the damage to the self representation that was produced by infantile impingements and assaults, the disruption of the continuity of being that Winnicott so often discussed. The reparative potential of the treatment setting may, on the surface, seem to resemble the corrective emotional experience but it is considerably different because it occurs spontaneously, and the interpersonal interaction is based on primitive mental mechanisms. Although their behavior may have been unruly, Alexander's patients still were able to maintain a moderate amount of reality testing in the consultation room, and their mode of relating was heavily punctuated with secondary process factors.

Current analytic settings are based on primitive psychic mechanism and are usually distorted replicas of the past. They can be viewed as the object relations aspect of the treatment process, which, if properly handled or if the therapist can survive the primitive ambience some patients create, can lead to progression on the scale of emotional development.

These treatment settings, the outcome of early object relationships, are either regressed states or reflections of fixated and distorted developmental levels. In cases of extremely severe psychopathology and psychoses, the ego state that characterizes the treatment process has little or no counterpart in any of the ordinary stages of development.

As patients regress and then progress up the developmental scale, they also recapitulate early psychic modes of relating that run the gamut from part-object relations, to fusion mechanisms, to emergence from fusion states, to eventually achieving whole-object relationships. This spectrum of progression can, in itself, be disruptive for a variety of reasons, many dependent on the type of psychopathology. It would be disturbing in any event, because to regress to an earlier stage of object relations is intrinsically threatening.

PAINFUL REGRESSED STATES AND EXTENSIONS OF TECHNICAL PERSPECTIVES

Patients often do not fear regression as therapists do, because they may be operating at the highest level possible, whereas therapists may feel some vulnerability as they regress and allow themselves to be the objects of primary process fused modes of relating. Furthermore, the early psychic mechanisms patients use are psychopathologically distorted, which means they are cathected with rage and destructive feelings. They impose a threat to any therapist who is about to enter the infantile arena that characterizes the treatment setting.

I am primarily referring to the fusion state, the earliest state of object relations. Therapists may sense the destructiveness that is embodied in the mechanism of merger and fear that patients will make inroads into their autonomy, which involves the professional self representation. In turn, the therapist's anxiety concerning letting the patient achieve fusion, an escape from an autistic or schizoid state, is also experienced as threatening and causes problems for the maintenance of a therapeutic stance.

In these instances fusion leads to confusion. Patients are reaching out for succor and in their own way are trying to create a holding environment, a therapeutic setting representing a rudimentary object relationship that can lead to contacts with the external world. Therapists' reluctance to enter this infantile world, because of the fear of the loss of professional autonomy, disrupt their therapeutic intent and treatment goals. This is a situation in which personal factors clash with therapeutic intent rather than propel it.

The impact of this situation is particularly devastating when the therapist reacts without knowing why; the silent elements of the interaction are occurring at an unconscious level.

To some degree, therapists have to support the patient's efforts to create a therapeutic setting based on the repetition compulsion as it attempts to adapt to or defend against infantile trauma. Nevertheless, there is always some resistance that analysts experience when they are forced to regress with their patients. This is especially true when the patient's orientation is paranoid. However, as therapists recognize that their patients are reliving early traumatic situations, they can be there for them without necessarily descending to their level of primitive emotionality. They can maintain their therapeutic stance without disturbing the patient's regressed state. They may be able to create a setting in which the patient can comfortably regress, a fairly good definition of the holding environment.

I have discussed a patient who had very painful regressions in another context in which I was dealing with various states of ego fragmentation (Giovacchini 1997).The resolution of my countertransference discomfort and the maintenance of therapeutic intent and treatment goals were associated with my feeling the patient's pain and not interfering with his misery. This was an extremely trying situation that had to be processed for the survival of the therapeutic relationship.

The patient, a middle-aged businessman, felt that no one—not his parents, wife, family, or former therapists—had ever been able to understand him. He complained bitterly that, especially in childhood, he had been treated as a nonentity or "fifth wheel." His biological parents were killed in an automobile accident when he was an infant, and he was raised by foster parents who had been friends of his parents.

He was obviously a very needy person. From the first session he cried a good deal and complained about the lack of love and affection in his childhood, which now as an adult caused him to feel inferior. He had very little self-confidence and felt that others thought he was ridiculous and incompetent. Actually, in his work he admitted he was doing fairly well, but he feared he would be fired because he would be "found out." During childhood he felt like an orphan and he often compared himself to Cinderella. His foster parents had six children of their own, who kept them quite busy. Since he was not biologically attached to them, he felt they never bonded, and therefore they did not respond to or even recognize his needs because of a lack of empathic attunement. He felt a profound resentment toward them, but, at the same time, he felt sorry for them because they worked hard and could hardly keep up with the demands, financial and emotional, that were heaped upon them.

His foster father was now a widower and frail and feeble, needing someone to look after him. The patient was assigned this role, which he felt was terribly unfair, but he tried to take care of him with the vain hope of gaining his love. At the beginning of treatment the father was living in the patient's home, which the patient's wife resented intensely.

Very early in treatment, he complained that I could not love him in the fashion and extent that he needed. I had my wife and children and did not have the capacity or intent to give him what he needed. I lamented to myself that he was right. I could not give him a mother's or father's love that an infant would need, and even if I could generate such feelings, they would not help because chronologically and in many other ways he was an adult. Mother's milk will not nourish an adult stomach.

Still, he had psychological sensitivities as evidenced by his evaluation of the other emotional problems of friends and relatives and of himself. In spite of his bitterness, there was an appealing waif-like quality about him, and his ironic, wry observations were often witty and humorous. I wanted to help free him of his anger at the world, which impeded the development of a capacity to enjoy himself and open himself up to relationships that could be eventually loving and intimate, such as with his wife and children. Basically, he seemed to want to be close to them, but he fled from them by burying himself in books or spending countless hours in front of the television set, which only made him feel worse about himself.

He told me of many instances in which he did something foolish, such as making an unwise purchase or letting himself be swindled in a minor way by responding to glib advertising for defective products that he did not need or even want. Afterward, he would viciously revile himself. It almost seemed that he indulged in such foolish behavior so he could take himself to task.

One particularly striking incident was responsible for his being very late for an appointment; only a few minutes remained. Standing on the sidewalk outside my office building was a scantily clad, attractive young woman with a tray of free sample packages of cigarettes. He queued up at the back of a very long line and patiently waited for his sample. At the end of telling me what had happened to him, he exclaimed in a high-pitched voice, "I don't even smoke." I could not help but smile, because there was something comical about this meaningless and ridiculous experience. Undoubtedly there was some hostile intent toward me in this, even as there must have been hostility toward others in all of his inappropriate or unwise actions and transactions. I, on the other hand, could only feel sorry for him, whereas I imagine others must have found him irritating. He said he was frequently referred to as a jerk.

During his sessions he spoke in a low, monotonous tone, but he was constantly complaining about every facet of his life. He also started complaining about our relationship in that he was not getting in touch with his feelings. I did not directly respond, but indicated that he would allow himself to feel when he felt it was safe to reveal himself. This would happen when he could trust the treatment relationship and feel that I could relate to him in a calm, accepting fashion. He apparently got my message, as he lost his poise and had an emotional explosion.

During one session about six months into the treatment, he started screaming and convulsively sobbing. The back of his neck turned beet red as he kicked and flailed on the couch. His body became stiff and he tightly clenched his fists. I could make out slurred words and sentences such as, "I want my Mommy," and "Please help me," in the context of extremely painful feelings. He groaned, moaned, and then shouted how badly everything hurt.

As his pain and misery intensified, I felt increasingly uncomfortable. I felt a need to help him and alleviate the torture that he had created for himself. I felt my motives were benign in that I wanted him to feel better, but, in retrospect, I believe I was trying to relieve myself of the pain I was absorbing from him.

To put matters in a favorable therapeutic perspective, I commented that he was being successful in reaching primitive painful parts of himself and that by so doing, he was trying to get rid of them by externalizing them. Evidently I was trying to give both meaning and purpose to behavior that was chaotic, painful, and self-destructive. It was also near the end of the session and I was trying to restore order and not let the turbulent feelings that were being expressed cross over the boundaries into my next session. To my relief, the patient completely regained his composure and quietly left.

I believed that my interpretation had hit its mark, and pointing out the adaptive significance of the patient's behavior had a calming effect and brought the patient out of a painful regression. Therefore, I was completely surprised when, at the beginning of the next session, he bitterly attacked me for having interrupted his attempts at reaching "important" feelings. He reviled me for not being with him at his moment of need. I had completely misunderstood him, and even though my interpretation might in some ways have been correct, it was inappropriate and intrusive. In essence, he told me that he was trying to get in touch with primitive feelings and frustrations and that instead of helping him, I wanted to intellectualize and avoid tumultuous feelings. He felt that interpretations were totally inappropriate because the use of words was at a much higher level of organization than what he was experiencing. His primitive feelings did not have the organization that could be explained by such secondary-process constructs as words and concepts. Furthermore, as soon as I moved up into a higher area of mental discourse, I abruptly thrust him out of an ego state that had to be experienced.

He emphasized that he wanted me to be with him, and I was to enhance rather than interrupt his regression. Interpretations were about the worst things to offer him. This caused me to feel some puzzlement, because within my technical armory interpretation holds an important position, and in this situation I did not know exactly what being there with him and for him meant. If words were out of the question, how could I be helpful?

It turned out that words were not completely proscribed. I mentioned that I could hear him cry for some kind of parental attention and nurture as he sounded like a child anxiously calling for his mother. He was using words the same way a small disturbed child would.

About a week later, he had a similar regressed episode. To some extent, I felt as if he were testing me to find out if I had learned anything from him since he had scolded me for my behavior during the first session in which he had regressed. I was careful not to make interpretations or in any way explore the meaning of his behavior. This meant that I remained attentively silent, but afterward the patient again expressed his discontent. This is similar to the clinical situation I have already discussed in which, because of the patient's fragile ego boundaries and lack of any protective shield, even the slightest impingement is felt as a violent assault and interpretations are experienced in a similar fashion. Reactive silence is understood as desertion or abandonment, and these therapies often end up as unresolvable impasses.

I felt a similar dilemma with this patient, although his dynamics are different. He was not particularly susceptible to impingements, but, in my mind, he had created a situation in which I felt, from a technical viewpoint, paralyzed.

I finally realized that the patient, as a child, wanted me to make my presence felt without intruding the adult world into the infantile world he had created. I also concluded that the only way I could permit myself to make contact with him was through words. Later, I learned that the patient wanted literally to be touched. I would not have been able to expand my therapeutic technique to include making bodily contact. I knew Winnicott, on occasion, touched and held his patients, but because of my training and my personal orientation and constrictions, I would not have been comfortable extending my technique into touching and holding activities. I wanted to keep our interaction on a verbal basis, but I also wanted to supply him with what he felt he needed.

When he pleaded for infantile succor during his states of extreme regression, I started commenting that I could hear and see how much pain he felt. At times I would add that he must feel he was a very bad person because he had to shout and scream for what he wanted. These were what I have called *phenomenological interpretations* because I was trying to describe what he felt but not why he suffered as much as he did. For example, he saw himself as a bad person, and in his garbled language he often referred to himself as bad, but I did not connect his sense of badness with his being abandoned. Because he was "bad," he had to scream for help and love, but I did not make a causal connection between his being abandoned and his then feeling there must be something wrong with him. He also indicated in less regressed moments that because he was bad, nobody loved or wanted him.

During regressed states he would not have been able to understand an etiological sequence because this was too complex a mode of thinking for the early ego states that he had produced. Even when he was relating at a more secondary process level, he doubted the value of that kind of insight.

If several sessions went by without painful regressed states, he felt that he and I were accomplishing nothing, that we were wasting our time and his money. He had to submerge himself in infantile feelings; he believed that then he could experience infantile gratifications that would make up for what he had lacked when he was a child. For the moment, my acknowledging, and thereby validating, what he felt sufficed and carried us through what he considered the barren moments of his therapy, in which he felt we were conducting an intellectual discourse that had little therapeutic potential.

He developed strongly ambivalent attitudes about therapy and would cancel his sessions several months at a time because he did not believe I could give him what he needed. He sought out other therapists who touched and held him, tried to hypnotize him, and otherwise manipulated the depth of his regression. Although he liked their experimental approach, he did not trust their integrity or intelligence and he was unable to regress.

He was in the midst of a dilemma. With me, he could achieve the regression to an early ego state, but I was not able to relate to him sufficiently at that level. Other therapists were not at all inhibited in trying to give him what he wanted, but he could not produce the regressed state in which he might have been able to respond to such ministrations.

I have often asked myself why I could not put my arms about him and hug him when he was crying like a needy, abandoned baby. He did awaken some such urge as I looked at his small, frail body convulsing with spasmodic sobs. He was a short, thin man who could be easily embraced, but my professional modus operandi would not allow me such liberties. Whether a less inhibited therapist could have been effective with him is a debatable question. In my case, my attempts to hold him would have been awkward and insincere, so I assume they would have done more harm than good. Furthermore, my ambivalence about the therapeutic validity of such actions would not have helped.

It is interesting, however, that the therapists he saw, who apparently readily practiced "hands on" therapy and were willing to use whatever was necessary to produce a regressed state, were unable to get him in touch with primitive psychic mechanisms and desires. By contrast, our treatment relationship, which had far more constraints than the radical therapies he was seeking, had been regularly able to reproduce early ego states and the conflict and turmoil associated with them. This was puzzling and became the central focus of our treatment.

Even though he eschewed what he called intellectual discussions, he could not help but be struck by what was an obvious discrepancy. He continued experiencing primitive ego states and accepted that I would not go any further in my responses than making phenomenological interpretations. After every such session, he felt relieved and "better," and he had changed in that he accepted that nonturbulent sessions also had some relevance to the treatment. We discussed at great length his mistrust, in that he felt most people would treat him the way his foster parents did. He could not count on anyone being interested in fulfilling his needs or acknowledging him as a worthwhile person. He acted out these attitudes with his provocative behavior, which represented a generalized paranoid attitude toward the world. In turn, external objects did in fact treat him like a bothersome second-class citizen, as his behavior became increasingly self-destructive. He had re-created the infantile scenario within the context of the repetition compulsion. He was contentious and litigious, often suing and being sued.

I believe that the sessions between the regressed states were analytic, as we were able to understand that his current provocative experiences were the outcome of defensive adaptations to his Cinderella-like position with his rejecting and negligent foster parents. Undoubtedly, the regressed states created a treatment setting in which we could explore his infantile conflicts as they continued to impact his relationships with the outer world.

He was also able to recover memories that had succumbed to repression, but this occurred in the in-between sessions. He remembered childhood episodes in which his foster father would beat him mercilessly with his belt. The act of recall was painful, and he sometimes cried as he remembered these terrible beatings. The so-called intellectually oriented sessions at times became less intellectual and more concerned with affect.

His sessions contained different degrees of regression. The in-between sessions, even when he regressed and uncovered repressed memories, had enough secondary-process organization so that we could communicate with words and make etiological connections. Later, he made it clear that this higher level of relating was possible because he had learned to trust me. This occurred because I was, in my own way, able to sustain him through his painful regression by being there with him, although I was not able to give him everything he wanted. Furthermore, he felt sufficiently safe with me so that he could express the depth and intensity of his infantile feelings without exposing himself to the risk of being annihilated. He did not have this type of security with the other therapists he sought.

At clinical seminars in which I have presented this patient, some colleagues have commented that the regressed states represented episodes of abreaction, which in later sessions led to higher levels of emotional integration that made it possible for him to utilize insight. His treatment was compared to Breuer's treatment of Anna O., who abreacted during regressed hypnotic states. In my case, it was postulated that the reliving of the traumatic situation made it possible to regain split-off parts of the self that had been embedded in traumatic experiences. These traumatic assaults had not been processed at the time of their occurrence. With Anna O., as discussed, Breuer called these traumatic split-off states hypnoid states that through abreaction could once again be incorporated in the main psychic stream.

The recovery of lost and split-off traumatic memories in my patient occurred during states that were less regressed, and even though their recovery was painful, in no way did it match the torment and misery of ego states that initially I tried to eliminate. In these deeply regressed states, he was undoubtedly reliving the pain of rejection, but he was also pleading for nurture and redemption. It was more than just the reliving of trauma, whereas in the in-between sessions, in which he still retained considerable secondary process, traumatic memories from the past emerged and left him with a sense of liberation.

The patient amply illustrates that the treatment model of the listening-interpreting analyst would have been totally inappropriate for his treatment. He did not disguise or hide his viewpoint. He openly expressed his view that interpretation was useless. Later he emended this viewpoint and became interested in understanding the effects of the infantile depriving environment on his behavior and the impact of the physically assaultive milieu on his pugnacious, provocative, and somewhat paranoid attitudes.

To achieve meaningful insight, he had to live out certain childhood constellations and his reactions against them in an almost preverbal context. I had become part of the failing environment and this became an especially precarious period of therapy. Not only was the patient threatening to terminate as he consulted other therapists, but I was also becoming disenchanted because I could not and did not want to give him what he demanded. In essence he was looking for infantile succor, not at the symbolic level; he demanded actual touching and holding and I did not want to conduct that type of treatment. On several occasions, I was on the verge of suggesting that since I could not comply with his wishes, perhaps he should see someone else. The fact that he could not find anyone made me hold back, but my countertransference feelings were impelling me to terminate our relationship.

I still wonder what would have happened if I could have expanded my therapeutic armamentarium to include holding and touching. Perhaps, deep in his unconscious, the patient had conflicts, possibly a phobia, about being touched and held, because of his tumultuous infantile environment. His treatment revealed a basic fear of intimacy, and this might have manifested itself in the somatic area of the skin. He begged for succor and to be held during his painful regressed state, but this might have been the expression of a conflict rather than just a simple wish. Possibly giving him what he cried for might have been disruptive and counterproductive.

In a sense, Freud's concepts of the treatment process are somewhat simplistic. True, there was considerable ingenuity involved in reading a patient correctly but he was operating more at the level of the dispassionate detective who can hold his feelings back rather than as a participant who is thrust into the emotional arena as transference–countertransference issues evolve.

Perhaps, as discussed in Chapter 1, these changes in therapeutic approaches are reciprocally related to social-cultural issues. As ego boundaries become more flexible, technique also becomes expanded, and therapists may permit themselves to make contact and reach out to their patients in ways that are not currently acceptable or considered appropriate. It is possible that in the future, touching and holding a patient may be considered part of standard technique.

Still, every technical innovation has to have a theoretical rationale, and it is difficult to understand how supplying infantile gratification to an adult can be beneficial. The ego may be regressed, but no regression is complete, because it occurs in an adult body, and the soma does not keep pace with the psyche. Even in the most regressed states, most patients can still talk, remain continent, and retain other functions that would not have been available to the infantile ego that the patient is reproducing in regression.

Nevertheless, techniques have changed in what might be considered to be a more liberal direction, and this is reflected in many areas. There is a greater acceptance of wide ranges of behavior, and the consultation room is more casual both as to how therapists and patients dress and how they relate to each other. Often therapists and patients are on a first-name basis, something that would have been unthinkable in Freud's time.

Concepts about psychopathology and what should be treated have also changed. For example, homosexuality was considered to be a manifestation of psychopathology, and therapists attempted to cure homosexual patients by resolving conflicts that caused them to repress their biological sexuality. Many contemporary clinicians do not think in terms of conflict when dealing with gay patients. They view their gender identity as an alternate lifestyle and the patient's choice of how to relate sexually is respected and not analyzed away because there is nothing to analyze. Homosexuality is no longer included in *DSM-IV*.

Concepts about psychopathology affect our therapeutic perspectives, which have changed considerably through the years. Formulations about emotional illness are no longer as rigid or absolute. They are made in the context of the social-cultural milieu, and what might have been shunned in the past, such as homosexuality, which was against the law, is, for the most part, accepted.

Treatment is directed toward the acquisition of maximum autonomy, and the patient has many more devices than in the past, when formulations were primarily psychodynamic.

Structural factors are highlighted as clinicians conceptualize patients, and the surrounding culture is a relevant variable. Clinicians investigate the patient's adaptation to the outer world, an approach that Freud (1924a,b) initiated. If an adaptation is reasonably effective and does not cause harm to the patient or society, then it is not included in the rubric of psychopathology. The chief indicator of psychopathology is how effectively, or rather how poorly, the ego's executive system's adaptive mechanisms relate to the outer world. If the psyche lacks effective adaptations, then many mental structures are disrupted, such as the sense of identity, narcissistic levels, and self-esteem.

This approach highlights the continuing importance of the environment, because a particular psyche might be able to reasonably function in one setting but not in another. This is an example of cultural relativism. I have described patients who could function in chaotic, turbulent settings but could not adjust to relatively calm conditions (Giovacchini 1979). The legendary master sergeant is a good example; he could thrive in battle, whereas most of us would be terrified, but he could not exist in peacetime conditions because he has the adaptive mechanisms to cope with the former but not with the latter.

These patients project their infantile environments into their contemporary milieu in addition to projecting their feelings and parts of the self into external objects. I call this type of projection *externalization* because the world of childhood is superimposed onto the current adult world, and an internalized past is externalized and shapes the patient's reality. The greater the similarity between the infantile world and the adult world, the better adjusted the psyche will be. The dissimilarities of these two worlds determine the intensity of psychopathology, as patients often seek realities that correspond to the infantile setting.

The master sergeant may have been raised in a turbulent, violent environment, and perhaps he had learned to survive under these traumatic circumstances. I recall an actual patient, a business tycoon, who was raised in the violent slums of the ghetto. Since he was physically and mentally well endowed, he was able to rise above his environment and replace the ghetto with the jungle of Wall Street, where he became immensely successful. He succumbed to intense panic states when a cardiac disorder forced him to slow down the pace of his hectic, frenetic existence. He, like the master sergeant, could not tolerate peace and tranquility. His breakdown occurred when he could not use the adaptive techniques he had learned in order to cope with his family and the ghetto, and that also served him in the warlike conditions of the world of finance.

Our therapeutic armamentarium has to supply clinicians with the technical adaptations to deal with what are basically structural defects. These patients attempt to construct the infantile ambience in the consultation room. Although therapists allow themselves to be receptacles for patients' feelings and parts of the self, the therapeutic ambience has to remain constant. It should not be influenced by patients' attempts to submerge it with the infantile milieu.

The business tycoon patient attempted to create a ghetto atmosphere by trying to provoke me. During a period of treatment, his usually well-bred manner and proper English deteriorated into a street accent, and he became boorish and belligerent, expressing biased and racist viewpoints that were not really his own. He tried to provoke me into arguing with him, displaying a chip-on-the-shoulder type of pugnacity. I did not waver in my professional stance because I recognized that he was trying to make me part of his infantile ambience and relate to me at the same turbulent level that characterized his early life. He did not succeed, and for a while he became so anxious that it seemed he would have to be hospitalized.

However, he weathered what appeared to be a serious decompensation and he was able to fulfill ego-ideals that, as a child, he had had to split off because they would have been dangerous handicaps in the world he lived in. He really loved literature and admired a particular poet, but he could not reveal these feelings either to his nuclear family or peers, because they would have ridiculed him for being unmanly and perhaps even attack him. In therapy, he was finally able to express the manifestations of a true self that had been buried by a more adaptive false self (Winnicott 1952, 1960a).

This type of patient is not usually a threat to the professional ego-ideal if the therapist recognizes that the patient is externalizing the infantile environment and indulging in defenses against and adaptations to that milieu. Therapists have to survive these attempts to bring them down to early and primitive modes of relating, but this can be achieved if they remain strictly in the professional frame of reference, which means they are nonparticipants, but at the same time understanding and nonjudgmental. These clinical instances are examples in which personal involvement is kept at a minimum with the aim of constructing a calm, constant, and reliable setting, permitting patients to construct or recover adaptations that are more syntonic with the adult world they live in.

These situations are the antithesis of clinical encounters that I have described in which patients need their therapists to be there with them in their regressed states. These patients are living out primitive ego states, that is, early levels of psychic structure, whereas patients who externalize are trying to create an outside world that shaped the course of their ego development. They also want the therapist to relate to them at the infantile level in contrast to other regressed states in which any activity of the therapist becomes an impediment to the maintenance of that state. Externalization, to some extent, is a universal phenomenon where the regressed states I previously described are comparatively rare and much more difficult to deal with.

In both clinical settings, however, it is essential that therapists are alert about their emotional responses, enabling them to assess what patients are trying to accomplish. With regressed primitive ego states, therapists are more likely to feel helpless, because usual technical procedures such as verbal interpretations prove to be useless, whereas therapists need not deviate from standard analytic practice with patients who externalize.

As clinicians learn more about the structural factors involved in psychopathology, there is less inclination to think in terms of standard analytic practice. The therapist's personal responses have become embedded in the treatment process, and there is an expansion of psychic structure in both therapists and patients.

Apparently the public has some awareness of changes of orientation in the practice of psychotherapy, if we accept that movies are reflections of social cultural orientations.

I believe that the first movie that extensively dealt with the psychotherapeutic process was *Spellbound*, directed by Alfred Hitchcock. The film was, in essence, a mystery in which the main characters had to work their way out of a dilemma by using techniques similar to those of a detective. The principal male character suffered from amnesia and was a murder suspect. The woman psychiatrist, who was also in love with him, had to help him recover his memory, and by so doing would be able to prove that he was innocent of any crime.

The specifics of the therapist's personality did not matter, except that she loved him and wanted to rescue him. Other than that, their interaction did not matter, and transference and countertransference were ignored.

The therapeutic relationship was collaborative and the conclusion could be placed in a psychodynamic frame of reference. The patient had experienced a trauma that was accompanied by considerable guilt, which led to repression of the traumatic incident. Once the repressed memory was recovered, all was well.

This was a somewhat simplistic portrayal of a single trauma causing a neurosis, much in the same way that traumatic neuroses have been depicted. Recovery of repressed memories and abreaction led to the elimination of the neurosis and its symptoms, similar to what Breuer and Freud (1895) wrote about in their *Studies on Hysteria*, although even then they did not make formulations in terms of a single traumatic event. It is true, however, that they did not pay much attention to the characteristics of the trauma-producing infantile environment.

In more recent movies, such as *Good Will Hunting*, which I mentioned earlier, the therapeutic climate is entirely different. There is no mystery to solve or clues to pursue. The problems that assail the patient are obvious, and the healing process is dependent on the strength of the relationship between patient and therapist.

When the hero was finally able to settle down in a therapeutic relationship, it was a highly emotional interaction and both participants achieved considerable growth. It was an informal situation. Both patient and therapist dressed down and there was considerable physical contact between them. During the first interview, the psychiatrist became angry at the patient, as had the other therapists, and grabbed him by the neck. Later in the treatment their emotionality was expressed by hugging each other.

This recent movie depicts treatment as a highly interactive process, which is in keeping with contemporary views of psychotherapy. Nevertheless, the patient–therapist relationship lacks dignity and professionalism. I cannot imagine a treatment relationship in which the therapist loses control and tries to choke his patient. Movies tend to be hyperbolic and this movie depicts a caricature of the treatment process. Still, the difference between *Spellbound* and *Good Will Hunting* recapitulates the evolution from the linear approach Freud postulated to the subjectivist preoccupation that is currently prevalent.

Techniques have changed as the interaction gains central prominence. Movies such as *Good Will Hunting*, as well as many treatment relationships, have very little if any technical rationale. They often are highly charged relationships, at best, based on common sense or intuitive humanism. Usually, there are two people emoting with each other, presumably involved in each other's welfare. Boundaries are often eliminated in what has been called "touchy-feely therapy."

I saw a patient in consultation who was very angry at her constantly unfaithful husband. She had seen a therapist, who was trying to be supportive. The patient would discuss with her therapist certain feelings she might express to her husband. For example, she would consider threatening him by saying, "You'd better not see your secretary again." The therapist would then add, "Or else." Many people, including the therapist, mistook this interaction for therapy.

This may have been an appropriate communication between two friends, but all therapeutic principles are bypassed in such a situation. There is no attempt to investigate what the patient is really protesting and why she had tolerated a masochistic relationship with her husband. Her dependency and vulnerability are totally ignored. Unfortunately, believing such a relationship constitutes treatment deprives the patient of the opportunity of having therapy.

THE OBSERVATIONAL PLATFORM

Granted that the interaction between patient and therapist has gained importance and significance, there has to be an orderliness and organization to the patient–therapist relationship and containment in the transference–countertransference axis that is based on the structure the therapist brings to the treatment process. Sterba (1934) was the first analyst to introduce the self-observing function as a quality of the patient's ego that facilitates the therapeutic process. As therapy loses its unilateral status, the self-observing function has to be put in a dyadic context. Both analyst and patient are observing each other and themselves at the same time. To put it more accurately, therapist and patient are viewing the interaction between them, which is assessed in terms of conscious and unconscious feelings.

To construct a metaphor, the patient and analyst can be considered to be on a platform that hovers above the patient lying on the couch and the analyst sitting on a chair adjacent to the couch. On the platform, the two participants are either standing or sitting and looking down at their counterparts below them. They are observing and listening to what is going on between the two persons they are looking at. Occasionally they may make some remark as to their conclusions about the interaction they are trying to understand, the analyst usually taking the lead as he discusses what he thinks with the patient. The patient participates in the discussion, agreeing or disagreeing, qualifying or amending what he has been told. Sometimes the patient takes the lead and may comment on what the two persons below are doing with each other. The focus is usually on the person lying on the couch, but frequently enough the therapist becomes the main topic.

This metaphor is similar to the one Bertrand Russell used to define his theories of classes. He called attention to the liar's paradox, in which a box or a square contains the statement that every statement in the box is false. Russell puts himself in a position above the box looking down. What is being said is about the falseness of statements in the box, but this assertion is in a different frame of reference than the statements and can be viewed as a meta-statement.

The position of the two persons on the platform is a meta-position. They are making statements about the analytic interaction, but they do not question the validity of what is being said. They only look for meanings that are not immediately apparent and they are also making observations about phenomena that are not directly visible to the participants at the lower level. In a sense, they have to get outside themselves to get a broader, clearer, and more objective picture.

To rephrase this process, the self-observing function has to be developed within the context of an object relationship. Without it, it would not be possible to understand the full implications of what is transpiring between the communicating participants, which in a practical sense means that transference and countertransference phenomena would remain hidden. What would seem invalid and sense-less at one level could be rich with meaning at another. The falseness of a statement would not be apparent if the statements were simply made within the box. Their validity or invalidity has to be determined in another class, as Russell would say, or from a clinical perspective they have to be reviewed on the observational platform. The surface irrationality between patient and therapist is elevated to another plane, where it can be rationally explained, but in terms of uncon-scious processes, which again brings clinicians to the transference–countertransference axis.

As patients associate, they are revealing derivatives of their uncon-scious, and within the transference context they direct their feelings toward their therapists. Therapists, in turn, maintain an attitude of ever-hovering or free-floating attention (Freud 1911–1914), which means that they are letting their unconscious respond to patients' free associations within the countertransference frame. This is happen-ing beneath the observational platform, the box level that contains various types of statements that are to be evaluated at another, higher conceptual level. The box level, the clinical connection, is the area of subjectivity, whereas the two people on the observational platform are viewing the intersubjective relationship below them in an objec-tive manner.

Spatial metaphors are meaningful for this description of the thera-peutic process. Higher and lower can also be applied to different lay-ers of the psyche as well as to subjectivity and objectivity. At the lower level, the mode of communication is, for the most part, primary pro-cess oriented, whereas on the observational platform communications are based primarily on secondary process orientations.

Ogden (1994a,b) views the treatment process as being based on the formation of "analytic thirds," which become embedded in the therapeutic ambience. I believe his ideas deserve attention because within the realms of intersubjectivity his formulations have been given considerable importance, as the various "faces" of the intrapsychic approach are increasingly interested in discovering the dynamics and the structural venues of the therapeutic process.

Ogden's approach to the understanding of the treatment interaction is popular because it emphasizes intersubjectivity. He describes the analytic third as "the experience of being simultaneously within and outside of the intersubjectivity of the analyst–analysand which I will refer to as the *analytic third*" (1994b, p. 64).

I believe that my metaphor of the observational platform depicts the same situation and relationship that Ogden has formulated. However, in therapy clinicians are dealing with two levels of relationship, which might better be conceptualized as containing four participants rather than three, as Ogden implies.

Perhaps Ogden preferred to think of this "third" as a supraordinate creation and wanted to emphasize its function rather than its relational and interpersonal aspects.

Muller (1998) refers to the "third" as relating to "members of another dyadic relation with one or each of the members of the dyad" (p. 4). Almond (1995) emphasizes the analytic role as being in another plane than the interplay of transference and countertransference. Crapanzano (1982) writes, "The signifying chain, the symbolic order, culture and grammar, we might say, serves to stabilize the relations between the Self and the Other by functioning as a Third" (p. 197). He is also discussing the analytic role and, in a sense, the holding and containing qualities of the treatment process.

Shapiro (1998) states, "[The] clearly structured framework created by the treatment process provides a safe, predictable, transitional space for therapeutic work" (p. 7). Again, this framework can be viewed as the essence of the holding environment that allows patients to comfortably regress. He relates this structuring function to the analytic third.

The concept of the analytic third has gained a foothold in the recent literature and contemporary thinking. It has been linked with semiotics, Lacanian concepts, and intersubjectivity, but, as so often happens in these areas, there is considerable confusion. Muller and Shapiro go beyond Ogden's (1994a) concept of a therapeutically generated intersubjectivity of the analytic pair. For them, the spatial framework of the therapeutic process has been incorporated in the formulation of the analytic third, whereas Ogden refers to this space as the transference matrix.

Ogden (1994b) states, "This third subjectivity, the intersubjective analytic third . . . is a product of a unique dialectic generated by/between the separate subjectivities of analyst and analysand within the analytic setting" (p. 64). Here, again, he is emphasizing that interaction creates meanings, which become essential ingredients of the therapeutic process. Still, the question has to be raised as to whether meanings are created or whether they are uncovered. The latter would be more in keeping with object related viewpoints of the treatment process, which also emphasize dyadic interactions.

Concepts about the analytic third have to be made more explicit and clarified by the various authors who write about it. Ogden's statement that I just quoted could also have been improved if he had defined some of his terms such as subjectivity, intersubjectivity, and dialectic. Dialectic, even among philosophers, has various and different meanings, especially when used by Socrates and Hegel. The analytic third can also be examined in terms of Sterba's (1934) self-observing function.

These concepts become relatively simple and clinically relevant if they are phrased in terms of transference and countertransference. Ogden (1994b) recognizes the influence of countertransference when he states that the concept of countertransference has to be "continually reground . . . in the dialectic of the analyst as a separate entity and the analyst as a creation of the analytic intersubjectivity" (p. 74). Again it would have been helpful if he had defined his terms, especially dialectic. I believe that if psychic processes are viewed in terms of a hierarchy based on a balance of primary and secondary process, it is more clinically useful to think in terms of transference–countertransference interactions than the philosophical concept of dialectic. I believe Ogden may be somewhat in agreement when he states, "Neither of these 'poles' of the dialectic exists in pure form and our task is to make increasingly full statements about the specific nature of the relationship between the experience of subject and object, between countertransference and transference at any given moment" (p. 74).

THE THERAPEUTIC VENUE: THE TRANSITIONAL SPACE

The transitional phenomenon represents a developmental stage, and the therapeutic interaction and treatment resolution occur within that space.

Many patients attribute the sources of their distress to the outer world—what has now been recognized as a victim mentality that ignores intrapsychic causation and exploration. Often these patients are dour, humorless types who are concretely oriented and mechanistic, as discussed in Chapter 1. The therapeutic task frequently consists of constructing a transitional space, often in a humorous or playful context. The therapist is invariably cast in the role of a transitional object that permits the patient to creatively enter the surrounding world, which had previously been seen as cruel and dangerous and the source of the patient's problems; it was viewed as being identical to the infantile traumatic environment.

According to Winnicott (1953), the transitional space is the area in which the capacity to play and construct illusions develops. It is also the space in which internal and external objects are differentiated. In therapy, patients have to replace the infantile milieu with the surrounding contemporaneous world, and they have to learn to relate to it as the sources of their problems become internalized. The problems are handled in the transitional space, often in a playful, somewhat humorous fashion, so that they are transformed from grim reality to playful illusion. Feinsilver (1980) has described a similar process.

The therapist becomes the catalyst for this transformation, as he is used as a transitional object, a task that can often be traumatic for the therapist. Again, narcissism may enter the picture, because being used as a transitional object can be a serious threat to the professional self representation and the narcissistic reservoir. Although the therapist may feel humiliated, debased, and dehumanized, he is nevertheless serving a useful developmental function in the same way as the mangled teddy bear and the shredded blanket.

I believe Winnicott (1969) was describing something similar when he discussed the use of an object in the service of identification. He was writing about the developmental pathway to the establishment of the identity sense or, in structural terms, to the formation of the self representation. He postulated that before you could use an object as an external object, that is, moving from the subjective object to the objective object, the child had to first destroy it.

I have taken issue with this theoretical position because I do not believe the external object has to be destroyed from the child's viewpoint. Instead, I concluded that the child decathects the external object, actually the caregiver, and this is a step on the way to the formation of object relationships and acknowledging that the source of nurture is not under the psyche's omnipotent control.

These processes can also be applied to treatment. Patients use their therapists at different levels, sometimes beginning by not acknowledging if and how they are being helped. Therapists are taken for granted, and there seems to be little or no investment in the person or function of the therapist. I would compare this to the stage of decathexis of the external object that occurs when the child is on the road to recognizing the meaningfulness of caregivers.

Even during the phase of seeming indifference, both infants and patients sometimes betray their dependence on the caregiver or the therapist. Winnicott (1958b) wrote about the capacity to be alone in the presence of someone else. The mother is there, creating a situation in which her child can ignore her. Still, she has to be there in order to be ignored. I have written about a child, who later became schizophrenic, who went into an inconsolable tantrum when his mother tried unobtrusively to leave him (Giovacchini 1997). The child wants it both ways. Part of the psyche is struggling to assert autonomy, free of dependence, which later contributes to narcissistic supplies and self-esteem; another part is aware of being helpless and vulnerable and has to hold the source of nurture and protection within the mind's territory.

The caregiving function is partially externalized in that it is held in the transitional space before it becomes part of the outer world. Then it can again be internalized as it further contributes to the strength and cohesion of the nurturing matrix that I have previously described as an essential element of the transitional phenomenon. The acquisition of the capacity to form object relationships and the acknowledgment of the outer world as separate from the psyche do not occur in a linear fashion in which internal parts of the psyche are relinquished to the realm of reality. Freud (1920) wrote about the amoeba extending and retracting its pseudopodia as it made forays into its milieu. In a similar fashion, psychic development occurs in similar back-and-forth forays that can be viewed as introjective-projective processes that lead to the creation of the transitional space. The latter develops further as it permits transitional objects to become incorporated in reality.

The therapeutic process has many parallels to what I have just described; the parallels emphasize the role of the transitional phase of development in the establishment of autonomy and object constancy. Even though therapists may be ignored as they are treated as transitional objects, patients often become very upset if a session is canceled or when their therapists leave for vacation. These responses are similar to those that are evoked when the mother who is being ignored leaves, the "environmental mother," as Winnicott labeled her. When therapists understand why and how they are used, the pain of wounded narcissism is considerably alleviated. Bringing infantile traumas and conflicts into the transitional space permits the construction of an observational platform and the therapeutic process is set in motion. In turn, the psyche gains the capacity to construct a transitional space as the horrors of the grim infantile reality that have structured the current milieu are internalized. The process of internalization requires a space in which traumas can be internalized and contained. When this occurs in therapy, the transitional space is constructed so that patients can internalize. This is a developmental achievement as well as an aspect of the treatment interaction.

The therapeutic process can be conceptualized in terms of sweeping spatial metaphors. At first, both the therapist and the infantile trauma are kept in the external world. The latter creates the grim reality I have frequently referred to and that defines many of the patients suffering from character defects. The therapist is also relegated to the external world and often placed within the context of noxious elements that have to be projected.

At this point, there are, for the most part, only internal psychic worlds and external reality that is riddled with projections of the infantile past.

As the transitional space begins to form, therapists are internalized and made into transitional objects. They are not yet introjects, nor have they been incorporated into the psyche for adaptive purposes, as occurs during more mature developmental phases when potentially helpful experiences can be introjected and enhance psychic functioning. When these experiences are incorporated into the psyche, I have referred to them as internalized functional introjects (Giovacchini 1967) in that it is the function of the external object that is amalgamated as psychic structure.

As a transitional object, the therapist is neither within the psyche nor outside of it, but rather in an in-between space, the transitional space. Children treat transitional objects as if they are part of the self when they use them to be soothed. As the target of their aggressivity and anger, they abuse them as if they were in the external world. Whether the transitional object is perceived as internal or external depends on how it is used.

Being able to form and relate to transitional objects is a structuralizing experience and leads to developmental advances. Similarly, as patients make therapists into transitional objects, the transitional space is constructed and psychopathology is dealt with in that venue. As resolution occurs therapists again become part of the external world. Patients, however, can now relate to them as objects in their own right and are able to incorporate their therapeutic function as a functional introject.

The internalization of the therapist as a functional modality culminates in the formation of an *analytic introject*. I believe that with successful treatment, patients continue the therapeutic process through the activities of their analytic introjects. After completion of treatment, some patients have to return occasionally to their therapists in order to recathect the analytic introject. It may require reinforcement from time to time so that self-analysis can continue.

To summarize briefly, therapists may be defended against as threatening objects. Then they are internalized as transitional objects as patients develop a degree of trust fostered by the formation of the holding environment and the constant reliability of the therapeutic setting. This happens simultaneously with the transport of the grim infantile external world into the transitional space, the playful area of illusion. Finally, the view of reality is modified as the therapist again is brought back into the surrounding world.

This is a schematic spatial account of the therapeutic process that can vary considerably, depending on the infantile background of patients and specific types of psychopathology. The movement from outside to inside and then back to the outside seems to be a constant feature of the treatment of fairly disturbed patients suffering from structural and developmental defects.

In the next chapter, I demonstrate how this movement is also found in some literary masterpieces, works that have incorporated the treatment process as the basis of their story line. In literature there is an interplay of imagination and reality. Consequently, concepts about the impact of reality and the function of fantasy and illusion might be highlighted in a good literary work of art. I also point out how the author's narcissism is involved in the plot and how it contributes to creative accomplishment.

A patient whom I have described in many different contexts had a psychotic episode in which he felt I had been paid by the Mafia to pick his brains. He meant pick his brains in a literal fashion, that I was driving an ice pick into his skull and macerating his cerebrum. For some reason, the situation struck me as funny and I chuckled. He was surprised at my response, and I explained that "picking his brains" was part of my job description and then he suddenly understood what I meant. He recognized that I was referring to learning about how his mind works.

Literally picking his brain meant that I was trying to steal his ideas and kill him. This was part of a plot to destroy him fomented by the Mafia and CIA, clearly a paranoid delusion. Making it into a metaphor took such an action out of the grim paranoid world he had constructed and placed it in the playful transitional space in which I could chuckle about it, and when he understood my viewpoint, he was also amused.

From a belligerent, paranoid orientation he quickly changed his frame of mind to one that had an amused, playful quality. He started describing his bizarre psychotic behavior as if he were talking about a series of striking but comic events. His narcissism caused him to enjoy himself, because he thought what he was doing was clever and bold, which, to say the least, was bold inasmuch as he was apprehended by security running down an esplanade completely naked.

He had clearly placed himself in the transitional space and instead of feeling persecuted and terrified, he was looking at himself in my presence. We were both back on an observational platform where he could playfully acknowledge how psychotic he had been, but he could also examine what he was doing in terms of infantile transference feelings.

When he was outside the transitional space, he adapted to and defended himself against destructively angry feelings by using paranoid projections. Play and humor are important ingredients of the treatment process. The patient's grimness suddenly disappeared when, in a sense, I played with his paranoid ideation and transformed it into an adaptive and constructive metaphor. The atmosphere in the consultation changed completely into fun-loving congeniality.

A young black woman in her early twenties wanted counseling because she was a battered wife. When asked the number of sexual partners she had, she replied that she had lost count. Apparently before the age of 6 she had been violated by her brother, father, and an uncle. She was also constantly physically abused. Around the age of 15 her father "sold" her to a pimp who used her sexually as well as financially. Practically everyone she had known as a sexual partner had been sadistic, so it was not hard to comprehend that she would have a physically abusive marriage.

It was interesting to hear that she felt that she had been rescued from a psychosis because of her institutionalization at a residential center. She was brought there at the age of 8 because of her disruptive behavior, especially in school, and her constant agitation. She was given Ritalin and related drugs, but her condition continued worsening. It was finally concluded that she could not be contained in an outpatient setting.

It seemed that she resisted therapy because she refused to talk. The therapist, from his experience with her, might have concluded that she was mute, because she was not belligerent toward him. After some weeks, she seemed to be comfortably quiet, although her behavior outside treatment was as turbulent as ever.

The therapist, however, was not disheartened. He believed that she was accomplishing something important. In his opinion, the treatment was providing a setting in which she could comfortably withdraw. The therapist was a devotee of Winnicott and he formulated that the patient was illustrating the capacity to be alone in the presence of someone else (Winnicott 1958a,b).

After several months, she started talking about the horrors of her infantile experiences as if they were common everyday events. Clearly, that was the only world she knew and she thought all children had been raised the same way.

Her behavior on the ward also changed. She attached herself to one attendant in particular. The staff concluded that she had fused herself with this staff person, as evidenced by her need to be constantly with her, and she felt anxious when her new caregiver was out of sight. Her behavior, generally, was considerably less disruptive and her mood became less confused.

In one respect, she acted in a bizarre fashion. When certain male personnel, doctors and attendants, entered the room, she would whoop like an Indian warrior and then jump into their arms. It was as if she were rejoicing in having men around and available. The effect her actions had on the observers was to stimulate the sense of the comic. True, it was a peculiar type of impulsivity but even though the targets of her behavior were unprepared for her physical impact, they were more amused than surprised or threatened.

On other occasions, she would jump on a bed and thrust her hips up and down imitating a coital rhythm, smiling and giggling at the same time. Frequently, she extended her arms to a male member of the staff, inviting him to climb on top of her and engage in sexual relations.

In spite of the strangeness of this behavior, she seemed to be enjoying herself as she playfully indulged in her erotic fantasies. In view of the brutality and sexual assaults she had suffered, she could still at this young age contemplate a sexual relationship as an enjoyable and playful experience. She was able to move out of the traumatic infantile reality into another space that she could control by pretending to have sex, but in this transitional space, she was the aggressor and in control of the situation, as happens when the repetition compulsion is reenacted.

This is another example of an attempt to work out conflicts and resolve trauma by converting grim reality into playful fantasy. In this case, she pantomimed the sexual act to master the terror that was part of her experience. Her hospitalization was successful in that her behavior in general was much calmer and not disruptive. She was also able to interact verbally in her treatment, which, unfortunately, had to be discontinued when she was discharged from the residential treatment center.

Being a child, she had to return to the grim reality that she had, for a while, been able to leave when she succeeded in converting the ward into a transitional area of playful reenactment. As she grew up, sex dominated her life, forcing her to make a masochistic adjustment. It is hoped the counseling she is receiving will help her find a less threatening world. Perhaps the protection she is getting from the law will also be beneficial. Her husband is forbidden to go anywhere near her.

To briefly summarize, therapy requires the construction of an observational platform in which the self-observing function of both participants is enhanced. This observational frame of reference focuses especially on the interaction between patient and therapist in terms of both conscious and unconscious factors. This is simply a restatement of the importance of examining the transference–countertransference axis.

I do not believe there is any advantage in postulating supraordinate organizations such as the analytic third or the coalescence of intersubjective dyads creating entities that go beyond individual boundaries.

The observational frame of reference cannot exist outside the context of transitional phenomena and the construction of the transitional space, which is both a developmental achievement and the venue of the curative factors of the treatment process. Within this space, there is a blend of subjective manipulations, and finally the acknowledgment of the self and external objects.

The activities going on within this transitional space, that is, the creation of illusion and playful fantasy, in particular, strengthen the intrapsychic focus and create a degree of psychological mindedness that enhance the therapeutic process. The distinctions between the inner and outer world are sharpened, although the capacity for creative fusion is also enhanced. The awareness of external objects is increased and knowledge about the self is expanded.

Knowledge of the self eventually leads to the establishment of an autonomous and valued self representation. To achieve such optimal resolution requires that therapists allow themselves to be used as transitional objects, reviled and abused, cast aside and thrown around as patients have been, but, nevertheless, therapists are indispensable in their capacity to soothe and offer solace.

Degrees of Narcissism and Creativity

As we have seen, narcissism can be beneficial as well as detrimental to the treatment process. At times, a good analysis can be compared to a creative achievement, as the analytic process and creativity are somewhat similar. Thus, there may be important connections between narcissism and creativity.

The expression of grandiosity by creative people is not offensive. In fact, the listener often identifies with what might appear to be boasting and feels enhanced rather than offended, as usually happens in response to ordinary arrogance. I believe that truly creative persons are narcissistic but their narcissism is a variety that can be labeled *humble narcissism.*

The therapeutic process focuses on the unconscious and primitive feelings and modes of thinking. In creativity, there is a blend of primary and secondary process (Giovacchini 1960, 1993). In structural terms, early developmental levels and ego states are operating simultaneously.

In the previous chapter, I discussed something similar occurring in therapy. On the observational platform, higher levels of cognition are operating with and examining earlier types of relating and communicating. Creativity is associated with a novel product or discovery of something that was previously unknown. In therapy, patients make discoveries about themselves that lead to the acquisition of psychic structure and novel modes of relating to the world. This can be considered the consequences of a creative endeavor.

THE THERAPEUTIC JOURNEY

The therapeutic process as well as endeavors to progress scientifically can be viewed as journeys of discovery. Frequently the course of analysis is depicted in dreams as a trip, often in automobiles, ships, and other vehicles of transportation. The driver or pilot usually represents the analyst and the passenger is the patient who is frequently in a passive relationship to the therapist and is being led around. Anxiety about the therapeutic process is frequently depicted in such dreams, patients being afraid of their passivity and the power they have attributed to their therapists.

A patient, a middle-aged woman, compared analysis to riding in a taxi. The passenger paid the driver for performing a function that could go beyond just transportation. If the passenger wanted to talk, she could say practically anything she pleased, because the driver did not fit, in any way, into her reality. What occurs in the cab is separated from the real world, and whatever personal impressions the driver might have would be essentially irrelevant to the practical welfare of the passenger.

Often the reverse happens—the cab driver does most of the talking and unloads himself on the passenger. I understand that this also happens frequently enough in therapy.

I felt that my patient's comparison of treatment with a cab drive was clever and creative. Good metaphors are the products of creative activity. She had been able to conceptualize the treatment relationship as being relatively safe, and, to a large extent, under her control.

Transportation dreams almost invariably raise questions of autonomy. Therapists threaten some patients at the same time they are trying to help them construct a cohesive and autonomous self representation. To many patients this can mean being made over and being cast in the therapist's image. Instead of achieving autonomy, many patients fear that they are being swallowed and submerged in the treatment process. Freud (1923) referred to this situation as the negative therapeutic reaction, in which the patient feels vulnerable to the powerful therapist.

Most of the patients I have discussed have problems relating to both the inner world of their psyche and the outer world of their current reality. As the patient establishes autonomy and gains self-esteem, both these worlds become less threatening. Self-knowledge creates a sense of stability in the same way that creative discovery leads to greater mastery of the forces of nature. Thus, the creative process and the intrapsychic focus of psychotherapy have many similarities.

The narcissistic gratification that is gained from creative accomplishment and therapy that seems to be going in the right direction (again an allusion to a journey) may lead to or impede further accomplishment. Increasing degrees of narcissistic gratification in therapy may stimulate the negative therapeutic reaction because, as the therapist feels enhanced, the patient may feel diminished. This often represents a repetition of the patient's position in the infantile environment.

The patient who created the metaphor of the taxi ride reported a dream in which she was riding in a taxi. In the dream, the patient is in a dangerous area. She is able to find a taxi and is safely removed from this threatening place. To the patient's dismay, the driver suggests that they go somewhere and have a drink. She somehow eludes him. She now finds that the cab driver wants a date. Her husband insists that she stay in the protective confines of their apartment and not go out.

Her first association to the dream was to equate the taxi driver with me. She was mildly surprised because she firmly believed that our relationship, though friendly, was strictly professional. In no way could she see me stepping out of the boundaries of the treatment relationship and suggesting that we move into another frame of reference. She would have expected that the taxi driver would have let her talk and would have taken her to her destination without suggesting a stop at a tavern on the way.

Her husband telling her not to go out represented his wish fulfillment because he was threatened by her increasing independence. He wanted her to remain an as-if character (Deutsch 1942), as she and a former therapist had described her. It also partially represented a wish fulfillment of her own because she also feared becoming a whole person. Being separate would bring her in conflict with her mother and husband, and in the transference she believed that I wanted her to fuse with me and make her part of myself.

This conflict about structuring an authentic self, something that she had already achieved to a considerable degree, manifested itself in the transference in her belief that she felt I was trying to get her to have my thoughts. She referred to the story of the robin swallowing the worm. As the worm is being swallowed it begins to think as a robin does by saying to itself, "Well, robins must eat."

The patient was well aware of the fact that I was not forcing her to fuse with me, although there is considerable evidence that her previous therapist was intruding certain parts of himself and his perspectives into her—oddly enough, perspectives about fusion and being psychically swallowed up.

NARCISSISTIC NEED TO CREATE STRUCTURE

My patient was experiencing a paradox in that the curative factor of structuring a self representation meant that she had to be swallowed in a fusion state. The cab driver was also sabotaging the treatment by trying to convert it into an erotic union. Part of her feelings were reactions to her first course of treatment with an analyst who was depressed and who also needed to fuse with her. He suffered from low self-esteem and guilt. Fusing with certain patients added to his depleted narcissistic supplies. He had to repair his patients in a Pygmalion fashion, but his attempts caused patients, and especially my patient, to feel as if she were being submerged by the treatment, a feeling she more completely discovered in her second course of treatment.

Clearly, the first therapist's need to create a person, that is, to structuralize an as-if amorphous personality into a whole person, was based on his need to regain parts of himself and to restore a narcissistic balance.

The first therapist had asked the patient early in the treatment to read a Chekhov short story, "The Darling," about a successful as-if personality. The heroine of the story was a perennial widow, but with each marriage she was able to adapt and help her husband in his work, although they were in widely different vocations or professions. The protagonist's capacity to identify with her husband's occupation caused the therapist to label her an as-if personality whose object relations were based on fusion states.

The patient objected because, unlike the heroine of the short story, she did not feel happy about being an as-if personality. She constantly felt humiliated and lamented her unformed identity, which made me suspicious of the initial diagnosis of an as-if personality.

She was too concerned about the lack of an identity, something that would not be expected in a true as-if character configuration, which Chekhov seemed to intuitively understand. Presumably there would not be enough structure to be aware of her amorphous state. She did not, however, voice her conflicted feelings.

I finally concluded that she was a pseudo–as-if character who had to keep her potential true self buried. As others fused with her, she would feel as if she were swallowed up in the manner that the worm accepted the robin's viewpoint, but she was not comfortable with her response. To survive, she learned to accept a state of not being acknowledged, which, at the deeper level, meant a state of nonexistence. She once stated that if God did not recognize her, then she did not exist. Though this was an adaptation, she was not able to accept·it and maintain a narcissistic balance.

Some analysts believe that the goal of analysis is to create a personality, to gain psychic structure de novo. This is, of course, the antithesis of the aims of classical analysis, which is concerned with what might be considered a rearrangement of the psyche. The basic organization of the mind remains intact, and developmental problems, structural defects, and the vulnerability of the self representation are not viable issues. Rather, the treatment is concerned with intrapsychic conflicts that have to be resolved so that patients can deal with the vicissitudes of the oedipal past.

The construction of a new personality could be an aim for patients suffering from primitive mental states with primarily structural problems rather than psychodynamic conflicts. It could certainly be a goal for as-if characters who adapted to a variety of false selves depending on with whom they are relating.

Creating a personality de novo is not really the goal of any therapy. Such treatment would have to create a virtual reality based on grandiosity and dominated by the therapist's narcissistic needs. If patients were so amorphous, unstructured, and unaware of themselves as discrete entities, it is doubtful that they would ever seek treatment and understand the operations or purpose of the therapeutic process.

My patient certainly had a true self but she had trouble bringing it into her sphere of awareness because of specific problems inherent in the infantile environment that are not particularly relevant to this discussion. She was aware of her first therapist's narcissistic needs and ambivalence. On the one hand, he wanted to "remake" her, a need he had toward some other patients as well, which I knew about. On the other hand, he also clung to conservative beliefs about treatment based on the patient's structural integrity. Regarding the latter, he sometimes lamented to the patient that he never should have accepted her for treatment in the first place.

The patient soon realized that the two of them had fused with each other, which later was experienced as destructive, because, apparently, the therapist absorbed the patient as the robin did the worm, enhancing himself and depleting the patient. However, this was not absolute and not entirely unidirectional. The patient gained sharper concepts about her feelings and beliefs and less of a need to intrude herself into her therapist's psychic space, which probably was what he was complaining about when he said he should not have accepted her as a patient in the first place. The patient was sufficiently able, at times, to achieve separation from the fusion and gain some boundaries. She was then able to state that she had now become the patient he would have wanted.

This did not mean he had reconstructed her in his own image. She had found parts of herself that were always there, at least potentially, but that had been submerged for defensive and adaptive purposes. It was because of this inner potential that I believe she was a pseudo–as-if character rather than an as-if character. The as-if qualities were on the surface, covering a formative true self, whereas in an as-if character there is no inner core; the self representation is all as-if. Therapists, according to their narcissistic needs, are either attracted or threatened by patients who have severe identity problems.

The analytic process has, at times, been compared to a creative endeavor, both of discovery and the creation of something new. The novel product would be the patient's new persona. This creation of a new person is frequently found in literature, such as Frankenstein's monster and Pygmalion's Galatea. The latter is the subject of a myth and of George Bernard Shaw's play *Pygmalion*.

PSYCHIC BIRTH AND NARCISSISTIC INVOLVEMENT: SHAW'S PLAYS

In analytic treatment, a new person is not created, but at times it may seem that there has been the birth of a personality. I will equate the extent of narcissism involved in the creative or therapeutic process with how much the newly created character is new, in contrast to how much of the made-over personality is simply a modification or revision of what had already been there. The latter is a more frequent situation in successful psychotherapeutic treatment.

Pygmalion

Many novels and plays can be interpreted as allegories of a psychotherapeutic journey. This is especially true of some of Shaw's works if treatment is viewed in terms of a structural progression or the acquisition of psychic structure. In *Pygmalion*, the relationship between Professor Henry Higgins and his ward and student Eliza is similar to one between therapist and patient. In the myth of Pygmalion, the artist Pygmalion, who is King of Cyprus, sculpts a statue of a beautiful woman and falls in love with his creation. He asks Aphrodite to give her life, which she does, and he marries her. This has an incestuous ring.

In *Pygmalion* and in the musical *My Fair Lady*, which is based on it, creativity is not as extensive as in the myth. Pygmalion had to create de novo when he conceived of and produced the statue of Galatea. There was no previous woman. She had to be created from scratch, so to speak. In fact, the final act of creation had to come from the heavens, as life was conferred to the statue by a goddess. Thus, the creation of life is the ultimate act of creating.

Artistic products to a large measure are externalizations of various parts of the creator's personality. The artist's personality in various guises is embedded in his works, and creative activity enhances narcissism. In Greek myths the externalization of the self is a narcissistic experience. Pygmalion had a statue brought to life because he had fallen in love with it, obviously a self-love expressed in erotic terms because he married his creative product. It is fitting that Aphrodite was the goddess chosen to make a statue into an erotic partner, which in the case of Pygmalion was a narcissistic object choice. The other famous myth of falling in love with what has been externalized, is, of course, the myth of Narcissus as he falls in love with a reflection of his image.

In Shaw's play, Professor Higgins takes a waif, a girl who sells flowers, into his house to prove to his colleague that he can improve her speech and comportment so that no one will be able to detect her humble cockney origin. He boasts that he will move her out of the poor, tumultuous world she was born in and make her into a new person.

Higgins is superbly self-confident, bordering on arrogant and smacking of grandiosity. His narcissism is obvious and his derogatory view of women, as evidenced by the way he verbally attacks Eliza, could be quite offensive. However, the reader or the audience is usually amused rather than offended.

I have postulated that the creative person exhibits a form of narcissism that I called humble narcissism but Higgins's orientation is somewhat puzzling. He is aggressive and insulting, which would make the adjective *humble* inappropriate. In *My Fair Lady* he excludes women from his life when he sings about the misery they cause men and laments the fact that they cannot be more like men. Both the play and especially the musical were extremely successful, and even feminists seemed to like them, although many of them are not particularly fond of Shaw.

In spite of Shaw's obvious misogyny, many women are impressed more by his wit than his sentiments, and Alan Jay Lerner's lyrics and dialogue in the musical are also typically Shavian—witty, ironic, and given to hyperbole. The hyperbole is often so well developed that it may be momentarily shocking, but it is experienced as caricature.

Higgins, as Pygmalion, wanted to create a new person. Though Eliza existed before Higgins met her, his intention was to create a new woman who had no connection to the world she came from or resemblance to the person he initially brought into his house. This would be a tremendous narcissistic achievement.

Pygmalion marries his creation, which has incestuous implications and certainly puts him in the position of a father. Galatea is also an extension of himself. She is a narcissistic object choice and a reflection of his projected narcissism.

In the play, the outcome is different, and controversial. Higgins's reaction to his creativity seems to be similar to the attitudes many creative scientists have (Giovacchini 1960, 1993). They seem to have lost interest in what they have created once they are finished with it. They still care about it, but not with the same fierce enthusiasm they once had or, to state it differently, with the same narcissistic investment. This seems to have been Higgins's position regarding Eliza's future.

Higgins created a person who fit in his world, the world of the aristocracy and the rich. She cannot go back to the world she came from because she is an entirely new person. She simply would not fit, now that she had been reborn.

Higgins tampered with the course of emotional development. By teaching her to speak like a lady, he was furnishing her with adaptive techniques that were appropriate to a certain segment of the current adult milieu, but not to the world of the flower girl. A good narcissistic balance depends on how well the techniques of perception and adaptation acquired in the infantile milieu operate in the current adult environment a person has to live in. I call this process externalization, in which defenses and adaptive techniques learned during childhood lead to the seeking and constructing of a reality that is synchronous with such adaptations.

Eliza was not an entirely new creation, because even during what might be called a period of indoctrination, she retained a vestige of individuality by fighting back. She resisted some of Higgins's outrageous demands and took umbrage at his insults. She was far from being an as-if personality and as the worm had robin's thoughts, she was not completely overwhelmed by Higgins's thoughts. Higgins was narcissistically offended at Eliza's rebellious attempts to maintain some level of self-esteem. In the myth this struggle did not exist and the narcissism associated with the creative act flowed only in one direction, since the product, Galatea, being created de novo, had no background, that is, no infantile environment to interfere with the creative process. Pygmalion worked with an unformed piece of stone, an amorphous mass, whereas Higgins had to undo an already existing personality before he could build something new.

Shaw had a problem in deciding what to do with Eliza now that she had gained a new autonomy. While she could not go back to the world she came from, she did not fit in Higgins's aristocratic world. She did not have the background even though she now had the personality that would fit in upper-class society.

In *My Fair Lady*, Lerner avoided the problem. Eliza remained in the Higgins's household in a servile position. This would be an incompatible situation for a person who has achieved a new, more expansive, autonomy.

Shaw understood that Eliza could not remain with Higgins because of the incompatibility of their personalities, which would have resulted in a clash for narcissistic dominance on Higgins's part, struggling with Eliza's attempt for narcissistic survival.

Galatea had no such problem regarding distributions of narcissism. Pygmalion was able to let Galatea enter his narcissistic sphere. The sculptor had been able to go beyond his own boundaries and create a dyad, which I assume was mutually rewarding as the relationship established a narcissistic balance that in turn strengthened the bond between Pygmalion and Galatea.

Because Eliza existed as a person before she was created, the problem Shaw faced is somewhat more complicated and perhaps there cannot be a satisfactory solution (see Vesonder 1977, Weissman 1958). In the play, Eliza moves out of the household and marries Freddy, a good natured but inadequate young man. She is also set up in a boutique by Colonel Pickering, Higgins's friend and colleague.

Galatea did not go into the external world, separate herself from Pygmalion, and establish her autonomy. Eliza, because it was part of her development, had to maintain her autonomy, so she had to move away from Higgins and establish herself in the external world. Otherwise, she would have been simply an extension of Higgins. Galatea was able to establish herself as an extension of Pygmalion. Although she was of the opposite sex, she was, in essence, his clone. This can be better expressed by stating that she was a clone of the feminine parts of Pygmalion.

I believe that the discussion of Shaw's play and the short myth of Pygmalion and Galatea highlight that the creative process involves enormous narcissistic shifts. These works of literature also indicate that there are similarities between therapy and the events depicted by Shaw, which deal with narcissistic problems as they might emerge in the countertransference.

In a long, eventful analysis, therapists and patients may establish exceptionally strong bonds that may interfere with the termination of therapy. I do not recall many cases in which made-over patients cannot find a niche that can accommodate their greater autonomy. I recall many therapies, however, in which therapists were unwilling to let their patients leave and be independent of the treatment interaction. In one instance, it became apparent that the therapist was jealous of his patient's new lover, a relationship that in itself was the outcome of therapeutic resolution. In the musical and in the 1938 film of *Pygmalion*, Eliza remains with Higgins, as would occur in interminable therapy, but Shaw's approach was more sensitive and subtle in that he recognized that the ending of the relationship between Eliza and Higgins represents a problem that is difficult to solve.

Levine (1997a) states, "The story of Pygmalion has enormous potential both as an elaboration of our understanding of narcissism in development, and, more immediately, as a parable for the psychoanalytic process itself" (p. 3). Unlike Silvio (1977) and Weissman (1958), Levine does not concentrate on Shaw's infantile neurosis to explain his plots. Rather, she examines the interactions of the characters in the film *Pygmalion* to enhance our understanding of psychological processes that clinicians frequently encounter in the therapeutic process.

A careful reading of works of literature will give us some insights about the authors' personalities, including their biases as well as the visions that are characteristics of their ego ideals. In addition, some knowledge about their childhoods and significant events in their lives will help us understand the implications of their oeuvres in greater depth.

Instead of being primarily concerned with the personality of the author, as occurs in psychobiographies, I am more interested in how processes involved in therapy and creativity can be explained in some of Shaw's writings. I believe his plays help us understand rather subtle interactions in a context that is made enjoyable by his wit and humor. His degradation of women in *Pygmalion* was made palatable by his shrewdness and sophistication. He appeals to our aesthetic sense as well as our need to expand our clinical dimensions.

To generalize, many artistic and scientific works are created by people of integrity and sensitivity. Shaw appeals to the sense of the aesthetic as well as to unconscious orientations. He was able to bring various feelings and attitudes to the surface that are in resonance with the audience's unconscious, and what he writes, though it may be disputed at a reality level, has validity in terms of intrapsychic processes. This ability may be an intrinsic quality of a truly creative person.

I believe that Shaw's caustic wit and ideas that may have been offensive to a fin-de-siècle culture were later accepted because of cultural shifts and changes that were accelerated by the First World War.

He did not shock his audience as he might have intended or directly assault their narcissism, because the surrounding culture met him halfway.

In Britain, the late nineteenth and early twentieth century society was fairly stable, conservative, and static. For the most part, people were resistant to change and intolerant of ideas that threatened to shake their fundamental beliefs and traditions. There were niches for almost everyone, a stratification of society in contrast to our present period. There was a certain security in that culture, but there was also a static rigidity that kept people in their place. What Higgins accomplished in *Pygmalion* would have been most unlikely in real life.

It was a culture, however, that was beginning to engage in self-scrutiny, and to show some signs of rebellion and restlessness. Shaw's culture had many repressive elements, but there were movements that might be considered to belong in the realm of the "return of the repressed." Shaw's shocking pronouncements, such as punishing victims rather than the criminals who assaulted them, his outrageous stance against doctors, and many other satires that were direct assaults against traditional, unquestioned beliefs, were often accepted as amusing rather than offensive. His attitudes frequently were the direct antithesis of Victorian morality. Still, this morality was crumbling, and Shaw was riding on top of the wave of the liberation of the repressed.

Because of cultural changes, Shaw lived in an era that found his plays fascinating and that was also eventually favorable to psychoanalysis. This is in contrast to the modern era, which, as discussed in Chapter 1, moves away from the intrapsychic focus.

Besides the receptivity of his culture, his literary genius and skillful, deceptive wit were certainly involved in the positive responses of his readers in spite of their prejudices. His penetrating perceptiveness undoubtedly pierced some of his readers' defenses, and yet somehow left them amused instead of anxious. This is the function of wit and humor, and many truths that would otherwise be unacceptable and rejected can be clothed in a joke (Freud 1905b). Shaw's style was based on a very enormous talent in communicating through humor, satire, and wit.

Undoubtedly, Shaw knew how to deal with both his and his audience's narcissism, which, in some of his plays, such as *Pygmalion*, was displayed in the remaking of a person or a personality. Many of Shaw's plots consist of a teacher and a student, although they may not appear as directly as they did in *Pygmalion*. His preoccupation with creating a new person, which, in a sense, was a concretization and a metaphor for the creative act, also had an appeal for many of his readers. The creative process has an inherent appeal for many sensitive, potentially creative persons (Giovacchini 1960, 1993). I have noted at many conferences that papers and symposia on creativity attract the largest audiences. Since Shaw was indirectly writing about the creative process, I believe he attracted a wide audience similar to those at psychoanalytic meetings.

Demonstrating his creativity enhanced Shaw's narcissism and also elevated the audience's narcissism. This is, in itself, an achievement, because attempts to enhance narcissism often take place at the expense of others. The narcissist needs to step on someone; to demean another person, institution, or ideology; to strengthen a feeble self representation, emphasizing the pejorative aspects of narcissism. By contrast, creative narcissists are humble narcissists and the audience can identify with them rather than feel overwhelmed by grandiosity and arrogance. In these instances writing about their own creativity and the creative process is, in itself, a creative act.

Major Barbara

In *Major Barbara*, Shaw again writes about the creation of a new personality, a process that resonates with the findings of psychoanalysis. I place *Major Barbara* in the middle of a continuum, with *Pygmalion* at one end and *Caesar and Cleopatra* at the other. I have selected this sequence because I believe that within the context of the play, there are varying degrees of narcissism. In *Pygmalion*, there is an almost complete re-creation of a personality, whereas in *Major Barbara*, Barbara modifies certain defensive patterns, alters her outlook, and is to some degree a remade person but not anywhere to the extent of the rebirth of Eliza. In *Caesar and Cleopatra,* there are extensions to Cleopatra's personality that are defined by executive functions and adaptations.

In terms of gradations of narcissism, the protagonist's narcissistic achievement is the greatest in Henry Higgins's creating of the "fair lady," intermediate in Undershaft's influence on Barbara, and the least in Caesar's tutelage of Cleopatra.

Since, in *Major Barbara,* I will be making comparisons of how Undershaft, Barbara's father, deals with his daughter and what might occur in an analytic session, I have to raise the question of whether the play is psychologically plausible. I stressed that the remaking of Eliza could also be viewed as a therapeutic experience, but I was not trying to make direct connections between the course of treatment and the course of elocution that Eliza was subjected to.

I believe that in *Major Barbara* the relation between father and daughter is in tune with reality and that most of the characters are real and not synthetically constructed. In *Major Barbara* specifically, I conclude that the relationship is realistic because it can be interpreted from a psychoanalytic perspective, and here I believe Shaw is demonstrating his intuitive grasp of human nature and psychodynamic connections.

Ordinarily, it is not important whether the characters are realistically constructed. Many basic psychoanalytic truths have been uncovered in works where the characters or situations have no counterparts in reality and the plot is highly elaborated or impossible, as, for example, in myths or fairy tales. Shaw also had a talent for converting a fairy tale or myth and finding a home for it in the world of reality, although, at times, he could also convert reality into a fairy tale, as occurred at the felicitous ending of *Major Barbara.*

I place *Major Barbara* next to *Pygmalion* on the continuum of how completely the protagonist is made over. This is dependent on the degree of restructuring of the self representation and the amount of narcissistic investment the teacher or father has in his endeavors to create a new person. In *Major Barbara,* the father, who owns an immensely successful munitions empire, is able to persuade Barbara to accept his lifestyle and live according to his standards. Although Shaw was somewhat ambivalent about psychoanalytic processes and had very little conscious knowledge of them, he is guided by psycho-analytic principles in the father's quest to change his daughter, an experience that will enhance Barbara's autonomy. Undershaft's tech-nique and mode of communication is very similar to an interpreta-tion. Obviously, Undershaft is proud of his achievement and derives considerable narcissistic pleasure in giving Barbara what he consid-ers to be a better balanced and healthier viewpoint, but, I conjec-ture, not as much as Pygmalion or Professor Henry Higgins.

In *Major Barbara*, the interaction between Barbara and her father can be viewed similarly to a treatment interaction. As is his custom, Shaw begins his play with a rather lengthy preface in which he ex-pounds his viewpoint. He is particularly concerned with morality and considers all the usual and standard virtues, such as family unity, re-ligion, peace, temperance, charity, and love of God, to be vices. Still, his arguments are clever and witty, and he does not appear irresolute in his attitudes. He is being pointedly blasphemous and irreverent.

In his irreverence he is leading to a point about the essence of morality which is, to put it simply, a straightforward belief in hon-esty, in uncompromising sincerity, with the ability to look inward and outward without self-delusion.

The main character in the play is Barbara's father, who embodies and personifies Shaw's ideology. Shaw (1941) states, "in Undershaft, I have represented a man who has become intellectually and spiritu-ally as well as practically conscious of the irresistible natural truth which we all abhor and repudiate" (p. 305). The natural truth is not in itself necessarily good, but to avoid it is hypocrisy and rank idiocy according to Shaw.

This attitude about the natural truth fits well with the credo of the principles of psychoanalysis, and I suspect that many clinicians would find the subject matter and characters in Shaw's play engaging.

Undershaft was charitable but in a unique way. He did not give to the weak and vulnerable and he did not believe in charity for its own sake. He expected achievement for what he gave. Analysts have similar expectations, but they are not overtly expressed. Rather, they are intrinsic expectations based on faith in patients' developmental potentials and their capacity to achieve autonomy and find their true selves. In many clinical instances, this attitude must remain implicit because the patient does not yet have a sufficient degree of psychic structure to be able to integrate it into the ego's executive system.

Barbara, on the other hand, initially believed in charity for its own sake and pursued her mission in the Salvation Army zealously. The play represents a struggle between Barbara, who has a well-defined ideology based on faith and altruism, seeking good in the weak and helpless, and her father, who is the devil's advocate.

Barbara's ideology is firmly entrenched and is the fundamental basis of her sense of identity. Undershaft will make inroads on the surface elements of her self representation, but these are modifications, and Barbara's core personality remains intact and is basically similar to that of her father. They are not afraid of the natural truth, and are unencumbered by hypocrisy, duplicity, or an unswerving conformity to their culture. Barbara's outlook is more in tune with the times, but she is highly individualistic, dedicated, and uncompromising. The play, in essence, is built around the differences and similarities between Barbara and her father and their struggle with each other.

There are various layers and stratifications to the identity sense, as has been frequently discussed. In general, Barbara, at the deepest layers of her self representation, has the same ideologies for the welfare of the world as does her father. She differs from him, however, as to how good can be accomplished. He abhors poverty, whereas she wants to work through it with sympathy and understanding, but their weltanschaaungs are similar. Only the surface levels of their self representations are different.

Barbara and her father have reached an agreement near the beginning of the play. She challenges him to come and observe her work at the mission, with the purpose of winning him over to her viewpoint. She emphasizes the universality of charity by telling him all he needs to do is ask anyone on Westham Street and they will direct him to the sign of the cross under which the mission is located. He responds in kind to her challenge by accepting it, provided she will return the visit by coming to his factory. Similarly, he also tells her in a grandiose fashion to ask anyone in Europe and they will direct her to the sign of the sword. It is apparent that they both have strong narcissistic investments in their work but not to the exclusion of accepting the challenge of looking at reality from a broader perspective. They agree to keep an open mind and examine the other's domain fairly.

In Barbara, Shaw creates a character who is willing to look at herself and her world unflinchingly, again qualities that make good analysands, as Levine (1997b) has noted. Levine also points out that Undershaft attaches himself to persons who have potential and energy even if they are not achievers when he meets them. He cultivates Barbara's fiancé who is just a poor, impractical Greek scholar, but who has a fierce determination to have Barbara. He is a philosopher with a keen sense of humor. Again, this type of personality makes for good analytic patients.

By contrast, Undershaft has no feelings for his son, who is a caricature of the indolent Englishman. His son admittedly cannot see himself in any profession and has no capacity for the arts, and yet he still maintains the pretension that he knows the difference between right and wrong, a claim that Undershaft finds astonishing because this has been a question that has baffled scholars and philosophers throughout the course of history.

Undershaft's son is different from Barbara, who is interested in the souls of men and women and the world they live in. Her brother lacks energy, insight, and interest, and rests his laurels on clichés, as might be typical of concretely oriented, mechanistic characters who are not good candidates for psychodynamically oriented therapy that focuses on intrapsychic processes. His narcissism is the extreme antithesis of humble narcissism, because it is all pretension and has no substance.

Undershaft is attracted to his daughter, the good potential patient, and dismisses his son with witticisms that suggest that since the son has no adeptness for anything and has no interest in the arts or sciences, he would make an excellent politician.

Undershaft visits the mission and observes how Barbara manages to subdue an angry, violent man by making him feel guilty. She is not aware of inducing guilt. Rather, she believes that she has shown him the error of his ways, but Undershaft knows better. He knows that the provocation of guilt does not have any lasting effects, an important clinical insight, but he does not argue with Barbara. As a good therapist, he waits until Barbara has become more receptive and vulnerable, a state of mind that often occurs in a therapeutic regression.

While at the mission, he engages some of the people in conversation and banters back and forth with them. The dialogue is typically Shavian and clothed in wit. For example, an elderly, somewhat pious man rebukes him by stating, "I wouldn't have your conscience for all your money." Undershaft, who views poverty as a disease, perhaps as a form of psychopathology, retorts, "I wouldn't have your money for all your conscience." This is a particularly effective use of the mechanism of reversal that not only changes meaning but makes an effective point. Undershaft is also pointing out that a strong conscience may be a liability, especially if it is at odds with dealing with the exigencies of reality.

In terms of current therapeutic exchanges, this interaction could be viewed as a transference–countertransference encounter in which the therapist maintains his narcissistic balance while primitive angry feelings are directed toward him, and implicitly telling the patient that it is more of a virtue to be rich than poor. If this elderly man had been a patient, he would have been told that his orientation was self-defeating and self-destructive, and a response to a harsh superego. Undershaft could respond to him because his superego was in synchrony with the external world and he could use it to make money and be successful. His self-esteem was sufficiently established and was enhanced rather than compromised by his wealth.

Shaw was able in this pithy exchange to describe rather involved technical treatment processes, which he was able to expand further in his next communication. Undershaft is asked what is his religion.

He calmly, but emphatically, replies, "I am a millionaire, that is my religion," bringing together apparently incompatible frames of reference. He is also indicating that he is fulfilling his ego-ideal and feels comfortable in the world he lives in.

Undershaft is not a man without scruples, and he is not at odds with the surrounding world. On the contrary, he is happy with the world he has created, the community that surrounds his munitions empire. His wife says that she finds her husband infuriating because he preaches immorality but practices morality. Undershaft does not believe that his viewpoints are either wrong or impractical. His treatment of poverty as if it were pathological is in cadence with his quest for independent initiative and ultimately autonomy.

The Salvation Army is in financial straits and needs help desperately. Barbara's superior immediately plays up to the multimillionaire, Undershaft, and entices him into contributing a large sum of money. She mentions that Blodgett, the owner of a huge whiskey empire, is also going to make a large contribution. Barbara is horrified that the Salvation Army will accept money from an institution that manufactures the ingredient that has led so many of its clients to ruin. She further resents that her father, a dealer in war, should also be approached and fawned upon.

Undershaft is aware that his daughter is becoming upset as he allows himself to be maneuvered into giving the Salvation Army a check. As he gives the check to Barbara's superior, she exclaims, "Thank God." Undershaft, the relentless realist, and perhaps because he wanted to keep matters focused on himself, as occurs in the transference, retorts, "You don't thank me?" This series of events causes Barbara to be disillusioned. At this point Undershaft finds her more pliable and he talks convincingly about his viewpoint.

I believe that Barbara had, to some extent, regressed as she became disillusioned. The usual confident, self-assured person became uncertain of her stance. Her narcissistic containment had been threatened, and she might have felt somewhat needy. At this juncture, a psychologically minded person might become more receptive, although initially she would show some signs of resistance (Kris 1950).

As would be expected, Barbara is, at first, angry at her father, a reaction similar to those analysands who have been forced to recognize the untenability of their defensive position. She reviles her father because his giving money to the Salvation Army has caused one of her converts at the shelter to return to drunkenness, as his belligerence and anger about his miserable condition emerged once again. She says, "I could forgive you if my forgiveness would open the gates of heaven to you. But to take a human soul from me, and turn it into the soul of a wolf. That is worse than murder." Actually, the person she was referring to was an impulsive, instinct-ridden person, who, under Barbara's tutelage, was beginning to control his acting out.

Undershaft, however, feels that an emotionally meaningful experience is not so fleeting in its effect, so he replies, "Does my daughter despair so easily? Can you strike a man to the heart and leave no mark on him?" He recognizes that Barbara's sincerity had succeeded in creating what clinicians could refer to as a holding environment and this could not be completely destroyed by disillusionment. There would be some lasting character changes.

Barbara momentarily feels better as her father's comment restores some of her self-esteem. Her self representation remains intact, but deep down her soul is troubled. She is depressed. She feels empty and lost, but is beginning to be aware of her father's wisdom. She replies, "You may be a devil but God speaks through you sometimes." I believe this statement indicates that Barbara's unconscious idealization of her father is emerging and makes her more amenable to his ideology.

Undershaft directs his next remark to his daughter's state of mind. After she admits how empty she feels, he says, "You have learnt something, that always feels at first as if you have lost something." The removal of a defense or the loss of a defensive position, at first, creates a vacuum, a state of suspension preceding the integration of the newly acquired insight. Undershaft's reply to Barbara, is, in itself, an interpretation that paves the way for Barbara's altered view of reality and the acceptance of her father's beliefs that power and wealth are not really evils.

Undershaft succeeds in winning Barbara over and showing her that her "faith" and her devotion to the Salvation Army are not reality oriented or particularly effective for helping mankind. At first, he shakes her by directly confronting her with certain corruptible features in an organization that she thought was incorruptible. There is considerable verbal exchange, which serves to loosen up and cut through her rigid orientations. The next step is the actual demonstration, the pragmatic application of his principles, by showing her how much good can result from such a titanic enterprise as his.

The content of Undershaft's ideology is not particularly important for this study. It is somewhat simplistic and the play has the happy ending of a fairy tale. Rather than dealing with the substance of the play, I wish to focus on the psychodynamic processes that characterize the interaction between Major Barbara and Undershaft, which invite a comparison to the analytic process.

Their interaction is patterned after the interpretative process. Undershaft, similar to the therapist, encourages Barbara to look at her attitudes. He leads her to examine them, and by so doing makes inconsistencies apparent. What was previously accepted by her without question she now sees as not altogether rational. Her reactions were part of a defensive system that replaced part of her reality.

To be made aware of the defensive nature of her feelings threatened her psychic stability. Her father had disrupted her tranquillity at the mission and she felt angry at him. The anger is often rationalized and projected. Barbara blames Undershaft for having ruined the life of one of her wards. Possibly this rationalization covers up Barbara's apprehension that her beliefs are being ruined and she displaces her attention to the unruly man whose impulses were being controlled by the guilt she generated in him.

I am conjecturing in psychodynamic terms about a series of events occurring within the context of an interpersonal relationship. What I have described could have easily happened in a well-conducted therapy emphasizing the intrapsychic focus.

To briefly summarize, Undershaft wishes to induce a character change in his daughter so that she will accept his weltanschauung.

He uses money rather than words to show her that she had falsely idealized poverty and charity. By explaining her reactions as the consequence of newly found insights, this explanation, in essence, being itself an interpretation, she shifts her idealization to her father.

The flow of behavior can be formulated in technical terms as first resistance, then rationalization, denial, and displacement, and finally an awareness of a moving emotional experience as she begins to accept her father's world. The insight Undershaft provided caused Barbara to feel sad and empty, a frequent response to a correct interpretation in the context of treatment. Undershaft, therefore, followed the principles of good analytic technique, but just as important is the fact that Shaw somehow recognized the precise steps that a person must go through to effectively communicate, as occurs in the therapeutic setting.

In the analytic setting, the positive transference is usually the vehicle that makes effective communication possible. Undershaft was not Barbara's therapist, any more than Henry Higgins was Eliza's. Barbara did not have a transference toward her father in the same sense a patient has toward a therapist. However, good rapport existed between father and daughter. Whatever fantasies she had about her father were not encroached upon by reality. He was not present during her childhood, so she could construct his image in whatever way her unconscious dictated without the necessity of having to deal with him realistically. She had felt positive toward him before he had reentered her life.

I believe that Undershaft's success in getting through to Barbara's defenses was because he knew the technique of effective interpretations, which led to effective communication.

The question remains, however, as to why Shaw was equally effective with his audience, since he was espousing morally reprehensible and unpopular principles. *Major Barbara* enjoyed an early success, and, although times were changing when it was first presented and the reactionary foundations of society were crumbling, there must have been other factors that had an impact on the individual psyche that might have reached a collective level.

There is a parallelism between the changes occurring in Barbara's character and what was happening in the early twentieth-century milieu. The relationship between father and daughter was a micro-cosmic reflection of the changes that were occurring in society in general, especially in England. Shaw apparently was echoing the latent forces that were gradually fomenting to change the static structure and stratification that characterized the fin-de-siècle culture of Western Europe. His play was congruent with the latent ideology of the time.

Freud found no such acceptance. Freud was dealing with conscious and unconscious sexual impulses, whereas Shaw emphasized the violent and destructive nature of man and how it can be harnessed. Were these destructive feelings more familiar and less frightening in Shaw's era than the sexuality Freud was describing?

Levine (1997b) speculates that the acceptance of *Major Barbara* was enhanced by a collusion between Shaw and his audience regarding what was not talked about. Shaw might have said, according to Levine, "I will leave sex out of this, if you think seriously about your society, your hypocrisy, and your aggression, and I will seduce you with my irresistible wit, humor, and intelligence." I believe that if Freud had limited himself only to the destructive components of human-kind's nature, he would not initially have been so hostilely received.

Shaw's audience could easily identify with Barbara. More specifically, like Barbara, they had a strong sense of right and wrong and tended to polarize issues. However, in spite of a rigid morality, there was a sense of uneasiness and a need for revision of strict standards. Social and cultural upheavals were already taking place, because the price of repression was too high. The audience might have sensed that the evil Barbara was trying to excise was a fundamental part of hu-man nature, the part of the personality the psychoanalyst calls the id. Barbara's defensive system was designed to deny the biologically intrinsic aspects of what she considered bad. The audience had simi-lar defenses, but they were uncomfortable with them.

Within Shaw's culture, narcissistic shifts were occurring that tended to break down the barriers of the different levels of society and class barriers. The aristocracy was isolated from the lower classes and either overtly or covertly considered itself a superior group. The aristocracy was narcissistically preoccupied with class distinctions, maintaining an aloofness patterned after monarchical protocol. If narcissism is viewed in a collective sense and part of a group phenomenon, then it was concentrated in the upper classes, with the lower classes clinging to the few pitiful remnants that were left over as crumbs.

Barbara tried to elevate self-esteem. All she had to offer was a religious-like faith. Undershaft, on the other hand, gave the lower classes jobs, elevated their material status, and generated their self-respect. In his world, narcissism was more equitably distributed. Undershaft, himself, came from humble origins and anyone who would succeed him also had to come from modest circumstances.

At first reading, the rise from rags to riches by Undershaft and his finding that Barbara's fiancé also came from humble origins, and therefore could become his successor, smacks of fairy-tale simplicity. The ending of the play has a deus-ex-machina quality. Viewed in terms of narcissistic shifts and societal changes, it is both clever and subtle.

The circumstances Shaw created are different from the usual fairy tale and from the complicated uncovering of true identities in many of Shakespeare's comedies. In both, an apparently humble person is recognized as a prince and member of a royal family. He is not really a peasant, whereas Undershaft and Barbara's fiancé were really poor and their ascent represents upward mobility. In pre–World War I Europe, children usually remained in the same work and social strata as their parents. Undershaft has broken through these barriers and, as a result, his workers have enhanced self-esteem. The working class now has narcissistic supplies that once were allowed only to the aristocracy.

This, of course, happens with every revolutionary movement, but in Shaw's society it was occurring in a covert fashion, and Shaw did not exhibit the bombastic qualities of the revolutionist. After all, he was a Fabian socialist, but through his wit he was contained and maintained considerable decorum.

Again, Shaw's effectiveness invites a comparison with Freud. Freud wrote from the viewpoint of the clinician. He recorded direct observations and his inferences from them. His descriptions of the unconscious were extracted from his patients' material and were not artistically elaborated. His writings are descriptions of basic raw material, which is not intrinsically appealing or artistic. Shaw, on the other hand, does not face his audience with the id head on. He, too, felt no necessity for avoiding the "ugly" side of human nature, but as in all artistic expression, he was able to communicate aspects of the unconscious without making his audience directly aware of what he was communicating.

The differences in the modes of communication between Freud and Shaw are those that distinguish the scientist and the artist, although Freud was also quite capable of artistic expression. In fact, the only prize he ever won was the Goethe award for literary achievement.

Still, Freud was referring to what he considered to be the truth in the sense of having made a new discovery, whereas Shaw was proselytizing a point of view, which, to some extent, required the creation of Barbara's new personality because she had abandoned her previous viewpoint. Shaw intuitively recognized certain basic psychoanalytic principles, especially demonstrated by his using the technique of interpretation in order to convince Barbara of his "truth." It is Shaw's intuitive grasp of psychoanalysis that makes him an effective communicator, and such unconscious knowledge, combined with his wit, is responsible for the appealing quality of his work.

In spite of Shaw's intuitive capacities, critics have raised the objection that he had many defenses and did not come to terms with his unconscious. The foolishness of some of his attacks, particularly on antivivisection, his need for power, his later adulation of Mussolini and Hitler, and his eccentric behavior and self-denial in oral and sexual areas, indicate the existence and extent of his characterological peculiarities.

While much of what Shaw said can be understood in terms of specific instinctual conflict patterns, the fact is not altered that there is an autonomous creative talent that has to be primarily viewed at the level of ego operations. For the defensive reaction to or the sublimation of an unconscious conflict tells us very little about a person's creative activity. Many times, such an investigation becomes an ad hominem attack.

It must be remembered that Shaw and Undershaft are not the same person. Undershaft is a character created by Shaw, not Shaw himself. Rather than creating a character that embodies all aspects of the personality, including intrapsychic conflicts and defensive attitudes, it is much more likely that Shaw portrayed in Undershaft only one aspect of his psychic structure, his ego-ideal. He created an ideal character, who embodied the qualities of abhorring hypocrisy, avoiding reaction formations, as well as having a positive outlook toward humankind's inner nature, an ideal that Shaw never attained. So it is Undershaft who has come to terms with his unconscious, not Shaw. To speak of Undershaft's neurosis is to introduce items in the play that have been gleaned from what one knows about Shaw and that are not found in the content of the play.

Other characters in the play may represent different aspects of Shaw's personality, perhaps the more neurotic components. I am only interested in the relationship between Shaw's and Undershaft's narcissistic investment in their wish to remake Barbara according to their own image, and how this may parallel the distribution of narcissism in the therapeutic process. However, it is well known that authors in their works, as persons do in their dreams, make multiple identifications according to the mechanisms of the primary process. In both cases, a character can contain one part of his psyche, such as an instinctual impulse as might be seen in an impulsive, demanding person. Another character can represent the personification of a different aspect, such as the superego, as might be depicted by a harsh, punitive, unforgiving person. In a play, in contrast to a dream, the conscious, more organized aspects of the personality can be depicted as well as other parts that stand in contrast with the author's ideology and that are held in a state of repression. In a dream, the reverse often occurs—the unconscious irrational parts of the psyche may intensify and produce a nightmare.

To briefly summarize, in *Pygmalion* and *Major Barbara* Shaw created Professor Higgins and Undershaft who, in turn, have narcissistic needs to create persons as an expression of their creativity, and they demonstrate that they have special skills to accomplish the task they have set for themselves. Higgins practically creates a new person, what he would have considered a de novo product and as I have indicated in the myth of Pygmalion, this is apparent.

By contrast, Undershaft begins with an intact personality with a well-organized, cohesive self representation. He merely wants to change and modify her surface attitudes, and he is especially skillful, as a therapist should ideally be, in knowing when his daughter would be receptive to incorporating his ideology, which in therapy would be considered to be an interpretative exchange. In fact, by giving money to the Salvation Army, he is creating the most propitious conditions for introducing his viewpoint.

His impact does not intrude into Barbara's fundamental character. He was quite different from Higgins, who pounded away at Eliza's characterological organization. Basically, he did not want to change Barbara. He was only interested in changing a particular outlook that involved her perception of and reactions to a segment of the outer world. Otherwise, he respected her autonomy. He liked her as she was, and was sufficiently attracted by her that he wanted her as an ally.

Barbara's self representation remained intact. Undershaft simply enlarged her horizons. In terms of ego psychology, her perceptual system was altered and became more in tune with reality. She no longer wore the rose-colored glasses of blind faith and religious zeal. The ego's executive system also underwent modification in that she constructed new adaptive techniques that in Shaw's mind would be more effective in dealing with the vicissitudes of the external world.

Caesar and Cleopatra

The final play on this continuum is *Caesar and Cleopatra*. I selected this play because it represents another instance in which a father figure helps in the maturation and development of a personality that can be compared to the treatment process and creative accomplishments. In both successful treatment and creativity, there is considerable narcissistic enhancement. In *Caesar and Cleopatra*, Cleopatra's personality remains intact. Whatever changes occur are accretions, primarily at the behavioral level. There is an expansion of psychic structure rather than modifications.

Caesar teaches Cleopatra how to be a queen, but she already is a queen. That role had been established for her since birth. She may feel some apprehension about her exalted position, but she never has any doubt as to who she is.

As the play opens, Cleopatra reveals her immaturity and her childish anxiety. She views Caesar, who is on his way to Egypt, as an ogre who will devour her. However, these reactions are far from grim. There is a charming, seductive quality in how she expresses herself, even her fear and anger. Her childishness almost seems appropriate for a queen.

In constructing a continuum of Eliza, Barbara, and Cleopatra, I am making distinctions on the basis of the degree of structural changes in the ego's subsystems, as occurs in treatment, and the gradations of narcissism that are involved in the therapist and the creator, both as an author and as a character in his play. Eliza was completely made over; Barbara made some changes in the perceptual sphere and the ego's executive system; and Cleopatra had an educational experience, which sometimes happens in therapy, especially in the treatment of children.

From a clinical viewpoint, Eliza required the most extensive character change. This could mean that she was suffering from the most severe psychopathology, and as we move to Barbara and Cleopatra, they are progressively suffering from less, with Cleopatra the healthiest of the three. It is tempting to make such comparisons after making formulations about teacher–pupil, father–daughter, and mentor–ward relationships, all of which are patterned after the treatment relationship.

Unfortunately, these evaluations do not ring true. Even though Eliza was the most rambunctious of the three heroines, the reader does not get the impression that she is a disturbed person. In fact, she shows considerable strength in putting up with the tyrannical discipline that Higgins imposed on her. She stuck to the task rather than running away from it, as she often felt tempted to do.

Although clinicians can speculate about the degree of character change that occurred in these plays, it is much more difficult to make judgments about the severity of psychopathology. All three of the heroines responded well to the ministrations of their mentor, so this would speak well of their degree of psychic stability. Eliza might have shown some problems with her self representation, whereas Barbara and Cleopatra had well-established senses of identity. But even with Eliza, the reader gets the impression that she was a fairly well-adjusted flower girl. It seems as if her problems began when she agreed to become Higgins's pupil.

There is a hint, however, that she might have had some problems adjusting to the lower-class, impoverished world she lived in, and Professor Higgins's offer was a godsend. She might have been ambivalent about accepting it, but nevertheless she did, indicating that she was not too happy living at the level she did.

Barbara and Cleopatra had no such ambivalence toward their mentors. Cleopatra had the imperious qualities of a queen, but she had no model after which she could pattern herself. A slave, a strong-willed woman, acted as a factotum and made most of the decisions, dominating the royal palace.

There were also divisive forces in the court, because some of the nobles favored Cleopatra's brother, still a young boy, as the monarch. Cleopatra was the queen, but she had many vulnerabilities, both personal and political. Caesar, a powerful general and a shrewd politician, supported Cleopatra and was responsible for her gaining the throne.

As was customary, she married her younger brother, Ptolemy XII. With the aid of Julius Caesar, she won the kingdom, but it remained the vassal of Rome. Her husband died, and she then married another brother, Ptolemy XIII, but by this time she had become Caesar's mistress and she bore him a child.

In Shaw's play, she relates to Caesar as a daughter. After she overcomes her childish fear of him, she eagerly accepts him as her mentor. Clearly, she idealizes him and he has become her ego-ideal.

Caesar, however, is not as didactic as Professor Higgins and Undershaft. His very presence secures her throne and curbs the outbreak of violence and disruption. He teaches Cleopatra how to deal with her underlings, but more by his manner than by overt instruction. Her introjection of the regal position is smooth and seems effortless.

In the plays I have discussed, the sexual factor is underplayed or omitted. This is especially noteworthy in *Caesar and Cleopatra*, because history has taught us that he was Cleopatra's lover. Inasmuch as Caesar related to Cleopatra as a mentor, it would be expected that a sexual relationship would be incestuous and interfere with her capacity to absorb his teachings.

Shaw apparently did not deal with what possibly might have been a conflict, but without precise knowledge of the sexual mores of Egypt, it is difficult to assess the role of erotic factors. After all, in the royal household, brother–sister marriages were common in order to preserve political unity, so incestuous relationships might have had a different kind of impact than they did in Shaw's world.

Shaw avoided such questions and concentrated, as in his other plays, on how Caesar contributed to Cleopatra's psychic development, beginning with a somewhat frightened, childish young girl who turns into a spirited and capable queen. Before meeting Caesar, Cleopatra had little knowledge about the world and the complex political climate she lived in. She was a queen and felt it in her bones, so to speak, but functionally she did not rule because she did not know how. The slave guided the household and the nobles ran the government as they pleased.

Caesar changed all this by taking over the government with his military strength and showing Cleopatra how to rule. He made her into both a queen and a woman, but Shaw kept sexuality implicit rather than confronting it.

Higgins also made Eliza into a woman and Aphrodite gave life to Galatea, making her into a sexual being. Higgins made Eliza into a beautiful, charming woman, but he did not relate to her at the erotic level. Although Caesar actually had a sexual relationship with Cleopatra, he acted only as a teacher in the play and did not get personally involved, keeping an optimal distance as a good therapist should.

In *Major Barbara*, there is a romance between Barbara and a young Greek scholar. Undershaft is interested in his daughter's fiancé and covertly encourages the relationship. Shaw, at the end of *Pygmalion*, and after considerable soul-searching, has Eliza marry Freddy, a dim-witted, but good-hearted young man who adores her. Shaw introduces a sexual relationship but keeps it in the background. Perhaps he realized that the construction of a self representation and the achievement of a good narcissistic balance means that the psyche has acquired the capacity to form intimate object relationships, and is thus able to love and to be loved.

However, this cannot happen with the therapist or the parent and mentor. In the play *Caesar and Cleopatra*, Caesar has a handsome young hero by his side, a model of jubilant masculinity. He is there as a presence and there is no overt intimate relationship between him and Cleopatra, although, as a hero, he swears his devotion to her and to be her champion.

Here, I believe Cleopatra is being idealized as she has idealized Caesar and made his ideals her own. Her sexual development goes no further in the play, although historians tell us that she had an affair with Caesar, and sometime in that period she married her brother, although it is debatable whether the marriage was consummated. It is interesting that Caesar, as he is leaving Egypt, tells Cleopatra that he will send her a beautiful young man, Mark Antony. Apparently, Shaw recognized that if Cleopatra were to be a queen and a complete woman, she would have to establish a solid and stable sexual relationship.

Shaw distorted history by omitting details of Caesar's and Cleopatra's sexual life because it would have made it difficult to pursue his thesis of the creation of a person, or, to be more precise, the blossoming of an identity. The incorporation of an ego-ideal as it expands its idealizing potential can be hindered or distorted by erotization.

Apparently Cleopatra was able to have an idealized and sexual relationship with Mark Antony, which in reality ended tragically with their suicides. The latter does not mean that they did not have a basically good relationship. Shaw would have us believe that Cleopatra was ready to have a good love object relationship.

I do not wish to further mix up history and fiction. I am simply interested in Shaw's perspective in creating in these three plays three narcissistically well-balanced women.

In *Caesar and Cleopatra*, he alters history by not describing the sexual relationship between mentor and ward. It is possible that Caesar had not yet started an affair with Cleopatra when he first met her, but he certainly did later. This, of course, is unacceptable between therapist and patient, even if the formal treatment relationship has ended. Again, this may be an example of Shaw's intuition that recognized that the therapist has to stay on the observational platform and maintain boundaries.

This did not happen in the myth of Pygmalion, but it does in Shaw's three plays. The birth of a new psyche varies in extent in the three heroines. I wonder which of these plays gave Shaw the greatest narcissistic gratification. I have heard that *Pygmalion* was one of his favorite plays. If this is true, I would conjecture that there was some parallelism between the amount of Shaw's narcissism and the totality of his creation, which would be determined as to whether he had to start from scratch, relatively speaking, or how much he had to work with when he started. I would doubt that there is such an absolute parallelism, but, in general, the harder the task or the more complex the problem, the greater the satisfaction derived from creative accomplishment.

Returning to the clinical sphere, do clinicians gain greater satisfaction, that is, narcissistic enhancement, from the successful or moderately successful treatment of severely disturbed patients than from the treatment of patients who seem to belong at higher levels of psychic development? Perhaps, in some instances, a therapist may feel profound pride as might occur in the rehabilitation of a schizophrenic. I can infer from the discussion in Chapter 1, that Frieda Fromm-Reichmann must have felt both gratified and proud after her treatment of Hannah Green as described in *I Never Promised You a Rose Garden*. Still, being able to help any patient, no matter the degree of psychopathology, to achieve further character integration, is creative and self-rewarding. It is hoped that as clinicians become further involved in in-depth treatment, the intrapsychic focus will be revitalized.

References

Adler, G. (1983). *Borderline Psychopathology and Its Treatment*. New York: Jason Aronson.

Akhtar, S. (1992). *Broken Structures: Severe Personality Disorders and Their Treatment*. Northvale, NJ: Jason Aronson.

Alexander, F. (1961). *The Scope of Psychoanalysis*. New York: Basic Books.

Alexander, F., and French, T. (1946). *Psychoanalytic Therapy*. New York: Ronald.

Almond, R. (1995). The analytic role: a mediating influence in the interplay of transference and countertransference. *Journal of the American Psychoanalytic Association* 43:404–494.

Arlow, J., and Brenner C. (1964). *Psychoanalytic Concepts and the Structural Theory*. New York: International Universities Press.

Atwood, G., and Stolorow, R. (1984). *Structures of Subjectivity*. Hillsdale, NJ: Analytic Press.

——— (1993). *Faces in a Cloud: Intersubjectivity and Personality Theory*. Northvale, NJ: Jason Aronson.

Bader, M. (1994). The tendency to neglect therapeutic aims in psychoanalysis. *Psychoanalytic Quarterly* 63:246–270.

——— (1998). Post modernism, the problem of validation and the retreat from therapeutics in psychoanalysis. *Psychoanalytic Dialogues* 8:1–37.

Boyer, L. B. (1983). *The Regressed Patient*. New York: Jason Aronson.

Boyer, L. B., and Giovacchini, P. (1967). *Psychoanalytic Treatment of Characterological and Schizophrenic Disorders*. New York: Jason Aronson.

—— (1980). *Psychoanalytic Treatment of Characterological, Borderline, and Schizophrenic Disorders*. New York: Jason Aronson.

Breuer, J.,and Freud, S. (1895). Studies on hysteria. *Standard Edition* 2:1–307.

Cocks, G. (1994). *The Curve of Life*. Chicago: University of Chicago Press.

Crapanzano, V. (1982). The self, the third and desire. In: *Psycho-Social Theories of the Self*, ed. B. Lee, pp. 179–206. New York: Plenum.

Cushman, P. (1995). *Constructing the Self, Constructing America. A Cultural History of Psychotherapy*. New York: Addison-Wesley.

D'Abro, A. (1951). *The Rise of the New Physics*. New York: Dover.

Deutsch, H. (1942). Some forms of emotional disturbance and their relationship to schizophrenia. *Psychoanalytic Quarterly* 11:301–321.

Ehrensaft, D. (1998). Child psychotherapy and intersubjectivity theory: ode to Anna Freud *Fort-Da: The Journal of the Northern California Society for Psychoanalytic Psychology* 8:5–15.

Eissler, K. (1953). The effect of the structuring of the ego on psychoanalytic technique. *Journal of the American Psychoanalytic Association* 1:14–143.

Erikson, E. (1956). The problem of ego identity. *Journal of the American Psychoanalytic Association* 4: 218–235.

—— (1959). *Identity and the Life Cycle*. New York: International Universities Press.

Fairbairn, R. (1941). A revised psychopathology of the psychoses and psychoneuroses. *International Journal of Psycho-Analysis* 22:250–279.

—— (1954). *An Object Relations Theory of the Personality*. New York: Basic Books.

Farber, S., and Green, M. (1993). *Hollywood on the Couch*. New York: William Morrow.

Feinsilver, D. 1980. Transitional relatedness and containment in the treatment of a chronic schizophrenic patient. *International Review of Psychoanalysis* 7:309–318.

Feynman, R. (1989a). *What Do You Care What People Think?* New York: Norton.

—— (1989b). *Surely You Must Be Joking Mr. Feynman: Adventures of a Curious Character*. New York: Bantam.

Flarsheim, A. (1975). The therapist's collusion with the patient's wish for suicide. In *Tactics and Techniques in Psychoanalytic Psychotherapy*, ed. P. Giovacchini, 2:155–196. New York: Jason Aronson

Freud, A. (1936). *The Ego and the Mechanisms of Defence*. New York: International Universities Press.

Freud, S. (1895). Project for a scientific psychology. *Standard Edition* 1:291–392.

—— (1900). The interpretation of dreams. *Standard Edition* 4/5:1–626.

—— (1904). Fragments of an analysis of a case of hysteria. *Standard Edition* 7:1–123.

—— (1905a). Three essays on the theory of sexuality. *Standard Edition* 7:123–244.

—— (1905b). Jokes and their relation to the unconscious. *Standard Edition* 8:9–236.

—— (1909a). Analysis of a phobia in a five-year-old boy. *Standard Edition* 10:1–148.

—— (1909b). Notes upon a case of obsessional neurosis. *Standard Edition* 10:153–193.

—— (1910). The future prospects of psycho-analytic therapy. *Standard Edition* 11:139–155.

—— (1911). Psycho-analytic notes on a case of paranoia. *Standard Edition* 12:1–82.

—— (1911–1914). Papers on technique. *Standard Edition* 12:85–172.

—— (1914a). On narcissism: an introduction. *Standard Edition* 14:67–105.

—— (1914b). On the history of the psychoanalytic movement. *Standard Edition* 14:1–67.

—— (1914c). Remembering, repeating and working-through. *Standard Edition* 12:145–157.

—— (1917). Mourning and melancholia. *Standard Edition* 14:237–259.

—— (1918). From the history of an infantile neurosis. *Standard Edition* 10: 1–123.

—— (1920). Beyond the pleasure principle. *Standard Edition* 18:1–65.

————— (1921). Group psychology and analysis of the ego. *Standard Edition* 18:65–145.

————— (1923). The ego and the id. *Standard Edition* 19:1–60.

————— (1924a). Neurosis and psychosis. *Standard Edition* 19:149–153.

————— (1924b). The loss of reality in neurosis and psychosis. *Standard Edition* 19:183–191.

————— (1933). The new introductory lectures. *Standard Edition* 29:1–183.

————— (1940). An outline of psycho-analysis. *Standard Edition* 23:141–209.

Fromm-Reichmann, F. (1950). *Principles of Intensive Psychotherapy*. Chicago: University of Chicago Press.

————— (1959). *Psychoanalysis and Psychotherapy: Selected Papers*. Chicago: University of Chicago Press.

Gedo, J. (1997). *Spleen and Nostalgia: A Life and Work in Psychoanalysis*. Northvale, NJ: Jason Aronson.

Giovacchini, P. (1958). Mutual adaptation in various object relationships. *International Journal of Psycho-Analysis* 39:1–8.

————— (1960). On scientific creativity. *Journal of the American Psychoanalytic Association* 8:407–426.

————— (1965). Psychopathological aspects of the identity sense. In *Psychoanalysis of Character Disorders*, pp. 3–10. New York: Jason Aronson.

————— (1967). The frozen introject. *International Journal of Psycho-Analysis* 48:61–67.

————— (1979). *Treatment of Primitive Mental States*. New York: Jason Aronson.

————— (1984). *A Narrative Textbook of Psychoanalysis*. New York: Jason Aronson.

————— (1986). *Developmental Disorders: The Transitional Space in Mental Breakdown and Creative Integration*. Northvale, NJ: Jason Aronson.

————— (1989). *Countertransference: Triumphs and Catastrophes*. Northvale, NJ: Jason Aronson.

————— (1993). The ego-ideal of a creative scientist. *Journal of the American Psychoanalytic Association* 34:79–101.

————— (1997). *Schizophrenia and Primitive Mental States*. Northvale, NJ: Jason Aronson.

———— (1998). The intrapsychic focus and its vicissitudes. *Fort-Da: The Journal of the Northern California Society for Psychoanalytic Psychology* 4:17–31.

Giovacchini, P., and Boyer, L. B. (1975). The psychoanalytic impasse. *International Journal of Psychoanalytic Psychotherapy* 4:15–27.

Gleick, J. (1992). *Genius: The Life and Science of Richard Feynman*. New York: Vintage.

Goldberg, A. (1998). Self psychology since Kohut. *Psychoanalytic Quarterly* 67:240–256.

Greenberg, J. (1964). *I Never Promised You a Rose Garden*. New York: Signet.

Greenson, R. (1965). The working alliance and the transference neurosis. *Psychoanalytic Quarterly* 34:155–181.

Grinker, E. (1975). *Psychiatry in Broad Perspectives*. New York: Behavioral Publications.

Grotstein, J. (1981). *Splitting and Projective Identification*. New York: Jason Aronson.

———— (1993). Boundary difficulties in borderline states. In *Master Clinicians on Treating the Borderline Patient*, vol. 2, ed. L. B. Boyer and P. Giovacchini, pp. 107–141. Northvale, NJ: Jason Aronson.

Grotstein, J., and Rinsley, D. B. (1994). *Fairbairn and the Origins of Object Relations*. New York: Guilford.

Hartmann, H. (1939). *Ego Psychology and the Problem of Adaptation*. New York: International Universities Press.

———— (1950). Comments on the psychoanalytic theory of the ego. *Psychoanalytic Study of the Child* 5:74–96. New York: International Universities Press.

Hegel, G. W. (1801). *Phenomenology of Spirit*. London: Oxford University Press.

Heidegger, M. (1977). *Basic Writings*, ed. D. F. Krell. New York: Harper & Row.

Horney, K. (1937). *The Neurotic Personality of Our Time*. New York: Norton.

———— (1942). *Self Analysis*. New York: Norton.

Jackson, W. C. (1998). A piece of my mind: in a word. *Journal of the American Medical Association* 280:493–494.

Karasu, B. (1996). *Deconstruction of Psychotherapy.* Northvale, NJ: Jason Aronson.

Kardiner, A. (1977). *My Analysis with Freud.* New York: Norton.

Kardiner, A., Karush, A., and Ovesey, L. (1959). Methodological study of Freudian theory. *Journal of Nervous and Mental Diseases* 11:129–168.

Kernberg, O. (1975). *Borderline Conditions and Pathological Narcissism.* New York: Basic Books.

Kernberg, O., Selzer, M. A., and Koenigsberg, H. W. (1987). *Psychodynamic Psychotherapy of Borderline Patients.* New York: Basic Books.

Klein, M. (1946). Notes on some schizoid mechanisms. *International Journal of Psycho-Analysis* 27:99–110.

Kohut, H. (1971). *The Analysis of the Self.* New York: International Universities Press.

——— (1977). *The Restoration of the Self.* New York: International Universities Press.

——— (1979). The two analyses of Mr. Z. *International Journal of Psycho-Analysis* 60:3–27.

Kris, E. (1950). On preconscious mental processes. *Psychoanalytic Quarterly* 19:540–560.

Kuhn, T. (1962). *The Structure of Scientific Revolutions.* Chicago: University of Chicago Press.

Laplanche, J., and Pontalis, J. B. (1973). *The Language of Psychoanalysis.* New York: Norton.

——— (1982). Self, ego, affects and drives. *Journal of the American Psychoanalytic Association* 30:893–918.

Lasch, C. (1991). *The Culture of Narcissism: American Life in the Age of Diminishing Returns.* New York: Norton.

Lehman, D. (1991). *Signs of the Times.* New York: Poseidon.

Levine, S. (1997a). Unpublished manuscript.

——— (1997b). Unpublished manuscript.

Lipton, S. (1977). The advantages of Freud's technique as shown in the analysis of the rat-man. *International Journal of Psycho-Analysis* 58:255–273.

Lohser, B., and Newton, P. M. (1996) *Unorthodox Freud: The View from the Couch.* New York: Guilford.

Masson, J. (1988). *Against Therapy: Emotional Tyranny and the Myths of Psychological Healing.* New York: Atheneum.

Masterson, J. (1976). *Psychotherapy of the Borderline Adult.* New York: Brunner/Mazel.

Matthis, I., and Szecsödy, I., eds. (1998). *On Freud's Couch.* Northvale, NJ: Jason Aronson.

McDougall, J. (1985). *Theaters of the Mind.* New York: Basic Books.

——— (1989). *Theaters of the Body.* New York: Basic Books.

Meissner, W. W. (1980). A note on projective identification. *Journal of the American Psychoanalytic Association* 29:43–61.

Mitchell, S. (1980). The intrapsychic and the interpersonal: different theories, different domains, or historical artifacts? *Psychoanalytic Inquiry* 8:472–496.

——— (1988). *Relational Concepts in Psychoanalysis: An Integration.* Cambridge, MA: Harvard University Press.

——— (1993). *Hope and Dread in Psychoanalysis.* New York: Basic Books.

Modell, A. (1963). Primitive object relationships and the predisposition to schizophrenia. *International Journal of Psycho-Analysis* 44:282–292.

——— (1990). *Other Times, Other Realities.* Cambridge, MA: Harvard University Press.

Moss, D. (1975). *Narcissism, empathy and fragmentation of the self: an interview with Heinz Kohut.* Recorded at the Chicago Institute for Psychoanalysis. H. Dunlop Smith Center for the History of Cartography. Chicago: Newberry Library.

Muller, J. (1998). A holding context for the therapeutic dyad. *The Austen Riggs Center Review* 11:3–5.

Ogden, T. (1982). *Projective Identification and Psychotherapeutic Technique.* New York: Jason Aronson.

——— (1986). *The Matrix of the Mind: Object Relations and the Psychoanalytic Dialogue.* Northvale, NJ: Jason Aronson.

——— (1994a). The analytic third: working with intersubjective clinical facts. *International Journal of Psycho-Analysis* 75:3–19.

—— (1994b). *Subjects of Analysis*. Northvale, NJ: Jason Aronson.

Ornstein, P. (1972). *On narcissism: beyond the introduction*. Paper presented to the Divisional Meetings of the Western Psychoanalytic Societies, San Diego, CA.

—— (1979). The borderline self in the psychoanalytic treatment process. *Journal of the American Psychoanalytic Association* 27:353–374.

Paris, B. J. (1994). *A Psychoanalytic Search for Self-Understanding*. New Haven, CT: Yale University Press.

Racker, H. (1968). *Transference and Countertransference*. New York: International Universities Press.

Reichard, S. (1956). A re-examination of "Studies on Hysteria." *Psychoanalytic Quarterly* 25:155–177.

Robbins, M. (1993). *Experiences of Schizophrenia: An Integration of the Personal, Scientific and Therapeutic*. New York: Guilford.

Roudinesco, E. (1997). *Jacques Lacan*. New York: Columbia University Press.

Schafer, R. (1968). *Aspects of Internalization*. New York: Internalization Universities Press.

—— (1992). *Retelling A Life*. New York: Basic Books.

Schulze, R., and Kilgalin, B. (1969). *Case Studies in Schizophrenia*. New York: Basic Books.

Searles, H. F. (1959). The effort to drive the other person crazy: an element in the etiology and psychotherapy of schizophrenia. In *Collected Papers on Schizophrenia and Related Subjects*, pp. 243–283. New York: International Universities Press, 1965.

—— (1961). Phases of patient–therapist interaction in the psychotherapy of schizophrenia. In *Collected Papers on Schizophrenia and Related Subjects*, pp. 521–559. New York: International Universities Press, 1965.

—— (1965). *Collected Papers on Schizophrenia and Related Subjects*. New York: International Universities Press.

—— (1986). *My Work with Borderline Patients*. Northvale, NJ: Jason Aronson.

Shapiro, E. R. (1998). Renegotiating the therapeutic frame. *The Austen Riggs Center Review* 6–13.

Shaw, G. B. (1941). *Selected Plays*. New York: Penguin.

Shur, R. (1994). *Countertransference Enactments* Northvale, NJ: Jason Aronson.

Silvio, J. R. (1977). George Bernard Shaw's *Pygmalion:* a creative response to early childhood loss. *Journal of the American Academy of Psychoanalysis* 23:234–256.

Spence, D. (1982). *Narrative Truth and Historical Truth.* New York: Norton.

Spezzano, C. (1993). A relational model of inquiry and truth. *Psychoanalytic Dialogue* 3:177–208.

Spitz, R. (1945). Hospitalism. *Psychoanalytic Study of the Child* 1:53–74. New York: International Universities Press.

———— (1946). Hospitalism: a follow-up report. *Psychoanalytic Study of the Child* 2:113–117. New York: International Universities Press.

———— (1965). *The First Year of Life.* New York: International Universities Press.

Spruiell, V. (1975). Three strands of narcissism. *Psychoanalytic Quarterly* 44:577–595.

Sterba, R. (1934). The fate of the ego in psychoanalytic therapy. *International Journal of Psycho-Analysis* 15:117–126.

Stolorow, R., Brandchaft, B., and Atwood, G. (1987). *Psychoanalytic Treatment: Intersubjective Approach.* Hillsdale, NJ: Analytic Press.

———— (1994). *The Intersubjective Perspective.* Northvale, NJ: Jason Aronson.

Stone, L. (1954). The widening scope of psychoanalysis. *Journal of the American Psychoanalytic Association* 2:561–594.

———— (1963). *The Psychoanalytic Situation.* New York: International Universities Press.

Strachey, J. (1934). The nature of the therapeutic action of psycho-analysis. *International Journal of Psycho-Analysis* 15:127–160.

Sullivan, H. S. (1953). *The Interpersonal Theory of Psychiatry.* New York: Norton.

Thompson, M. (1994). *The Truth About Freud's Technique.* New York: New York University Press.

Vesonder T. G. (1977). Eliza's choice: transformation myth and the ending of *Pygmalion.* In *Fabian Feminist: Bernard Shaw and Woman,* ed. R. Weintraub, pp. 39–45. University Park, PA: Pennsylvania State University Press.

Volkan, V. (1995). *The Infantile Psychotic Self and Its Fate*. Northvale, NJ: Jason Aronson.

Weber, M. (1956). On charisma and institution building. In *Selected Papers of Max Weber*, ed. S. N. Eisenstadt, pp. 286–324. Chicago: University of Chicago Press.

Weissman, P. (1958). Shaw's childhood and *Pygmalion*. *Psychoanalytic Study of the Child* 13:541–561. New York: International Universities Press.

Winnicott, D. W. (1952). Psychosis and child care. In *Collected Papers: Through Paediatrics to Psycho-Analysis*, pp. 219–228. New York: Basic Books.

———— (1953). Transitional objects and transitional phenomena. In *Playing and Reality*, pp. 1–26. London: Tavistock.

———— (1956). Primary maternal preoccupation. In *Collected Papers: Through Paediatrics to Psycho-Analysis*, pp. 300–315. New York: Basic Books.

———— (1958a). *Collected Papers: Through Paediatrics to Psycho-Analysis*. New York: Basic Books.

———— (1958b). The capacity to be alone. *International Journal of Psycho-Analysis* 39:416–440

———— (1960a). Ego distortion in terms of the true and false self. In *The Maturational Processes and the Facilitating Environment*, pp. 140–155. New York: International Universities Press.

———— (1960b). The theory of the parent–infant relationship. In *The Maturational Processes and the Facilitating Environment*, pp. 198–217. New York: International Universities Press.

———— (1963). The mentally ill in your case load. In *The Maturational Processes and the Facilitating Environment*, pp. 217–230. New York: International Universities Press.

———— (1967). The location of the cultural experience. In *Playing and Reality*, pp. 95–103. London: Tavistock.

———— (1969.) The use of an object and relating through identification. In *Playing and Reality*, pp. 86–95. London: Tavistock.

———— (1971). *Playing and Reality*. London: Tavistock.

———— (1974). *The Maturational Processes and the Facilitating Environment*. New York: International Universities Press.

Yalom, I. (1996). *Lying on the Couch*. New York: HarperCollins.

Zetzel, E. (1956). Current concepts of transference. *Journal of the American Psychoanalytic Association* 1:526–557.

❖ ❖ ❖

Index

ABOUT THE AUTHOR

Peter L. Giovacchini, M.D., is Professor Emeritus, Department of Psychiatry, University of Illinois College of Medicine. He is a training and supervising analyst and founder of the Center for Psychoanalytic Studies in Chicago. Dr. Giovacchini has published more than 200 papers and 25 books. He is in the private practice of psychoanalysis in Chicago.